Expanding Welfare in an Age of Austerity

Changing Welfare States

For quite some time, a key finding and theoretical puzzle in comparative welfare state research was welfare states' remarkable stability. In the last decade, however, it has become clear that advanced welfare states were (far) less immovable than they seemed at first. In fact, speaking of *changing welfare states* captures much better the actual reforms that were taking place. This series is about the trajectories of those changes. Have there been path-breaking welfare innovations or are the changes incremental instead? Are welfare states moving in a similar or even convergent direction, or are they embarking on divergent trajectories of change? What new policies have been added, by which kind of political actors, how, and with what consequences for competitiveness, employment, income equality and poverty, gender relations, human capital formation, or fiscal sustainability? What is the role of the European Union in shaping national welfare state reform?

This series answers these and related questions by studying the socioeconomic, institutional and political conditions for welfare state change, its governance, and its outcomes across a diverse set of policy areas. The policy areas can address traditional "old" social risks like old age, unemployment, sickness (including the health care system), disability and poverty and inequality in general, or "new" social risks that have arisen mainly due to post-industrialization, such as reconciling work and family life, non-standard employment, and low and inadequate skills. In addition to focusing on the welfare state more narrowly defined, the series also welcomes publication on related areas, such as the housing market. The overriding objective of the series is tracing and explaining the full trajectories of contemporary welfare state change and its outcomes.

Expanding Welfare in an Age of Austerity

Increasing Protection in an Unprotected World

Anthony Kevins

Amsterdam University Press

Cover illustration: Wired Canvas (reproduced here without alteration under a Creative Commons license – https://creativecommons.org/licenses/by/2.0/legalcode)

Cover design: Coördesign, Leiden
Lay-out: Crius Group, Hulshout

Amsterdam University Press English-language titles are distributed in the US and Canada by the University of Chicago Press.

ISBN 978 94 6298 021 1
e-ISBN 978 90 4852 939 1 (pdf)
DOI 10.5117/9789462980211
NUR 752

Printed and bound by CPI Group (UK) Ltd, Croydon, CR0 4YY

In memory of my father

Table of Contents

List of Tables and Figures

Tables

Figures

Acknowledgements

This book project has benefitted from a wide array of support over the years. The research contained within was developed at McGill University and substantially revised and expanded at Aarhus University, with generous financial support from the McGill Institute for Health and Social Policy, the Faculty of Arts at McGill, AU Ideas, and the Guy Drummond and Nathan Steinberg Fellowship Programmes.

First and foremost, I owe a sincere debt of gratitude to Stuart Soroka, who served as my PhD supervisor and mentor since my time at McGill. His continual feedback, guidance, and support have been truly invaluable, both for the development of this book and my career as a researcher. I cannot thank him enough. This project also benefitted greatly from the helpful comments and suggestions of my dissertation committee members, Antonia Maioni and Hudson Meadwell, whose diverse interests dramatically improved the quality of the manuscript. I am grateful as well for all of the support I received from professors and colleagues at McGill's Department of Political Science, the Centre for the Study of Democratic Citizenship, and the McGill Institute for Health and Social Policy. I am especially indebted to Dietlind Stolle, Maria Popova, Michael Smith, Stephen Saideman, Naomi Lightman, Marc-André Bodet, Alessandra Radicati, Quinn Albaugh, Clare Devereux, Sarah Malik, and Virginie Lasnier.

The book also benefited greatly from the insights and comments of researchers at Aarhus University's Department of Political Science, where I have held a post-doctoral position for the past three years. I have been positively impressed by the friendly and extensive culture of peer feedback at the department. I am especially grateful for the assistance of Kees van Kersbergen and Carsten Jensen, who have been instrumental in enabling me to refine my manuscript and integrate into Aarhus. The book has also been improved by the comments of Bruno Oliveira Martins, Philipp Pechmann, Lisa Wewerka, Suthan Krishnarajan, and Alexander Horn, as well as by the technical assistance of Annette Bruun Andersen.

In addition, I have been lucky enough to receive extensive external feedback, and the manuscript is much improved as a result. Steve Hellman has been an endless source of encouragement and advice since my time at York, and I am very thankful for his many years of support. At the Institute for Qualitative and Multi-Method Research's summer programme, early comments from Patrick Emmenegger were central to setting in motion the rest of this project. Furthermore, he also provided key feedback for the development of this book in his role as external examiner for my dissertation defence. My visits to the Università degli Studi di Milano, the European University Institute, and Sciences Po were also formative, with Maurizio Ferrera, Stefano Sacchi, Matteo Jessoula, Hanspeter Kriesi, Paul Marx, and Bruno Palier offering important insights and suggestions that would prove essential to the book's research design and analysis. Their generosity with their time and expertise was truly impressive. Similarly, I have also received helpful feedback on the manuscript from Bernhard Ebbinghaus, Mélanie Bourque, Jon Kvist, Daniel Béland, and Barbara Vis.

The staff at Amsterdam University Press – in particular Vanessa de Bueger, Jaap Wagenaar, and Kristin DeMint Bailey – have also been incredibly helpful over the past several years. The manuscript benefited greatly from the comments of the editorial board and anonymous reviewers at the AUP and the *Journal of European Social Policy*, where some of the book's ideas and analysis have previously been published ("Political Actors and the Extension of Welfare Coverage", 2015, *Journal of European Social Policy*, 25(3): 303-315).

A special thanks also to the busy interviewees who set aside hours of their time to answer my questions and decipher my French and Italian. Our conversations were eye-opening, and I feel lucky to have met all of you.

Finally, my most heartfelt thank yous go to my family, for steeping me in familialism since childhood, and to my partner Morgan, for her boundless patience, support, and love – here as elsewhere, *sine qua non*.

1 Struggling with Persistent Gaps

Since their creation, welfare states have had to distinguish between individuals who should be given access to social programmes and those who should be excluded. The metrics of exclusion that governments have employed vary widely, from citizenship to residency to occupation, with often dramatic implications for the lives of individuals. While this means that the division between welfare state insiders and outsiders is in some sense a longstanding issue, countries that opted to structure benefit access around occupational and employment status have confronted additional challenges: in recent decades, the rapid expansion of atypical employment has created a growing group of not just labour market outsiders, but welfare state outsiders as well. This situation has been made all the more difficult by an economic climate that has generally been unfriendly towards generous welfare state benefits and coverage; as a result, governments have faced a trade-off between either extending coverage and retrenching the 'good' benefits given to 'insiders' *or* maintaining the protection, coverage, and benefits of the relatively well-off at the expense of a growing class of excluded 'outsiders'. In other words, they have had to choose between either providing lower-quality benefits for everyone or entrenching a 'dualistic' welfare state with two major, divergent sets of benefit levels.

This gives rise to a particular conundrum for the left, whose egalitarian and solidaristic ideological claims end up crashing up against the protection of the privileges of much of their core constituency (or membership, in the case of leftist trade unions). How do they balance the trade-off between coverage levels and benefit generosity, between leaving outsiders unprotected and increasing levels of welfare state dualisation? When, in the face of broader economic austerity, do governments actually extend welfare coverage, and why do they take different routes in doing so? Indeed, these questions are especially pertinent in today's Europe, given that coverage gaps persist and can contribute to a cycle of exclusion that will long outlast the current crisis.

In answering these questions, we build most directly on research examining welfare state dualisation: that is to say, insider-outsider divisions based on welfare state access rather than labour market status per se. It is worth noting at the outset that increasing (or decreasing) dualisation can be the product of a number of different kinds of policy change, and the link between dualisation and the quality or quantity of social support is not straightforward. Table 1.1 sets out some illustrative examples. As an illustration, we might envision a hypothetical welfare state in which access to a given benefit programme is available only to 80% of the population – leaving the remaining 20% (the welfare state 'outsiders') with no access whatsoever. The first approach extends access to the programme to all residents in a country (universalisation), erasing the welfare state dualism in the process. While ideal with respect to addressing dualism, it is also likely to be financially burdensome for the state (even granting that in some instances economies of scale may offset some of the costs). The second and third approaches, coverage extension and coverage restriction, clearly decrease and increase levels of dualisation, respectively. The former might involve, for example, including new occupational groups within the social insurance system – an approach that was popular prior to the age of austerity, but has since fallen out of favour. The latter, in turn, while less central for our purposes, might involve introducing citizenship (rather than simple residency) requirements to gain access to benefits.

Table 1.1 Conceptualising Dualisation

	Universalisation	Coverage Extension	Coverage Constriction	Residualisation	Inaction
Impact on Level of Dualisation	Dualisation Eradicated	Decreased Dualisation	Increased Dualisation	Increased Dualisation?	No Impact?

The fourth and fifth approaches, however, are more difficult to assess in terms of their comparative impact on welfare state dualisation. 'Residualisation' creates a two-tiered system by introducing a less generous residual benefit programme for outsiders. At the very least, this approach entrenches welfare state dualisation by likely reducing the political demand for providing outsiders with access to the primary benefit system. By some formulations, this might be viewed as a prime example of welfare state dualisation, since it institutionalises the dualism. Despite the fact that inaction has no impact on dualisation levels, it is certainly worse for outsiders (in the short-term at least) than residualisation, since at least with the latter they would gain access to modest benefits.

In light of this conceptual difficulty, instead of concentrating on dualisation as a process, we focus on approaches to dealing with pre-existing welfare state dualism, defined as unequal programme access and benefit generosity. Specifically, we will address both changes in access to a particular family of benefits (e.g. for the unemployed) and whether these benefits are standardised. In this way, universalisation is seen as dealing more completely with already existing dualism when compared to residualisation, while inaction is considered the least desirable option. Note also that, from a policy change perspective, this approach maps onto that of Hall (1993): universalisation addresses dualisation via revolutionary reform (what Hall refers to as 'third order' change), residualisation addresses it via piecemeal change (e.g. 'second order' change), while inaction of course leaves the status quo as is.

Overall, we will analyse the determinants of these three responses to a dualised system (though incremental coverage extension and restriction will also be discussed). We begin this investigation by focusing upon healthcare and benefits for the unemployed in the French and Italian cases, and then proceed to test the relevance of these findings in a broader context. The trajectories in France and Italy are such that they offer us valuable leverage on our topic. While both countries start out with relatively similar Bismarckian institutions in the two policy domains, we in fact see contrasting results: in unemployment, France gradually fills the many insurance-based gaps by building up benefit coverage via universally available means-tested benefits (shifting away from insurance principles, primarily from 1989 onwards), while in Italy the insurance approach remains paramount and large coverage gaps persist; in healthcare, by contrast, Italy makes a complete switch to a Beveridgean model in 1978, while France sticks to and expands its insurance model.

This chapter will lay the groundwork for the rest of the book, situating our research in the field and indicating what we will add to the current scholarship. This will include a brief summary of scholarly debates and consensus on the relationship between welfare state institutions, parties, and the public, focusing on research that directly touches upon our key questions and building upon it as we go along. Here we pay particular attention to work on: partisanship and welfare state reform; labour market dualisation; welfare state dualisation and the left; and public opinion and the welfare state. The chapter will then outline the questions to be addressed in this book – along with a set of general expectations – after which point it will present a brief justification for the use of France and Italy as case studies. It will conclude by providing an overview of the subsequent chapters and the structure of the argument.

Studying the Welfare State

Partisanship and Welfare Reform

We begin with the work on partisanship and welfare state reform in the age of austerity. Although much of the research this inspired was most interested in welfare state retrenchment, it nevertheless offers an obvious starting point for our investigation, given our focus on welfare state expenditure and generosity.

Central to this wave of literature is Pierson's (1994) *Dismantling the Welfare State? Reagan, Thatcher, and the Politics of Retrenchment*, which sparked considerable debate. Here, Pierson argued that the relationship between the left and the welfare state is a variable one – that, while the left may have been responsible for welfare state expansion in the Golden Age, it is policy feedback, rather than partisanship, which matters most for welfare state reform (1994: 9). Thus, to label the left as the protectorate of the welfare state is to mistakenly extend the role of the left from welfare expanders to welfare defenders. Key here is the different logics of expansion and retrenchment: while the former involved directing benefits towards groups of voters, the latter involves taking benefits away from groups with a vested interest in organising to protect them (Pierson 1996). In tough fiscal times, then, benefit provision would become a zero-sum game, changing the cost-benefit calculations even among those with a desire to expand benefit coverage.

Research stemming from this analysis ultimately coalesced around three major arguments. First, a series of studies provide support for the Pierson's proposition that left-wing parties had become delinked from welfare state expansion, although authors disagreed when this shift occurred – with answers ranging from the 1970s to the 1990s (cf. Huber and Stephens 2001; Kittel and Obinger 2003). Explanations frequently point to the problem of the welfare state's economic unviability, caused by a combination of demographic and economic pressures as countries attempted to increase their economic efficiency and attractiveness to capital in a competitive global economy (e.g. Scharpf 2000; Burgoon 2001; Castles 2004).

A second group of scholars, however, argued that even in the face of demographic and economic pressures on the welfare state, the impact of the left on welfare state generosity has not significantly decreased. Arguing against the approach taken by many of the above authors, Allan and Scruggs (2004) pointed to the inappropriateness of welfare state expenditure as a dependent variable. The authors argued that entitlement data provides a more accurate measure of welfare state effort, and that when the dependent variable is properly specified, results demonstrate that the left does indeed continue to make a difference (Allan and Scruggs 2004). Similarly, work by Korpi and Palme (2003) concluded that a lack of left representation in cabinets was associated with an increased probability of social insurance programmes being retrenched. Perhaps most germane for our purposes, Levy (1999; 2001) argued that in systems where not all welfare programmes are progressively redistributive, the left has had occasion to eliminate regressive programmes and use the freed up revenue both to expand progressive programmes and balance the budget.

Finally, a third group of researchers turned claims about the continued salience of partisanship in the post-expansionary age on their head. Most notably, Fiona Ross (2000) argued that although partisanship has continued to be of import in recent decades, the left has been disproportionately associated with welfare state retrenchment, not expansion. For her (F. Ross 2000: 162), partisan dealignment trends have provided incentives for left-wing parties to move to the right, while their status as traditional defenders of the welfare state has given them the means to retrench more effectively than the right. This position has found support in studies such as that of Kitschelt (2001), which suggested that during fiscal and economic crises, it was the parties of the centre-right rather than the left which were the most likely to resist retrenchment and try to protect existing welfare programmes. Other authors, such as Green-Pedersen (2003), suggest that the left may in fact not even be particularly fond of broad, universalist benefits; according to this argument, the right often prefers universal welfare state programmes due to their market-conforming qualities, while the left often opts for narrow targeted benefits since they are more redistributive.

In light of the conflicting evidence and claims, one may well wonder how so much variation in results is possible. The most obvious answer is that omitted variables, changes in variable specification, and – to a great extent – different measures of welfare state change (i.e. social expenditure levels versus replacement rates) lead to quite diverse findings. That so much diversity in findings is associated with even slight changes in specification should make us nervous. There are two likely explanations here, which in fact have important implications as we move forward with our own investigation: first, the diverse results may indicate that measurement error is a serious problem in many of these studies, and that as a result we need to more rigorously investigate how we can best operationalise the pertinent variables; second, the diversity in findings may be the result of heterogeneity, suggesting that there has not been a uniform cross-national process which has affected all welfare programmes equally. In order to address the potential that measurement error severely complicates research findings in this field, our statistical analysis will employ various dependent variables, approaching coverage from different angles and even using policy change itself as a dependent variable. The apparent lack of a uniform cross-national relationship between the left and welfare reform, in turn, will serve as a central theme of this book, leading us to question what it is that explains variance in partisanship's impact across different programmes and policy reforms

Irrespective of how one thinks to answer this question (cf. Pennings 1999; Kitschelt 2001; Vis 2010), it seems clear that the dispute about the effects of partisanship on welfare reform has not been resolved and that we are unlikely to discover a universal relationship between the left and welfare reform *writ large*. As a result, we must accept that the relationship is heterogeneous and complex and narrow our focus to specific types of welfare reform, particularly those that are of theoretical interest. To that end, we concentrate on reforms that deal with the dualised nature of welfare states – i.e. those that serve to extend access to benefits and, in some cases, even standardise their generosity. This is a particularly interesting research area both because of its practical implications and because it gives rise to conflicting incentives and raises interesting ideological questions for the left.

Expanding Dualism

Recent decades have witnessed a considerable dualisation of labour markets and, as a corollary, welfare programmes – developments which have led to a considerable expansion of political science literature on the topic (cf. Rueda 2007; Häusermann 2010; Emmenegger et al. 2012). In addressing these developments, we lay out what *labour market dualisation* is, indicate its broad prevalence and distribution, and highlight why it matters for the welfare state. In doing so, we will lay the groundwork for the discussion of *welfare state dualisation* that is at the core of our investigation.

Labour markets are said to be dualised insofar as they exhibit a split between a primary sector which contains better, well-paying jobs and a secondary sector which is characterised by less attractive, low-paying jobs, which are typically temporary and/or part-time in nature (Berger and Piore 1980). Much of the earlier work on this topic examined the United States within this framework, looking at the relationship between disadvantaged groups and jobs in the secondary sector, as well as the division's impact on weakening and dividing the American working class (Gordon et al. 1982). This approach has subsequently been exported and applied to a variety of cases, examining the division between labour market insiders (those with protected jobs in the primary sector) and outsiders (everyone else). The purported source of this division has seen various conceptualisations: insiders may, for example, derive their preferential position from issues such as higher labour turnover costs (Lindbeck and Snower 1988; 2001), insiders'

Figure 1.1 Outsiders as a % of Total Labour Force

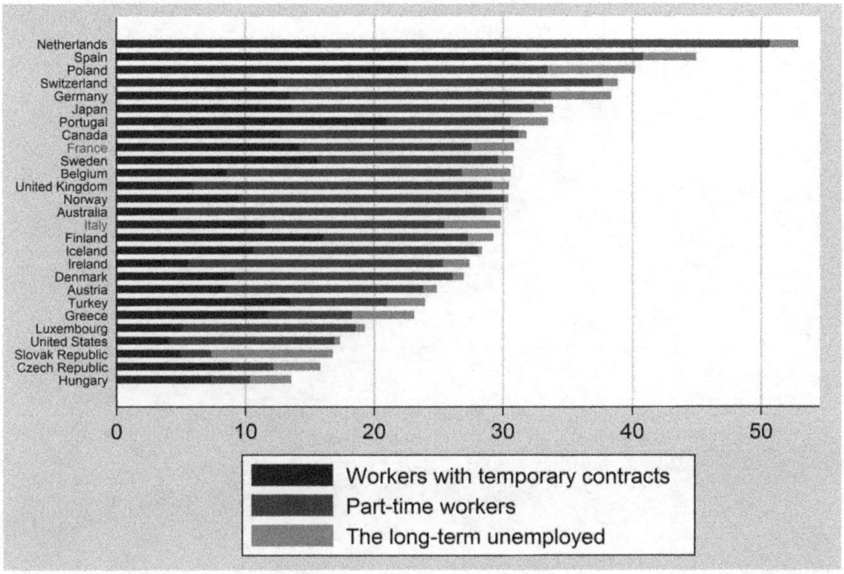

possession of firm specific skills (Solow 1985), or outsiders' lack of political representation by trade unions (Saint-Paul 1996; 1998).

Yet regardless of where one thinks this division arises from, the approach has become increasingly relevant as the prevalence of nonstandard employment relations (such as jobs which are part-time, short-term, and/or temp agency based) have increased cross-nationally in recent decades. This has occurred partly as a result of post-industrialisation in general (Kalleberg 2000), but also in an attempt to avoid strict labour laws (Mitlacher 2007). As King and Rueda (2008) point out, dualisation has been a particular problem in countries with strict labour regulations (such as those found in Continental Europe); the centrality of cheap labour in modern economies leads countries which prevent these types of jobs from developing within the primary economy to develop a large sector of non-standard employment aimed at filling this role.

The prevalence of labour market outsiders across the Organization for Economic Cooperation and Development (OECD) is demonstrated by Figure 1.1, which presents average percentages of temporary contracts, part-time work, and long-term unemployment (defined as unemployment lasting longer than a year) in the labour force over the 2000-2009 period.[1] As one notes from the graph, our two central cases, France (at 30.8%) and

1 Temporary contracts and part-time work are defined using the standard OECD definition.

Figure 1.2 Outsider Figures and Component Parts

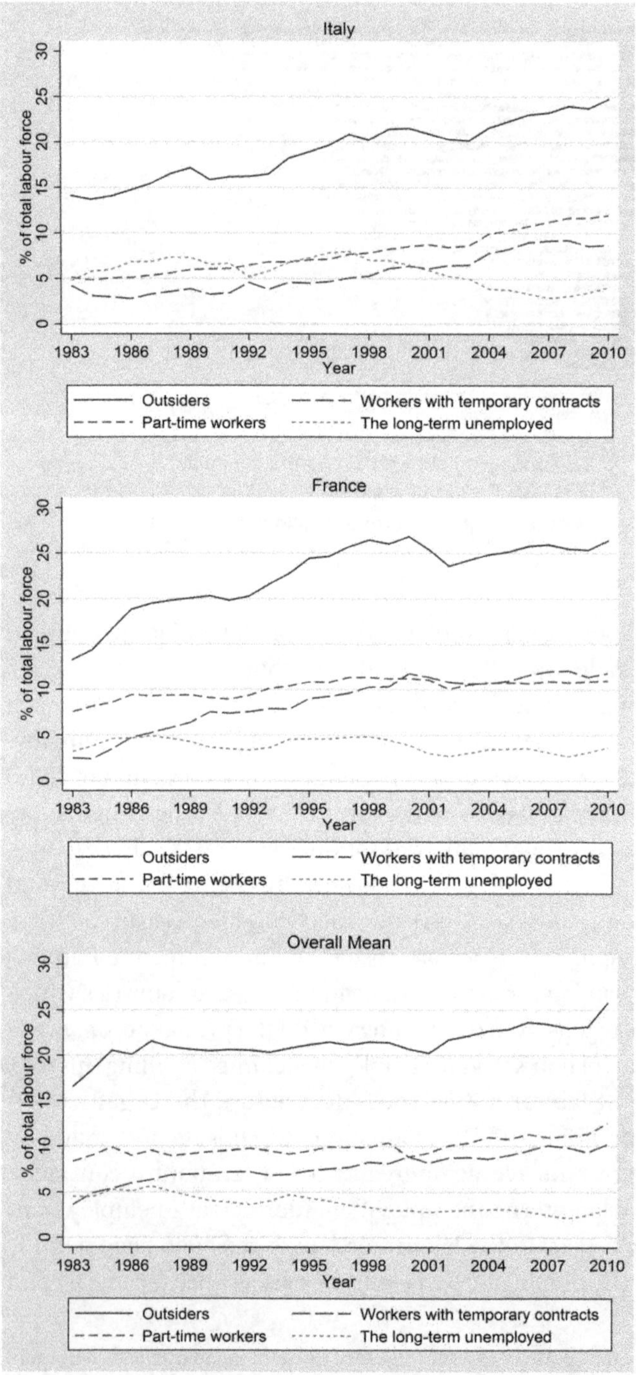

Italy (at 29.8%), are in fact quite typical – with their scores hovering around the median (29.9%) and just above the mean (29.4%).

Figure 1.2 then traces this measure of labour market outsiders (along with its component parts) as a percentage of the labour force, comparing developments over time from 1983 through to 2010; Italian and French trends are listed, alongside overall mean changes across the OECD.[2] Note that despite a general dip of long-term unemployment (defined as unemployment over twelve months), the overall number of labour market outsiders has consistently risen. As one would expect from Figure 1, Italy rounds out the period with a mean slightly below the broader average, while France's rate is slightly higher than the average. Although these numbers may only approximately track the actual number of welfare state outsiders (depending on the arrangement of welfare state programmes), they nevertheless indicate a broad pattern that is suggestive of the growing potential salience of insider/outsider divisions.[3]

It is also worth noting that these trends have not impacted all groups of workers equally, with women, youth, and immigrants making up a disproportionate percentage of labour market outsiders (Estevez-Abe 2006; Gash and McGinnity 2007; Lodovici and Semenza 2008). Furthermore, rather than serving as a stepping stone, these non-standard jobs have frequently lead workers into repeated bouts of non-standard employment (cf. Martin et al. 1999; Gash 2008; Lodovici and Semenza 2008). This is no small issue, since non-standard employment has often been associated with various negative consequences in addition to simple precarity (Booth et al. 2002; Blanchard and Landier 2002; D'Addio and Rosholm 2005).[4] Add to these factors the negative conditions associated with our other component group of labour market outsiders – the long-term unemployed – and it becomes clear that the gap between insiders and outsiders is a large one.

2 The OECD mean includes values for: Australia, Austria, Belgium, Canada, the Czech Republic, Denmark, Finland, France, Germany, Hungary, Ireland, Italy, Luxembourg, the Netherlands, Norway, Poland, Portugal, the Slovak Republic, Spain, Turkey, the United Kingdom, and the United States. Note that data for certain years are missing for some countries, however.

3 Furthermore, when examining the data on part-time workers, it is also important to note the prevalence of involuntary part-time employment: indeed, both France and Italy have considerably higher rates than the averages in the EU15 and the OECD. Italy in particular had its rates more than double in the 2000s, while France peaked in the 1990s (unfortunately pre-1993 data is missing in the French case, however).

4 Worse still, these negative effects often persist for workers who enter into this type of employment even after they gain standard employment; this is particularly problematic since these positions are prevalent among labour market entrants (Scherer 2004; Gagliarducci 2005; Bernardi and Garrido 2008).

Crucially for our purposes, this distinction between the divergent benefits accrued by labour market insiders and outsiders is (unsurprisingly) expected to lead to divergent preferences. This division is further complicated by the fact that in many instances, the benefits of insiders come at a cost to outsiders (and vice versa). It is this logic which underpins, for instance, Saint-Paul's conclusion that 'incumbent employees will favour policies that increase the exclusion of "outsiders" in order to increase their ability to bid up wages and other dimensions of their welfare associated with their insider status' (1996: 266). Similarly, active labour market policies may remain unpursued, even if costless to enact, as they would potentially allow the long-term unemployed to underbid insiders (Saint-Paul 1998; Gaston and Rajaguru 2008).

What is more, these divergent preferences go well beyond the labour market. Here it is key to note that in many instances (particularly across the corporatist welfare states of Continental Europe) the privileges associated with standard employment extend into the realm of welfare benefit provision. This is the case because occupation, employment status, and employment history (with regard to both occupation and the number of years spent in full-time standard employment) are often intricately tied up with access to welfare state programmes. As a result, even in instances where welfare state dualism is not already common, one notes two potential routes to welfare state dualisation: the first is through the increase in the number of labour market outsiders, which, without a commensurate policy change in the link between employment status and access to welfare benefits, leads to further dualisation (i.e. a greater number of welfare state outsiders); and the second, more direct route, is through welfare reform which trades the protection of benefits for welfare state insiders for increasingly poor coverage and benefits for outsiders.

The importance of benefit extension and standardisation to mitigate welfare state dualism (whether driven by economic developments or past policy choices) has thus become especially evident in recent decades. What is more, the distinction between the interests of welfare state insiders and outsiders raises the ideological dilemma for leftist actors highlighted above: in light of the circumstances, it would appear that they are forced to choose between either defending the insider privileges of many of their traditional supporters or upholding claims of broad solidarity and egalitarianism, reaching out to attract outsider support as well. Indeed, this growing division among workers gives rise to what Esping-Andersen (1999a) labelled one of the three new emerging class cleavages – that between welfare state insiders and outsiders – and it is here that the literature on dualisation and partisanship most clearly intersects.

Dualisation and the Left

At a broad level, there is evidence to suggest that social policy segmentation is intricately connected to party dynamics, with more parties and greater ideological polarisation associated with higher levels of segmentation (Picot 2012). Research focusing expressly on the left, however, has tended to concentrate on the connection between leftist parties/unions and insider/outsider preferences more generally. Looking at France, for example, Smith (2004) argues that parties of all stripes have purposefully directed resources towards insiders and that as a result, the French left (despite its own rhetoric) has been responsible for increasing inequalities between classes and generations. Rueda (2005; 2006; 2007) has made similar arguments using a cross-national approach, but with specific reference to employment policy – suggesting that Social Democratic governments have largely abandoned their commitment to egalitarianism, opting instead to represent the interests of insiders. Other evidence, however, suggests that Social Democratic parties may in fact be pursuing outsider support (Schwander 2013) or that insider and outsider preferences (at least around employment policy) may not in fact be notably different (Emmenegger 2009).

Despite this debate, at the very least it seems safe to conclude that leftist parties will likely vary in their pro-outsider orientation (see Marx 2014 for evidence of this). If we take the pursuit of outsider votes as a central element in explaining benefit extension and standardisation, the obvious next point of inquiry is why some parties pursue outsider support while others do not. Indeed, this question brings us back to our discussion about the variation in findings in the literature on partisanship and the welfare state. As we briefly suggested above (and will further discuss in the next section), electoral incentives likely explain a large part of this variation. We would therefore expect, *ceteris paribus*, that the substantial increase in the number of outsiders will impact party positions, at least past a certain tipping point (insofar as those outsider preferences conflict with those of the traditional support base). Note that since the policy has ideologically attractive characteristics (e.g. as related to solidarity and egalitarianism), the key factor here would appear to be the potential for the party to expand its vote share.

Before we proceed to discussing the opinion-policy link in more detail, however, we first turn to consider trade union preferences vis-à-vis dualisation. There are two reasons for doing so: first, work on the topic complements research on leftist parties, since trade unions are faced with similar conundrums around solidarity, egalitarianism, and the protection of insider privileges; and second, although our primary focus is on parties, trade unions will play a prominent role in our investigation thanks to their broader political role in many European countries. This latter relevance arises from the fact that, as Béland (2001) has observed (in a study on the French case), in countries where trade unions are involved in the management of social insurance schemes, these unions are accorded an 'ideological veto point' that augments their political influence. This is the case even when union membership is low. In many instances this influence finds its expression in mass protest – or at least the threat of mass protest – thus harkening back to Pizzorno's (1978) concept of 'political exchange' (i.e. the use of the political resources of labour to gain concessions from the state). Thus, while their influence can vary dramatically across time, space, and reform type (see, for example, Da Conceicao-Heldt 2008; Häusermann 2010), unions clearly have a potential role to play.

While this research suggests that trade unions can potentially have a strong influence over which social policy reforms are passed, what stances should we expect unions to take with regard to dualisation? Although union members within the standard economy are likely to favour dualism insofar as it protects their own benefit levels, many leftist unions have traditionally made 'mass-class' claims that contradict such a position. In addition, representing the interests of outsiders also offers a potential source of revitalisation for the union movement, presenting an opportunity to increase membership and, consequently, maintain broader relevance and sway.[5] As a consequence, cases in which unions reach out to precarious workers remain relatively common across Europe, with union ideology (specifically a focus on the working class) key in low-membership countries like France and Italy (Benassi and Vlandas 2016).[6]

Yet unions are faced with the additional problem of maintaining specific gains, achieved through bargaining, for their paying membership. As a result, as Palier and Thelen (2010) suggest, organised labour – generally hard-pressed to defend past gains – has in many instances been quick to ignore the needs of outsiders. What is more, trade union positions on the sorts of reforms we are interested in are shaped by strategic and institutional contexts that increasingly push them towards supporting

5 This can be thought of as akin to the vote seeking behaviour of left-wing parties.

6 Indeed, the conflict of interest between the 'old working class' and labour market outsiders creates a situation in which unions often struggle to redefine an encompassing working-class identity (see G. Ross 2000).

dualisation (Clegg et al. 2010). This is especially the case when they feel that the only alternatives are even less agreeable. Union leaders may well also feel compelled to defend the overall organisational interests of the union by defending its institutional position but acceding to otherwise problematic reforms (Davidsson and Emmenegger 2013). Yet, even where union leaders have a strong preference on a particular social policy reform, internal union democracy can lead lower-level representatives to wield considerable power in mobilising an alternative consensus (Baccaro et al. 2002). The result is a complex interplay of organisation and membership preferences, similar to the electoral incentives for left-wing parties – at least in their mass-class heyday – but with a generally more long-term focus (due to the absence of electoral competition for office).

Overall, then, we can separate past research into two broad camps: one which suggests that leftist organisations (whether parties or unions) turn in on themselves, ignoring the plight of outsiders and contributing to welfare state dualism, and another which avers that they pursue outsider support. That this general debate in the literature has been occurring underlines the extent of the problem, especially in insurance-focused systems, where generous benefits for those with standard employment biographies often exist alongside weak or non-existent coverage for those without. The pattern is visible across programme areas, ranging from unemployment benefits to pensions to healthcare (Freeman 2000; Palier and Martin 2007; Raitano 2007). While this process has occurred in all three of Esping-Andersen's (1990) worlds of welfare, it has been most acute and pervasive in on the European continent (Häusermann and Schwander 2012). Dualisation thus presents a particular challenge for the left in Continental and Southern European states.

Public Opinion and the Welfare State

Political actors do not exist in a vacuum, however, and we therefore finally need to consider the potential role of public opinion in this story.[7] While we are ultimately interested in how and when public opinion might matter for welfare state reform, the first point to note is that the relationship is clearly reciprocal: welfare states (e.g. Dallinger 2010) and their consequences (e.g. Milanovic

7 Note that although we can generally distinguish redistributive benefits (such as unemployment benefits) from life-cycle ones (such as healthcare) (e.g. Jensen 2012), the connection of healthcare coverage/benefit generosity to occupational status within the health insurance systems upon which we are focusing does suggest redistributive conflict.

2000; Lupu and Pontusson 2011) shape attitudes towards redistribution.[8] This is the case not only at the aggregate level of 'the welfare state', but also with regard to individual social policy programmes, which derive considerable continuity on the basis of their existing institutional design. As Pierson argues, the welfare state acquires its political strength from two principal sources: 'the electoral incentives associated with programmes which retain broad and deep popular support and the institutional "stickiness" which further constrains the possibilities for policy reform' (2001b, 411). Prospect theory is especially relevant here, as it suggests that, even where they are equal, losses elicit more opposition than gains elicit support (see Levy 2003). As a result, we might expect governments to avoid reforms that could be perceived as enacting broad losses on certain groups, even when public opinion supports major reorganisations of the welfare state (e.g. Boeri et al. 2001b).

At the same time, while these considerations potentially shape both opinions themselves and the attention governments give to different groups, it nonetheless leaves room for public opinion to impact policy change. First, reform is quite evidently still possible, even from an institutionalist perspective, whether through punctuated equilibrium (offering the potential for radical change) or subtler processes such as institutional drift, layering, or conversion (cf. Pempel 1998; Schickler 2001; Thelen 2003; Hacker 2004; Streeck and Thelen 2005). Second, there is a sizeable body of research suggesting that the public opinion/policy change connection is of considerable import in democracies (e.g. Erikson et al. 2002; Brooks and Manza 2007; Soroka and Wlezien 2010), even though certain groups may exert greater influence than others (cf. Downs 1957; Dahl 1961; Jacobs and Skocpol 2005; Enns and Wlezien 2011). Insofar as politicians are concerned about re-election, we should therefore expect public opinion to have at least some potential influence on social policy reforms.[9]

That leaves us with the question of what, aside from the welfare state, shapes the content of public opinion. For some, standard variables such as

8 Economic transformations also matter here, with the shift to post-industrialism arguably undermining traditional welfare state solidarity (e.g. Pierson 2001a; Taylor-Gooby 2011a).

9 Although some authors (e.g. Przeworski and Sprague 1986; Kitschelt 1994) have argued that left-wing, Western European parties in particular are policy- rather than office-seeking and are constrained by strong ties to the labour movement, we would contend that they are nevertheless still sensitive to public opinion. Especially in light of declining ties to the labour movement and a shift away from mass-class party structures, it seems reasonable to conceive of these parties as bundles of both ideological commitments and organisational incentives. This latter characteristic involves both short-term office-seeking behaviour and long-term concerns vis-à-vis the future of the organisation. While parties themselves clearly have an influence on public opinion and the way it is expressed at the ballot box (see, for example, Holian 2004; Meguid 2005), a reciprocal relationship remains.

age, income, gender, social class, and political orientation do most of the work in explaining variation (cf. Van Oorschot 2006; Bonoli and Haüsermann 2009; Busemeyer et al. 2009; Taylor-Gooby 2011b). There is also considerable evidence to suggest that the insider-outsider cleavage also matters (see Esping-Andersen 1999a; Boeri et al. 2001a). As numerous authors have argued, part-time and temporary employment (in addition to frequent bouts of unemployment) engender a sense of economic insecurity, which in turn increases support for social assistance, redistribution, and social investment (e.g. Burgoon and Dekker 2010; Schwander and Haüsermann 2013). (At the same time, however, outsiders may also be less likely to wield democratic influence than insiders [see Häusermann and Schwander 2012].[10])

In conclusion, we note that – even in the face of institutional inertia – public opinion (whether at the aggregate or group level) has the potential to shape the social policy reforms that governments enact, as parties seek office and policy influence. They do so both by appealing to voters with popular policy proposals and by attempting to attract further attention to somewhat salient issues already within their wheelhouse (see Petrocik 1996). This process plays out in a broader setting in which public opinion itself is being shaped by demographic factors, policy choices, and institutional arrangements that condition not only preferences, but also the relative influence of different groups in society. Our investigation will proceed by embedding this dynamic within a context of partisan politics and economic constraints, and welfare state dualism in order to examine attempts to extend and standardise coverage.

Methodology

As Davidsson and Naczyk (2009: 32) point out, the roles of parties in reforms that mitigate or exacerbate welfare state dualism has been comparatively understudied, as has unions' use of political influence or institutionalised

10 The potential weight of these opinions is likely compromised by some of the issues discussed above (regarding Prospect theory), particularly since political coalition building is affected by the comparative institutional advantages that welfare regimes afford certain sectors and factors of production (Manow 2001). A study of debates around unemployment in Italy by Baglioni et al. (2008) provides an excellent illustration of how this might impact outsider influence: although they find that debates around unemployment benefits arise when there are large number of unemployed persons, business and labour organisations have the loudest voices within this debate (forming a 'golden triangle' with national ministries). This is then reflected in the media, with the unemployed themselves largely absent from the discussion (Baglioni et al. 2008: 847).

roles in this regard. This book, by presenting an in-depth investigation of two cases in two policy domains and then turning to assess the generalisability of our findings, is intended to help expand our understanding of these processes. What is more, by including a specific consideration of reform itself in the quantitative analysis (as opposed to simply looking at incremental changes in outcomes), we hope to rectify a common failing in quantitative studies by more directly aligning the analysis with our qualitative research. Too often, quantitative analysis has focused on changes in spending or coverage levels that may not adequately reflect the timing or import of policy changes, which can in turn lead to an exaggeration of either continuity or change. We therefore hope to make a strong methodological point in addition to our substantive arguments about coverage extension and dualisation.

Before proceeding to an overview of the research project, however, a definitional comment should first be made, so as to clarify how the relationship between the left and insiders/outsiders will be conceptualised. In defining the distinction between insiders and outsiders we broadly follow Schwander and Häusermann's (2013) lead, treating the division between insiders and outsiders as more than a simple binary one. Instead, it is possible for an individual to be neither a full insider nor a full outsider, with three components comprising the division: labour market dualism, which 'refers to structural disadvantages of outsiders in terms of earnings possibilities, job mobility and access to training'; political integration dualism, wherein 'labor market outsiders are politically under-represented and alienated from democratic decision-making'; and social protection dualism, marked by outsiders who 'are structurally disadvantaged with regard to social right coverage and welfare benefits' (Häusermann and Schwander 2012: 30; Schwander and Häusermann 2013).

While it is this final division (i.e. welfare state dualism) that is at the core of this book, our investigation will pay close attention to the varying degrees of insider/outsider-ness that exist along different dimensions of dualism. This point is especially pertinent with regard to reforms that predate the massive rise in labour market segmentation, as it highlights the potential relevance of dualism to earlier periods. Most importantly for our purposes, this suggests that even in cases where the percentage of labour market outsiders is relatively small, we may still find a substantial divide in welfare state coverage. Moreover, this distinction makes it clear that, depending on the structure of the welfare state, even individuals not typically classified as labour market outsiders might accurately be considered welfare state outsiders.

With that in mind, we now turn to outlining the research to be carried out in this book. We will begin by delineating the questions that the study will attempt to address and presenting the potential relationships suggested by existing research. A justification of the cases selected will then be provided, after which point we present the general research strategy and methodology.

The Central Questions

The central research question which this book will attempt to answer is the following: what accounts for divergences, both within and across cases, in the approach of leftist parties to dualised welfare states (pushing for either universalisation, residualisation, or the status quo)? In other words, when, why, and how do governments, faced with economic constraints and limited protection for vulnerable populations, extend benefit access? Alongside this primary question, we also address the extent to which public opinion may have shaped government responses to growing gaps in welfare state coverage, as well as the contextual factors that have shaped those opinions.

Competing hypotheses will be listed in detail in subsequent chapters, as we deal with our different policy domains specifically, but the literature review suggests a broader framework from which we will, over the course of the book, extrapolate. Given that leftist parties have been in power in both France and Italy, yet their respective welfare state programmes have experienced different trajectories of reform, it seems clear that there is no consistent relationship between partisanship and reform vis-à-vis all dualised welfare state programmes. This observation points towards a number of potential relationships:

Scenario 1: The left may opt to maintain the backing of traditional (insider) supporters with pro-status quo preferences, leading partisanship to have a limited impact on the relevant party preferences. This decision may be based, for example, on the perceived feasibility of poaching more votes than might be lost by pursuing reform.

Scenario 2: The left may seek the support of outsiders where possible, but their preferences across countries may differ (being sometimes pro-reform, sometimes pro-status quo), with outcomes in line with those preferences. Outsider preferences might be shaped, for example, by the distribution of access to social programmes in society.

Scenario 3: The left may seek/oppose the extension and standardisation of benefits for reasons unrelated to insider/outsider cleavages – perhaps because it is of use to the leftist organisations themselves. This might be the case, for example, because leftist parties/unions prioritise the status quo to maintain political resources derived from the current institutional arrangement (or oppose it to undermine the political resources of rival parties/unions).

Scenario 4: Different relationships may dominate different policy domains. This could be the result of issues related to an issue inherent to the policy domain (e.g. is it dominated by life-cycle or redistributive characteristics?) or the specific institutional context of the relevant programme.

All of these relationships are likely conditioned by contextual factors alluded to in the broader literature, so the chapters will outline relevant theories within each of the two policy domains. In brief, we will argue that institutional factors play a key role in shaping the likelihood of benefit reform and standardisation, and that they do so by shaping partisan interests and influence. In many instances, especially with regard to benefits for the unemployed, the key factors are those that distinguish Southern European welfare states from their Continental counterparts.

As we will explore in subsequent chapters, there are two routes by which typically Southern European institutional characteristics might matter. First, they may have a *direct* impact on leftist parties and organisations, shaping their preference for either reform or the status quo, regardless of popular opinion (i.e. institutions → leftist reform proposals). In cases where the left is pro-reform, we would then expect benefit extension (and possibly standardisation) to come about once windows for change arise. Second, the impact of institutional factors may be *indirect:* rather than influencing leftist organisations directly, they may help to shape public opinion, which in turn has the potential to influence the reform proposals that leftist parties support and put forward. This mechanism (i.e. institutions → public opinion → leftist reform proposals) may play out at the level of aggregate public opinion and/or at the level of groups in society which might potentially press for reform. As we will discuss below, while this public pressure is enough to push the left towards forwarding reform proposals, the specific content of the reform pursued will depend on organisational incentives (e.g. the power resources that the left derives from a corporatist social programme). Taken together, these factors help us to understand when, why, and how governments extend benefit access in the age of austerity.[11]

11 Absent these pro-reform influences, external pressures for benefit extension are required – but in these cases both the implementation and the long-term prospects of the change are seriously at risk.

The Central Cases

In investigating the processes at work and attempting to answer our research questions, the study will focus half of its attention upon two cases: France and Italy. Both countries will be examined in the context of broad economic constraints on welfare state expansion and an increasingly dualised system (both due to changes in the economy and policy choices). The selection of these countries is based both upon: (a) certain institutional similarities that posed a challenge to the existent system; and (b) the cross-country and cross-domain differences in outcomes as the countries dealt (or failed to deal) with these challenges.

Turning first to similarities between the cases, both countries are classified by Esping-Andersen, originator of the dominant typological welfare state framework, to be central cases of the Corporatist-Statist welfare type (1990; 1999b). These welfare states are marked by their attempt to preserve rather than overcome status differentials tied up with, for example, class and gender differences; this leads them to be interventionist (except regarding family services) yet not particularly redistributive (Esping-Andersen 1990: 27). At the same time, both France and Italy may be considered atypical Continental welfare states, and both countries consolidated their welfare states considerably later than their neighbours (Schmidt 2000: 269).

Despite these similarities, the French and Italian welfare states are quite obviously not functional equivalents. Indeed, there are numerous other scholars who would place Italy into an alternate, Southern European world of welfare, which is in some ways characterised as an extreme version of the Corporatist-Statist model (Ferrera 1996b; 2000; Martin 1996; Rhodes 1996; Naldini 2003). The main characteristics of this Southern welfare type include (as delineated by Ferrera):

1. The peculiar 'excesses' in income maintenance: peaks of generosity accompanied by vast gaps of protection.
2. The departure from institutional corporatism in the field of healthcare and the (partial) establishment of national health services, based on universalistic principles.
3. The low degree of state penetration of the welfare sphere, in a broad sense, and the peculiar mix between public and non-public actors and institutions.
4. The persistence of clientelism and the formation – in some cases – of fairly elaborate 'patronage systems' for the selective distribution of cash subsidies. (1996b: 29-30)

In keeping with this broader picture, Italy is indeed much more fragmented and clientelistic in its service provision than France, with a strikingly large proportion of social spending directed towards pensions over other services, and is generally much more traditional – placing a high emphasis on traditional family structure and gender roles (Schmidt 2000: 269).

Yet crucially for our purposes, the countries do share two key traits: a historically insurance-based focus that has resulted in benefit rationing via occupational and contribution-based controls on access to benefits (whether within the unemployment insurance or social health insurance systems); and a broad, historical unavailability of universal benefits for those who lack access to the main system – with residual benefits traditionally both means-tested *and* categorical, thereby requiring recipients to belong to a protected category of individuals (e.g. the disabled). As a result, in-built welfare state dualism became increasingly exaggerated as the number of labour market outsiders began to expand in the 1970s. This division was then further reinforced by the protection of insiders via labour market protection not extended to outsiders.

Table 1.2 Outcomes across the Core Cases

	Benefits for the Unemployed	Healthcare
France	Two-tier system (evolutionary change)	Two-tier system (evolutionary change)
Italy	Status quo (no change)	Universal system (revolutionary change)

Not only were France and Italy relatively late to address these problems (to the extent that they have addressed them at all), but as was previously mentioned, they also employed divergent approaches (see Table 1.2). France ultimately pursued a process of residualisation in both policy domains, extending access to benefits for the unemployed (via the Revenu Minimum d'Insertion) and healthcare (via the Couverture Maladie Universelle). Italy, by contrast, failed to institute a comparable, nationally available benefit for the unemployed, while in healthcare it instituted revolutionary reform, replacing the social health insurance system with a universal one (the Servizio Sanitario Nazionale).

While the relevance of the dualism to benefits for the unemployed is clear, it is worth pausing for a moment to consider the value of the concept to discussions of healthcare. First, we note that healthcare has been a comparatively neglected domain within studies of dualisation. On the one hand, it is true that other, non-labour market-related factors – most notably age and illness – complicate the insider-outsider divide on healthcare access by affecting levels of concern about health benefits. Yet, as our investigation will demonstrate, there are nevertheless important welfare state insider-outsider divisions that have both health-status and monetary (via co-payments, lack of coverage, etc.) implications. Second, there is the question of timing, related specifically to our two healthcare cases: given that our reforms of interest started in 1978 and spanned several decades, it is clear that the context in which these programmes were introduced varies considerably over time. While the Italian healthcare reform was undoubtedly influenced by more straightforward class politics, the focus on austerity in the late 1970s and the debates around access across insiders and outsiders, as we shall see, in fact give the comparison considerable force.

The book will therefore explore, given certain similar problems, what led the two countries down different paths and, in the case of Italy, how we can understand different approaches across different domains. Lessons drawn from these case studies will then be tested on a broader sample of countries to explore whether and to what extent the conclusions drawn can be extended to other countries. We also employ a series of investigative case studies on six additional Continental and Southern European cases in order to better situate France and Italy within their welfare state and healthcare families. In doing so, we are able to further assess the extent to which our core cases are deviant, typical, or simply different.

The Approach

In carrying out this research, we employ a mixed-methods approach. For our qualitative analysis, we combine research from secondary sources, archival research, and elite interviews.[12] For our quantitative analysis, we utilise survey analysis (in both country-specific and multi-level model form), time-series analysis, and duration analysis.

The remainder of the book proceeds as follows. Chapter 2 will compare developments in France and Italy vis-à-vis benefits for the unemployed, using the French case as a foil for the Italian. In particular, it will contrast the residualisation of the French system, particularly via the 1988 Revenu Minimum d'Insertion, with the failed attempt at residualisation in Italy through the 1998 Reddito Minimo di Inserimento. The chapter highlights

12 The Appendix contains further details on how I obtained, conducted, and made use of the interviews.

the impact of certain Southern European characteristics on popular demand for benefit extension: namely, the prevalence of informal work, limited administrative capacity, and the central role of the family unit. Chapter 3 then examines how well the French and Italian cases reflect developments in other countries, using illustrative case studies from other Continental (viz. Belgium, Austria, and Germany) and Southern European welfare states (viz. Portugal, Spain, and Greece) on the introduction of broadly available social assistance. It then explores public opinion in Continental and Southern Europe, both in our two central cases and the others. Chapter 4 then builds on the findings of the previous chapter by investigating the determinants of attitudinal variation alongside the factors driving changes in outcomes in European and other OECD countries. This latter analysis is carried out first through examining changes in coverage levels over time (using time-series analysis), then through examining policy change directly (using duration analysis). Together with the results from the previous chapter, the findings serve as support for both the conclusions of Chapter 2 and the broader argument about the importance of properly defining the dependent variable in quantitative studies that seek to assess policy changes.

Chapter 5 then shifts our focus into the healthcare domain, again comparing the French and Italian cases. The analysis will centre upon the contrast between the transformative universalisation of the Italian system (with the 1978 Servizio Sanitario Nazionale) and the residualisation of the French system (with the 1999 Couverture Maladie Universelle), drawing out contrasts with the developments highlighted in Chapter 2. The chapter argues that the direct impact of institutions on party preferences is key to this divergence, here again noting the importance of defining institutional features of Southern European welfare states. Chapter 6 serves as a first step in examining the generalisability of the findings on healthcare, beginning with an investigation into developments across our other European case studies and then proceeding to a discussion of public opinion across our cases. Chapter 7 then broadens this analysis, expanding the list of countries under investigation and incorporating outcomes into the analysis. This begins with an analysis of public opinion and then turns to examine what shapes changes in healthcare coverage levels, exploring the factors influencing the likelihood of universalising reforms being introduced. This investigation provides support for the findings from the case studies: social health insurance systems and structural constraints are seen to have a notable impact. Chapter 8 will then draw out a series of conclusions from the findings as a whole, comparing the results of the analysis in the two policy domains in order to hypothesise about potential explanations for the contrasts. The book then concludes by stressing the implications of these findings for the possibility of rectifying coverage gaps in Europe today.

In accordance with the research questions laid out above, this investigation will be couched within a consideration of institutional factors that directly shape government responses (and thus, potentially, the role of partisanship) and/or shape them through an impact on public opinion. To preview our conclusions, we will ultimately argue that certain institutional arrangements (typically those associated with Southern European states) have had a considerable impact on the left's relationship to welfare state dualism. While public opinion helps to explain whether or not reform occurs at all (through the shaping of electoral incentives for parties to adopt pro-reform stances), institutionally derived party preferences appear to impact the type of reform pursued (through creating organisational incentives that are either pro- or anti-status quo).

Conclusion

This chapter has presented a framework for the remainder of this book, which will examine when and how partisanship matters with regard to the extension and possible standardisation of benefit access in dualised welfare states. In laying out this outline, the chapter began by drawing out lessons from the existing literature, focusing upon the scholarship on partisanship and the welfare state, labour market dualisation, and welfare state dualisation and the left. It then proceeded to present the research questions to be explored in the proposed study, as well as a justification for the use of France and Italy as our central comparative case studies. The chapter then concluded by outlining the structure of the book.

Overall, this research project aims to fill a gap in the literatures on dualisation, partisanship, and the welfare state by examining the relationship between public opinion, the left, and the extension of welfare coverage. It will do so by comparing two infrequently compared welfare state programmes and employing a more nuanced approach to combining qualitative and quantitative evidence than is typically used. In the latter instance, the goal will be to assess the likelihood of reform itself rather than the potential outcomes associated with policy change. In light of increased dualisation and the growing number of welfare state outsiders, particularly in Continental and Southern Europe, it is hoped that this research will provide some insight into an on-going political process which continues to affect the benefits available to millions of individuals in these countries.

2 A Tale of Two RMIs[1]

Unemployment benefits can be broadly divided into three categories: unemployment insurance, operating as a sort of insurance fund for workers who pay into them; unemployment assistance, which targets benefits towards certain groups that have exhausted their access to unemployment insurance; and social assistance, in which benefits are generally available for those who pass a means test, making them available to unemployed persons who lack access to other funds.[2] The difference between the first and the latter two programmes is best conceived of as a distinction between insurance and assistance, with unemployment insurance entailing horizontal redistribution (i.e. between different stages of an individual's life) and unemployment and social assistance involving vertical redistribution (i.e. between richer and poorer individuals) (Palier 2002: 11). Due to the nature of these benefits, financial stresses and the growing number of atypical employees (a group which is typically unable to qualify for unemployment insurance) over the past several decades have led to decreasing proportions of the unemployed being covered by the principal unemployment benefit scheme. As a result, the existence of a non-categorical social assistance benefit in particular has become increasingly essential in preventing large swaths of unemployed persons from falling through gaps in protection – though of course the benefit's wider availability is compensated by lower benefit levels when compared to unemployment insurance.

This process has been particularly acute in Continental and Southern Europe, where the insurance principle has historically occupied a central role across welfare state institutions. The extent to which these countries have largely corrected for declining unemployment insurance coverage rates, however, has varied dramatically. Exploring this process of coverage extension via social assistance, this chapter will contrast the French and Italian experiences surrounding the introduction of a national minimum income scheme, which is best conceived of as a benefit of last resort, designed

1 An adapted version of portions of the analysis presented here and in Chapter 3 has also been published at the *Journal of European Social Policy* (Kevins 2015).

2 Here we are interested only in non-categorical social assistance programmes, so we exclude discussion of social assistance benefits that are directed only at a specific subset of individuals who would otherwise pass the means test (e.g. benefits solely for poor elderly people). Of course this sets aside the fact that all benefits are, in a certain sense, categorically defined (e.g. by requiring citizenship or residency), but this does not undercut the basic contrast to which we would draw attention.

to combat poverty and target all unemployed persons rather than simply those who had made adequate unemployment insurance contributions. This analysis will be carried out in an attempt to explore why large gaps in coverage have been filled in some countries but persist in others. Focusing on a paired comparison in this way allows us to explore the factors at work behind a residualist (as opposed to universalist)[3] approach to dealing with welfare state outsiders under conditions of broad fiscal constraints.

While the two systems clearly have their differences, the reform trajectories of these countries are such that the French case provides an excellent foil to the Italian. Both countries started out with relatively similar, heavily insurance-centred systems in the post-Second World War period, which then suffered from fairly similar crises; both were relative outliers in their lack of a minimum income scheme late into the twentieth century. In France, the country's late development of broadly available social assistance placed the system more in line with Southern European welfare states than other Continental ones (Paugam 1993: 23). Although successive French governments initially dealt with coverage issues through ad hoc extension to certain categories of unprotected groups, they were eventually able to move past that stage – particularly with the 1988 introduction of a general minimum income scheme (the Revenu Minimum d'Insertion [RMI]). Italy, on the other hand, experimented with a comparable scheme ten years after the French (the similarly named Reddito Minimo di Inserimento [RMI]), but eliminated it entirely within a few years. The end result is an Italian system with comparatively low coverage, as well as the vast discrepancies in benefit generosity that entails (with an 80% replacement rate for some, via the Cassa integrazione guadagni straordinaria, and 0% for many others).

The question to be addressed in this chapter is thus how one can explain the contrasting fates of these attempts at residualisation via minimum income schemes (henceforth referred to by their shared RMI acronym). In exploring the issue, we test three potential explanations: the first two positing a direct relationship between partisanship and benefit extension, and a third focusing on outsider preferences vis-à-vis extension (as shaped by certain broader factors). By taking this tack, we explore the relationships between political actors, public opinion, and institutional factors in the hopes of ultimately uncovering the determinants of coverage extension across policy domains. Attitudes of outsiders – divided into Schwander

3 The former approach entails creating a residual system to extend access to benefits (though they are less generous than those in the primary system), while the latter extends access to the primary system.

and Häusermann's categories of labour market, political, and welfare state outsiders (as laid out in Chapter 1) – will be a recurring theme in the analysis (2012; 2013). Ultimately, our findings will be formulated using a combination of secondary sources, insights derived from interviews with party and union officials, and survey analysis.

In approaching this issue, we will first briefly situate the cases within their broader histories, in the process justifying their comparison. The three aforementioned theories that might give us insights into the extension (or lack thereof) of coverage in the cases will then be presented and subsequently used as a framework for the rest of our examination. As a test of partisanship-based theories of change, we will then proceed to analyse the political factors surrounding the development of the RMI in France and Italy, which will be followed by a consideration of the potentially relevant structural factors that may help account for the varying outcomes. The chapter will then briefly conclude with a summary.

To preview our conclusions, it will be argued that the different trajectories in France and Italy do not appear to reflect any consistent relationship between partisanship and benefit extension, in contrast to other work examining the pro-insider/outsider stances of parties and unions. Rather, we submit that the divergent outcomes in the cases are the consequences of contrasting levels of public pressure, with the relevant public preferences shaped by contextual factors – all of which ultimately shapes party preferences as they respond to electoral incentives. Using Ferrera's (2005) work on social assistance in Southern European welfare states as our framework, a case will be made for the importance of three factors in particular: namely, the prevalence of informal work in the Italian labour market, limited administrative capacity, and the centrality of the family in the Italian welfare state. The analysis presented below will suggest that these three Southern European traits can help us understand why Italy has been unable to follow in France's footsteps, more than two decades after France introduced universally available unemployment benefits.

Contextualising the Cases

This section will briefly provide some historical context for the French and Italian cases, in the process laying out some of the relevant similarities and differences in their reform trajectories. In broad strokes, both countries can be considered somewhat atypical corporatist states – though Italy's system is much more fragmented, traditional (particularly regarding gender roles and the family), and clientelistic, leading many to categorise it as specifically Southern European (cf. Ferrera 1996b; 2000; Martin 1996; Rhodes 1996; Naldini 2003). Yet the countries do share two particular traits that are central for our broader purposes: an insurance-centred focus that has led to a certain degree of rationing through occupational and contribution-based controls on who has access to benefits; and a general, historical inadequacy of social assistance benefits (with actual programmes both means-tested and categorical, requiring recipients to belong to a protected category of individuals (e.g. the disabled), thereby failing to fill in most of the gaps in the unemployment insurance system.[4]

The defects of this incomplete system became increasingly accentuated over time, as the rapid rise in unemployment following the oil crises of the 1970s brought the unemployment insurance funds under increasing pressure; this in turn often resulted in more restrictive eligibility requirements. What is more, changes in the international economic climate pushed the countries towards easing their labour market regulations, resulting in an increased number of workers in atypical employment (and therefore outside of the sphere of unemployment insurance coverage). As such, a growing number of workers were unable to qualify for benefits when they lost their jobs, creating a pressing need to reform a system ill-designed for the new realities of unemployment.

France

In the French case, these developments resulted in a growing crisis of legitimacy for the system, particularly as structural unemployment became a serious issue. Once the long-term unemployed became an identifiable group, one of the underlying principles of the unemployment insurance system – that the risk of unemployment is randomly distributed across society – became increasingly difficult to defend, as some excluded groups were in fact much more at risk than groups that had access to benefits (Béland and Hansen 2000: 54). The rise of atypical employment, in turn, further complicated the issue, given the occupational restrictions associated with accessing unemployment insurance.

Yet substantial developments in assistance benefits to offset this process would not begin in earnest until after the centre-left came to power in 1981 under Mitterrand's Socialist Party (PS) and subsequently abandoned

4 While some local-level minimum income schemes have long been in existence, their presence is far from ubiquitous and the benefits are quite variable in their generosity.

Keynesianism in 1983. The hope here was that welfare expansion would serve to maintain social harmony during a period of austerity and economic upheaval (Vail 2010: 148). While this initially involved the creation of a few new targeted state-financed benefits (i.e. the Allocation Spécifique de Solidarité and the Allocation d'Insertion),[5] the 1988 RMI marked a substantive shift from the old approach towards social assistance benefits (Paugam 1993: 105).

The introduction of the RMI significantly increased coverage, with huge sums of state funds directed at providing a minimum income to non-students over 25 (so long as they were willing to enter training or be placed in a job); benefit receipt was supposed to be tied up with *insertion* measures at the local level – but this aspect of the programme was more nominal than real, with the principle primarily serving to justify the introduction of the programme (Clegg 2011: 37). Although the RMI can in some respects be seen as a continuation of policies such as the Allocation d'Insertion, the former was nevertheless innovative in its near universality and its explicit construction as a right, as demonstrated by the first article of the law introducing it: 'any person who, as a result of their age, their physical or mental condition, or their economic and employment situation, finds themself unable to work has the right to obtain reasonable means of subsistence from society' (Lafore 2008: 122; France 1988]).[6] As Barbier and Théret note, unemployment under this new characterisation was not simply a risk, but also a potential status, entitling one to access benefits unrelated to insurance contributions (2001: 156). The result of these developments has been an expansion of the social safety net in France, 'stemming the rise of inequality and poverty through policies that compensate for trends unfolding in the market [...] guarantee[ing] that nobody can be left without any support' (Palier and Thelen 2010: 138-139).

Italy

Italy, by contrast, has long suffered from a general failure to implement broadly available unemployment assistance and social assistance style benefits. Although the 1947 constitution of the newly formed republic made social assistance a right, thereby calling for a shift of the burden for these

5 While the former was directed at the long-term unemployed whose unemployment insurance benefits had expired, the latter was for those transitioning into the labour market (e.g. single mothers, new refugees, etc.).

6 All translations, here and below, are my own.

programmes from private charities to the state, little headway was made. Indeed, there has been a longstanding general and persistent lack of clarity and division between the use of insurance principles and a system of welfare based on rights (Negri and Saraceno 1996: 34-35). As a result, the process of constructing the Italian welfare state was largely occupation-based, with benefits slowly expanded to various groups of workers (Paci 1987: 277).

On a more practical level, the inability of Italian unemployment insurance to respond to the crisis was arguably even more pronounced than in France, since even unemployment insurance programmes received relatively little public funding in Italy up until the early 1980s. The 'ordinary' unemployment insurance benefit (Disoccupazione ordinaria) had strict eligibility requirements and extremely low compensation rates. Generous replacement rates, by contrast, were available under special circumstances – namely for partial or total working time reductions without dismissals (i.e. layoffs) – via the Earnings Integration Funds (Cassa integrazione guadagni ordinaria and Cassa integrazione guadagni straordinaria, together referred to as CIG benefits below). Yet these 'wage compensation' benefits were only available to a limited number of workers, primarily those in highly unionized sectors such as medium- and large-sized industrial firms (since the social partners had to negotiate to have the benefit applied) (Jessoula and Vesan 2011: 143).

Broader attempts to correct for coverage gaps have been lacking, and the one national attempt to deal with the issue, via the Prodi government's 1998 RMI experiment in pre-designated municipalities, was eliminated by the subsequent Berlusconi government. Thus, significant long-term developments in the realm of unemployment benefits in Italy over the last several decades have been rather limited, involving: the introduction of the unemployment insurance with reduced eligibility benefit; the creation of the mobility allowance (*indennità di mobilità*); and gradual increases to the 'ordinary' unemployment benefit. This lack of advancement contrasts starkly with the fact that governments since the late 1980s have been placing reform of the unemployment benefit system on their agendas (Lodovici and Semenza 2008: 171). This failure to enact more substantial reforms is, in turn, reflected in Italy's abysmal record of using transfers to reduce poverty (cf. Baldini et al. 2002: 62; Fargion 2003: 336).

Explaining Benefit Reform

In general, research on the determinants of minimum income scheme introduction within this context of broader retrenchment has been limited, leaving us with few theories that might be applied in an attempt to understand our cases. There are good reasons to doubt that the literature on welfare state expansion more generally would be applicable during recent decades, as the circumstances surrounding welfare state policy decisions have shifted dramatically since the expansionary period; the result, according to some authors, is the rise of a 'New Politics' in which left-wing governments are no longer associated with safe-guarding and expanding the welfare state (cf. Pierson 1996; Scharpf 2000; Burgoon 2001; Castles 2004). Regardless of whether one accepts the New Politics hypothesis, welfare state extension since the 1980s seems self-evidently more zero-sum than in the immediate post-war decades, giving us good reason to expect that the dynamics have changed. Nevertheless, we may reasonably construct three potential explanations (the first two of which are mirror images of one another) using recent related research, thereby providing an initial framework with which to work. Note that this approach will also allow us to assess the capacity of these theories to help us understand the divergent outcomes in our cases.

Theory 1: Anti-Outsider Left

The first theory relates to the role of leftist parties and unions, as they attempt to court and/or maintain 'working class' voter support that crosses the welfare state insider-outsider divide (with the groups respectively composed of workers who either have or lack access to the protections gained through standard, permanent employment). Under what we call the *Anti-Outsider Left* theory, it is posited that centre-left organisations since the 1970s have abandoned their commitment to egalitarianism, opting (under conditions of fiscal restraint) to protect insiders instead of extending benefits. Leftist parties – rather than risking the ire of their traditional, well-protected supporters – are expected to hunker down and insulate these workers at the expense of those outside of the traditional labour market (Rueda 2005; 2006; 2007). Relatedly, unions are expected to accede to reforms that increase dualisation as a result of the power they derive from social insurance and/or the preferences of their (insider) membership (Clegg et al. 2010; Palier and Thelen 2010; Davidsson and Emmenegger 2013). The implication here is that since debates around unemployment, for example, are dominated by business and labour organisations, only labour market insiders will have their voices represented in the discussion (Baglioni et al. 2008).

While this theory has generally been applied to labour market policies, the logic of the arguments can reasonably be expected to extend to welfare state coverage as well. Within this framework, we would expect a consistent negative relationship between leftist government and benefit extension (at least over the past several decades, given fiscal constraints); right-wing parties, by contrast, may pursue policies designed to attract outsider voters, since doing so does not compromise their traditional voting bloc – and it might, in fact, facilitate concomitant cuts to other benefits. Alternatively, the right may also ignore welfare state outsiders, particularly where these outsiders are also disenfranchised politically. Although this theory has no direct implications at the level of individual preferences, it is assumed that welfare state outsiders are pro-reform, but that leftist parties are simply unable or unwilling to incorporate these preferences into their political positions.

Theory 2: Egalitarian Left

Conversely, the *Egalitarian Left* theory predicts the exact opposite relationship between leftist parties and benefit extension. Despite the research arguing that recent decades have been defined by a 'New Politics' of the welfare state, some authors maintain that partisanship retains an important, egalitarian influence on welfare policy. Rather than turning in upon themselves, leftist parties may view the increased exposure to risk felt by citizens in modern economies as an opportunity to expand support – thereby leading them to continue to pursue welfare expansion (Garrett 1998: 1). Indeed, there is some evidence to suggest that social democratic parties are specifically pursuing this option vis-à-vis labour market outsiders (Schwander 2013). The growing number of atypical workers and the long-term unemployed may therefore push leftist parties to pursue benefit expansion in order to shore up their electoral support.

This view also finds support in work looking at both benefit generosity and cuts in social insurance (cf. Allan and Scruggs 2004; Korpi and Palme 2003), though neither instance deals directly with benefit extension. It is of course possible that leftist parties protect existing benefit generosity and social insurance through a commitment to avoiding broader benefit extension, so the applicability of this theory must of course be investigated. The predicted action of this Egalitarian Left also depends on the preferences of outsiders, as they may or may not be supportive of expansion to outsiders at the cost of reduction of insider benefits (see discussion of Emmenegger 2009 below). Nevertheless, this theory provides for the possibility that, under circumstances where welfare state outsiders are supportive of extension, leftist parties will pursue that route.

Theory 3: Southern European Exceptionalism

The final theory, rather than pointing to the role of leftist actors, suggests that institutional factors unique to Southern European welfare states may be central to our story. This is particularly plausible since a lack of social assistance is presented as one of the characteristic features of the Southern European welfare model (Ferrera 1996b: 20). This body of literature on the Southern European model, which was developed as a response to Esping-Andersen's tripartite typological model (1990) that described Italy as having a Continental welfare state along the lines of Germany's, provides the basis for the theory of *Southern European Exceptionalism*. In particular, three factors are highlighted by Ferrera in his discussion of the delay and/or lack of development of assistance benefits in Southern European welfare states: the size of the informal economy, which may complicate benefit extension while simultaneously decreasing the perceived need for it; administrative difficulties, such as weak state capacity and clientelism, which may prevent social assistance programmes from being implemented for technical reasons and/or by fomenting public scepticism about the viability of such a programme; and the increased role of the family, with youth remaining at home much later than in other countries, which may decrease demand from young/female welfare state outsiders as well as the perceived need for reform more generally (2005: 8-10).

Implicit in this theory is the argument that the overlap between welfare state insider and outsider interests may be greater than that predicted by the Anti-Outsider Left hypothesis, such that the outsiders (under certain circumstances) may actually support policies that protect insiders. In work on labour market policies, Emmenegger argues that these preferences may result from the presence of an insider family member, expectations about future insider status, and/or ideas about the larger balance of power between capital and labour (2009: 132). Note that under this theory, left-wing parties may or may not be courting outsider voters; but even though leftist parties may be protecting the status quo, outsiders might actually be generally supportive of this move. The key point here is that we incorporate the impact of different welfare state structures on the extent to which we witness this particular partisanship mechanism – namely, that Southern European countries have been disproportionately affected by this phenomenon.

Note that while Theories 1 and 2 (which could be grouped together as the *Partisanship Matters* theories) are mutually exclusive, either is compatible with Theory 3, as it may be the case that leftist/rightist parties are concerned with welfare state outsider preferences, but that these preferences vary according to other factors. As such, while the Anti-Outsider Left predicts that the left will be unconcerned with benefit extension (but that the right may be), the Egalitarian Left theory may lead to the left to reform in circumstances where the outsiders are supportive of change. The Southern European Exceptionalism theory, in turn, highlights circumstances that lead welfare state outsiders to support or oppose reform of insider-centric systems.

With these three theories providing the framework for our analysis, let us now proceed to assess the ability of these theories to explain why France and Italy have reformed (or failed to reform) their systems in such contrasting ways. We begin by considering the potential role of partisanship in the divergent outcomes.

Politics and the RMIs

Given the central role of partisanship in the Anti-Outsider Left and Egalitarian Left theories, our first task must be to lay out the political motivations behind the creation of the French and Italian RMI programmes as a sort of preliminary test. The introduction of the respective RMI programmes was an important moment in both countries, though for contrasting reasons: in France it was a turning point, with the benefit significantly extending coverage to previously excluded groups through its near universality and marking the construction of unemployment benefits as a right rather than a privilege associated with having made adequate contributions; in Italy it was a missed opportunity for reform, the closest the country came to dramatically increasing coverage rates and providing unemployment benefits along universalistic (rather than categorical) means-tested lines. France then continued further down its path, while Italy returned to its previous relative stasis. So in what context were these two programmes adopted?

In France, public concern regarding *les exclus* – that is, unemployed individuals whose reintegration into the labour market and participation in society have been compromised by poverty and other barriers – made unemployment benefit reform a far more salient issue. Conceptions of egalitarianism in France during the 1970s gradually shifted away from a concern with equality of benefits and towards a simple correction of what would otherwise be vast inequalities in access to benefits (Bec 1995: 138). Here one notes the playing out of tensions between republican citizenship ideals (pushing towards equality) and the existing Bismarckian system (with its social segmentation and labour market focus) – but under increasingly constraining economic circumstances. With rising unemployment a serious problem by the 1980s, integration of *les exclus* had become a major issue in public debate as both the left and right criticised the government over increasing unemployment and the rise of the 'new poor' (Paugam 1993: 66; Béland and Hansen 2000: 55). In particular, youth and immigrant unemployment/integration increasingly became a central fixture of the debate as young people and *banlieusards* partook in a series of demonstrations against various reforms (Silver 1994: 533-534). The growing unemployment crisis, in turn, was exacerbated by high long-term unemployment rates; with an unemployment rate of 9.3% by 1988 (when the RMI programme was created), 46.2% of unemployed persons had been out of work for over a year (up from 7.7% and 41.3%, respectively, five years earlier) (OECD 2012c). Atypical work was also becoming increasingly common, with 11.9% of workers in part-time employment and 7.8% in temporary employment during the same period (up from 1983 rates of 9.6% and 3.3%, respectively) (OECD 2012c).

Initial attempts to deal with the crisis had involved use of special employment measures to combat social exclusion, but by the mid-1980s the shortfalls of this approach were becoming apparent, particularly with regard to its decentralized nature and concomitant reliance on local funds and resources (Clegg 2010: 91). Support then began to shift towards the introduction of a general minimum income scheme, albeit with some tentativeness, even on the left (Belorgey 1988: 105-106). It was in this context that Mitterrand's 1988 campaign promise to introduce a minimum income scheme to protect 'those that our society has abandoned to the throes of unemployment' came about (Mitterrand 1988 [my translation]). Popular concern about the issue was clearly substantial enough for Mitterrand to attempt to use the issue to try to tap into traditional Parti Communiste Français (PCF) voters (PCF vote loss had been proceeding quite rapidly by that point) and mobilise the left-wing of the electorate (in line with the Egalitarian Left hypothesis); he then carried through with the promise following his re-election (Clegg 2010: 91).[7]

The importance of the RMI was highlighted at a PS Executive Committee meeting a few months after the election, with then Prime Minister Michel Rocard declaring its creation one the 'three matters of urgency' facing the government (Parti Socialiste 1988). At the same time, however, the RMI was

7 The importance of the RMI in the PS platform was highlighted at an Executive Committee meeting a few months after the election, with then prime minister Michel Rocard declaring its creation one the 'three matters of urgency' facing the government (Parti Socialiste 1988).

evidently popular enough for it to pass quasi-unanimously in the National Assembly (albeit with the assistance of the reform's vagueness (Palier 2004a: 118-119)) and to prevent subsequent governments on the centre-right from eliminating it (although it has been retooled in numerous ways, most notably with its replacement by the Revenu de solidarité active (RSA)). Unions have broadly acquiesced, as Clegg (2012) argues, largely to the defensive role they have had to play in trying to maintain *paritarisme:* partly through not making too much of a fuss; and partly by stressing their central focus on benefits based on employee contributions.

Yet these developments have not been welcomed by everyone, with the PCF and leftist unions in particular expressing concern over residualisation. At the Confédération générale du travail (CGT), for example, a former national secretary asserted that the RMI constituted a 'deformation of the social protection system', arguing instead for an alternative route to coverage extension via 'a system that guarantees an individual's right to integration through employment' (Le Duigou 2012). Similar arguments were prevalent at the PCF, with the editor-in-chief of the PCF's *La Revue Économie et Politique*, stating that 'the RMI was the worst solution to a real problem [...] but a good solution for as long as there are no others' (Rauch 2012).[8] Note that these perspectives do not suggest a necessarily pro-insider or pro-status quo position, but they do rely on the feasibility of enacting the desired broader labour market reforms in order to avoid the exclusion of outsiders. Yet irrespective of these reservations on the left, the RMI has continued to maintain the bulk of the bipartisan support that has existed since its implementation. This raises questions about any kind of straightforward relationship between partisanship and reform more generally, as implied by the Anti-Outsider Left and Egalitarian Left theories.

The Italian RMI, on the other hand, came about in the context of a similar unemployment crisis, but the political motivations varied greatly from those in France. By 1998 (when an RMI programme would finally be developed) unemployment was even more of an issue than it had been in France, with both a higher unemployment rate (at 11.9%, up from 10.2% five years earlier) and more long-term unemployment (at 59.6%, up from 57.7% five years earlier); the seriousness of these problems was not a new development either, with these figures having historically surpassed their French counterparts for decades (OECD 2012c). Similarly, atypical employment was also on the rise in Italy, with 7.4% of workers in part-time employment and 8.5% in

8 His predecessor expanded upon the PCF's position, arguing for a two-pronged approach that deals with both access to benefits and the creation of non-precarious jobs (Morin 2011).

temporary employment (up from 5.6% and 6.0%, respectively, in 1993) (OECD 2012c). As the director of the Labour Division of the centre-left Italia dei Valori described the problem to me more recently,

> Italy is a country that is hardly European, since in contrast to better countries, such as France, Germany, and the Nordic states, it has an aberration in the labour market [...] We have created a grey, nebulous area in which there are four or five million precarious workers that wind up being labelled freelance workers because they have a fiscal code, but in reality are largely dependent workers and in other European countries would qualify as such [...] These four million [young] people are excluded from any social safety net, from any access to credit – from the fundamentals of European society. (Zipponi 2012)

In light of this picture, one would assume that, all else being equal, the potential purpose and beneficiaries of a programme similar to the French RMI would serve should therefore have been obvious.

In contrast to the French case, however, the creation of the Italian RMI in 1998 lacked both party backing on the right and the kind of public support that would have led to outrage at its dismantling in 2002. In the end, in fact, it is difficult to explain the experiment without reference to the influence of external factors relating to the European Union. As Graziano and Jessoula argue, the programme's creation was the result of two factors: first, European cognitive resources (specifically vis-à-vis policy ideas) and the wide availability of comparisons to other member states resulted in increased debate about gaps in the Italian welfare state, while also providing potential solutions to resolve them; second, and relatedly, the Prodi government attempted to use this opening, as well as claims about external constraints, to build a pro-reform coalition (2011: 164). Yet this approach lost much of its efficacy once Italy had met the Maastricht requirements and pressures from the European Union subsided – not least of all because divisions within the left coalition and between it and the unions became increasingly difficult to manage (Fargion 2003: 335). Furthermore, as public support for the European project began to wane, so too did the possibility of using the European Union (and comparisons with other European countries) as a catalyst for reform (Graziano and Jessoula 2011: 168).

At the same time, however, parties on the Italian left do appear to be more consistently in favour of an RMI-style benefit than their French counterparts, perhaps because the continued lack of coverage makes the potential compromise of the principal system seem less important.

When asked about the division between welfare state outsiders and insiders, for instance, the national director of the Work, Welfare, and Citizenship Policies section of the Partito della Rifondazione Comunista (PRC) pointed not only to the need for labour market reform to correct the issue, but also to an RMI-style benefit as essential for covering the long-term unemployed, arguing that it should be introduced alongside the extension of access to the primary system (Fantozzi 2012). Similarly, at the Partito dei Comunisti Italiani (PdCI), national director of Industry and Mass Organisations (and former senator) Dino Tibaldi did argue for the extension of standard benefits to outsiders, though he noted that this approach was currently not feasible financially, and pointed to the need to create a benefit for unemployed young outsiders in particular (Tibaldi 2011). These sorts of positions also extend to the major centre-left party, the Partito Democratico: the president of the PD Labour Forum asserted that the creation of a complementary RMI benefit was a priority for the party, while PD deputy Jean-Léonard Touadi pointed to the need to use an RMI benefit to 'support, reinforce, and increase social cohesion and inclusion' (Gabaglio 2012; Touadi 2012).

Yet despite the seemingly broad leftist support for the programme, there was nevertheless little advancement on the issue, including during the leftist coalition's return to power in the mid-2000s. This may partly be explained by the opposition of most of the major unions, as they were generally opposed to the RMI experiment. Indeed, two of the three largest unions (the Confederazione Italiana Sindacati Lavoratori and the Unione Italiana del Lavoro, but not the leftist Confederazione Generale Italiana del Lavoro (CGIL)) signed the 2002 Patto per l'Italia (Pact for Italy) that argued that the experiment had demonstrated 'the impracticality of using a State law to determine who has a right to [assistance]' (Patto per l'Italia 2002: 7). Even the CGIL, despite being 'very interested in [the programme] as an anti-poverty instrument', as the director of its Labour Market Department put it, was 'consistently critical of the actualisation of the [RMI] experiment, since [...] there was a lot of variation from municipality to municipality and a lack of the oversight needed to correct for these sorts of issues'; here, as in France, the preferred route was the expansion of access to CIG benefits (Treves 2012). Broad public support for the reintroduction of the programme might have counteracted these pressures by providing parties with electoral incentives to overcome these difficulties, but movements of the type seen in France were largely lacking and support faded once the run-up to the EMU had passed. Taken together, these factors help to explain both the failure of the centre-left to permanently institute major reforms before losing office in 2001 and their relatively uneventful (for our purposes) return to power from 2006 to 2008.

Unsurprisingly, the Berlusconi governments were no better, as their most aggressive attempt at reform – the region-based Reddito di ultima istanza (RUI) programme, instituted in 2004 to replace the RMI – was both optional and only partially funded (at 50%).[9] While it is true that the 2001 constitutional reform gave the regions the lion's share of control over social assistance (thus making central reform more difficult), the state nevertheless retains the right to set essential levels of provision and step in if regions fail to guarantee those levels (although it has thus far failed to do either) (Sacchi and Bastagli 2005: 98). Indeed, Jessoula et al. (2014) highlight the importance of political factors in right-wing opposition to a minimum income scheme. In particular, they argue that this opposition unfolded in two phases: first, from 2001 to 2006, driven by Northern League opposition to a benefit that would arguably mainly benefit Southern Italy; and second, from 2008 to 2011, driven by a resurgent preference on the right for subsidiarity, with the role of the family and civil society foregrounded (Jessoula et al. 2014: 140).

There are a few signs of hope for the future, however. First, faced with persistent high unemployment (especially among youths) and poverty rates since the start of the Eurozone crisis, public attention has recently begun to shift back to the failed project. This culminated with a signature collecting campaign for the institution of an RMI-style programme, referred to as Reddito minimo garantito, submitting over 50,000 signatures to the parliament in April 2013. Second, the current Grand Coalition government has recently introduced another limited minimum income project in the 2014 Legge di stabilità ([Financial] Stability Legislation); enacted as an anti-poverty measure for the next three years, it will be implemented in several major metropolitan areas. Nevertheless, this does not necessarily spell the beginning of a move to permanently institute a minimum income scheme. As the minister of labour and social policies, Enrico Giovannini, explained in November 2013: 'People who have been talking about the arrival of a minimum income [programme] have not read the text carefully [...] What the Senate has specified is a supplement of 40 million euro per year, for

9 When the CGIL attempted to pressure the government to continue with the RMI project, the administration countered that the Pact for Italy represented a general agreement illustrating the need, in the words of Welfare undersecretary Maurizio Sacconi, to replace the 'failed [RMI] attempt with a much more targeted instrument consisting of an income of last resort for situations of extreme need, for which the instruments of access to work are insufficient' (Riz 2002 (my translation)).

the next three years, to the Poverty Fund' (Patucchi 2013). What the future holds for the RMI project therefore remains quite unclear, especially once the Eurozone Crisis passes.

More broadly, how can we explain this general lack of advancement in Italy? Given that the push towards major reform of the Italian unemployment benefit system seems to have been driven more by external factors[10] than internal pressures for reform, the contrast with the French case suggests that certain, non-partisanship-based determinants of benefit extension may be missing in Italy. Although centre-left parties continue to appear open to the creation of an RMI-style programme, their failure to prioritise the issue while in government raises questions about a consistent relationship to extension; similarly, the centre-right's dismantling of the RMI experiment suggests that they too are not especially reaching out to welfare state outsiders. Indeed, this situation is directly contradictory to that which occurred in France, where the RMI enjoyed bipartisan support. As a result, there does not appear to be an observable, consistent, and strong partisan divide on the issue across the two cases, which suggests that partisanship-based theories cannot explain the divergence. Instead, we would argue that the key difference centres around demand for reform – thereby pre-empting, for example, the possibility that the feasibility of increasing vote shares by poaching outsider support from other parties might explain the different trajectories.

Both Italy and France have suffered from unemployment crises that put considerable pressure on their unemployment insurance systems, yet only in France do we see a forceful public debate about the nature of the benefit system and the strategic use of the issue for electoral purposes. The institutional arrangements favouring unemployment insurance in the two countries undoubtedly created groups of winners – workers who had access to generous benefits (i.e. welfare state insiders) and most of the unions who represent them – losers – workers ineligible for benefits (i.e. welfare state outsiders) – and even 'mid-siders' who fall somewhere in between (Jessoula et al. 2010: 579). Since there is certainly not a dearth of individuals in Italy who do not particularly benefit from the current system,[11] some

10 Namely, the run up to the EMU and, more recently, the impact of the Eurozone Crisis on unemployment and poverty levels.

11 Recent estimates suggest that approximately 19% of part-time workers with a permanent contract, 38% of workers with fixed-term contracts, and 48% of temp agency workers completely lack access to benefits in cases of unemployment (Berton et al. 2009: 55).

Figure 2.1 Italian Attitudes towards Government Responsibility for the Unemployed

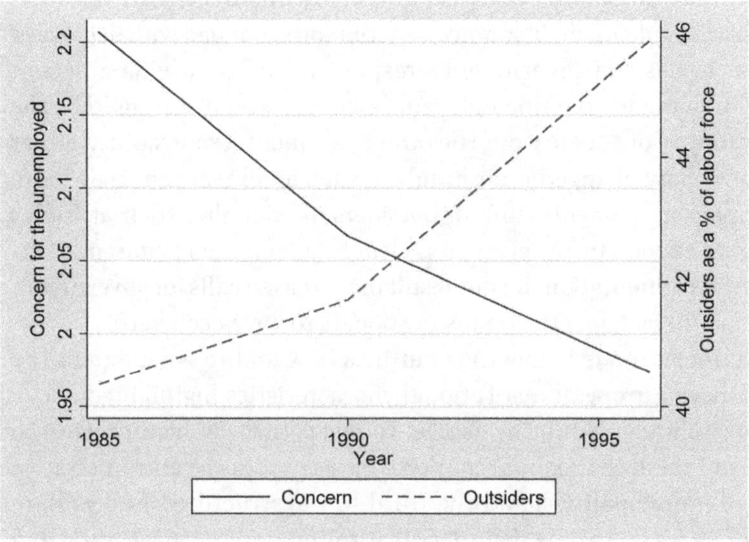

other factor(s) must explain the divergent outcomes.[12] Given that there is no uniform partisan divide across the two countries, the absence of substantial internal pressure for reform in Italy (despite the large number of welfare state outsiders) suggests potential support for the Southern European Exceptionalism hypothesis.

The extent of the underlying puzzle is illustrated by Figure 2.1, which tracks (over time) Italian attitudes about government responsibility to provide for the unemployed alongside the prevalence of Italian labour market outsiders. With regard to the former, respondents were asked 'On the whole, do you think it should or should not be the government's responsibility to provide a decent standard of living for the unemployed?', with four potential responses ranging from 'definitely should be' to 'definitely should not be'. Decreasing agreement with this statement[13] contrasts with the increasing numbers of labour market outsiders over the same period (calculated as the summed proportion of self-employed, part-time workers, temporary

12 Part of this may relate to the differing prominence of egalitarianism within conceptions of citizenship in France and Italy, but even in the latter case arguments for citizenship-based access to benefits are clearly not foreign (witness the example of healthcare reform).

13 The differences between the means are statistically significant (two-tailed tests were run on the three pairs of values). The number of observations in 1985, 1990, and 1996 were 1528, 964, and 1048, respectively.

workers, and the long-term unemployed), which – due to the UI-centric system and its contributory principles – provides a rough proxy of increases in welfare state outsiders.[14] As such, it appears that decreased access to traditional unemployment insurance benefits corresponded with decreased belief that it was the government's responsibility to provide a decent standard of living for the unemployed; since one would assume that the growing group of outsiders would be pro-government responsibility, either the rest of society changed their minds to such an extent that they more than compensated for this shift, or outsiders did not alter their attitudes as one would expect. In any event, it is clear that increased labour market/welfare state segmentation did not result in increased calls for government intervention (in fact, just the opposite appears to have occurred).

The argument made below thus outlines how and to what extent the three Southern European institutional characteristics highlighted above can help us to understand this puzzle. To recap, the first factor relates to the nature of the Italian labour market, the second to the administrative capacity of municipalities, and the third to the structure of its welfare state. Overall, we will argue that these institutional factors have mitigated what would likely otherwise have been substantial public pressure on the Italian government to reform (either by welfare state outsiders or by broader groups).

Southern European Characteristics and Public Pressure

Starting with the first of these characteristics, the prevalence of work in the informal economy has arguably created an environment in which the actual employment status of a formally 'unemployed' worker is easily called into question (Ferrera 2005: 9; Gough 1996: 15). Indeed, one can easily understand how this factor may well contribute to a lack of sympathy for unemployed persons who are ineligible for benefits, as well as creating administrative difficulties when it comes to determining eligibility. While it is difficult to measure the informal economy, Italy is widely regarded as having one of the largest in the OECD, with Schneider estimating that it represents 26.2% of the Italian GDP (compared with 14.8% in France and an OECD average of

14 Due to data limitations, values are calculated with different denominators: part-time labour is a % of total employment; temporary employment is a % of dependent employment; and long-term unemployment (over twelve months) is a % of the civilian labour force). Nevertheless, the values are adequate for our purposes and are indicative of the general increase.

16.4%, and second only to Greece) (2005: 611).[15] Given these circumstances, Italians may understandably believe that many individuals who purport to be unemployed are actually working under the table. This issue is further complicated by the belief that many of these individuals are foreigners. As a report by Antonietta Barone, a manager at one of the province-based agencies charged with monitoring local labour markets, (later cited in the *Corriere della Sera*, one of Italy's major newspapers) stated:

> There is no shortage of [agricultural] businesses established expressly to fictitiously employ foreigners, that in reality are created out of a sort of empty box, established only on paper so that they can hire individuals once a year [...] [with the foreigners then becoming] the recipients of unemployment, maternity, and sickness benefits [...] [while continuing] to work under the table as housekeepers or nannies. (Stella 2010)

With concerns about scheming immigrants thrown into the mix, it is not difficult to imagine the scepticism that surrounds the provision of benefits.

At the same time, however, the policy-based difficulties created by rampant undeclared income do not seem paralysing at the administrative level, in light of numerous attempts to deal with this issue. Such efforts include the recalibration of means testing in 1998 via the introduction of the Indicatore della situazione economica equivalente (which looks at both wealth and income, thereby attempting to move beyond means testing based solely on declared income) and the various efforts by municipalities involved in the RMI (e.g. bringing in claimants during times when informal work would likely be occurring, assuming a basic level of income, looking at standards of living) (Sacchi and Bastagli 2005: 124). Furthermore, at least among the left-wing party directors/deputies with whom I spoke, the assumption remains that the programme is workable (Fantozzi 2012; Gabaglio 2012; Touadi 2012; Zipponi 2012). As such, while the prevalence of the informal economy likely contributes to a lack of popular support for benefit reform by calling into question the actual needs of 'unemployed' individuals, technical complications related to the issue do not appear in and of themselves to actively pre-empt reform.

Second, it has been suggested that the administrative difficulties from which many municipalities suffer, combined with fears of clientelistic behaviour on the part of local administrators, have also impeded the development of means-tested benefits in Southern Europe (Ferrera 2005:

15 Estimates from 2002/2003.

10). This is of particular concern given the well-known lack of administrative capacity in certain Italian regions (cf. Putnam 1993; Milio 2007). Indeed, this issue is connected with the previous one, as low administrative capacity to determine legitimate benefit recipients helps to explain, for instance, the historical preference in Italy towards category-based benefits (Dell'Aringa and Lodovici 1996: 182).

More recently, the experience with the Italian RMI experimentation would also seem to confirm this, though only up to a point. The insertion portion of the RMI, particularly with regard to employment integration, required significant coordination and resources at the municipal level, which many of the poorer areas lacked (Alti 2001: 5). This was a well-known issue, with the Berlusconi government referring to local governments' 'lack of capacity in designing and implementing social insertion measures' as one of the central problems with the RMI; yet even that government did not appear to have believed this was an insurmountable issue, given its assertion that one of the advantages of its new RUI programme would be overcoming this issue via the introduction of 'incentive schemes for local administrations to operate synergistically' (Ministero del Lavoro e delle Politiche Sociali 2003: 27-28). Whether the introduction of such improvements could simply have occurred under the RMI is up for debate, but the assumption that administrative difficulties can be overcome appears widespread.

That is not to suggest that the problem is a trivial one, however, and the belief in the challenges posed by administrative issues is not simply found on the right end of the political spectrum. When asked about the persistent delays in re-implementing a national RMI-style benefit, the president of the PD Labour Forum, Emilio Gabaglio, pointed firstly to the current lack of resources and secondly to, as he put it, 'structure':

> You know, in a country such as ours – I am thinking primarily of the Southern regions, but not only them – there is a problem of efficacy, transparency, control. These mechanisms [such as the RMI] can quite quickly become clientelistic tools, or even worse. As such there are somewhat cerebral reservations, a sort of fear – and we need to get over this – but we [also] need to create organisations capable of guiding and managing a process of this type. (Gabaglio 2012)

Concerns with these sorts of problems thus clearly extend beyond party boundaries, and it is easy to understand how attempts to institute social assistance might be met with popular scepticism (despite the apparent belief among politicians that they can in fact be addressed).

Nevertheless, moving away from abstract conceptions of a general lack of capacity across municipalities and looking instead at the issues that were actually encountered under the RMI, it becomes obvious that administrative difficulties have not in and of themselves thwarted reform. Rather than suggesting a complete lack of competency or capacity on the part of municipal governments, many of the concrete problems that arose (e.g. a lack of access to documents needed to verify eligibility, low involvement in insertion programmes, a limited number of occupational programmes due to low levels of private sector involvement) had practical, workable solutions that did not necessarily require inordinately greater administrative capacity (Sacchi and Bastagli 2005: 122-124). To be clear, this would have undoubtedly required some retooling and even organisational improvements, as well as a rebalancing of existing policies to prevent functional overload (Matsaganis et al. 2003: 646-647). Yet such changes need not have been revolutionary, and as such there does not appear to be any reason to assume that administrative limitations have doomed Italian minimum income schemes from the start. As such, while technical administrative issues have indeed played a role – most notably by making improvements considerably more challenging than they otherwise would have been – it is difficult to conclude that they have actively prevented governments from attempting substantial unemployment reform. It is easy to understand, however, how these sorts of problem might engender scepticism among the public with regard to the feasibility of such a programme, thereby potentially further decreasing pressure for reform.

The last factor, and arguably the most important in our case, involves the family-centred nature of Southern European welfare states such as Italy's, with state protection concentrated on the risks that the family cannot deal with by themselves (Mingione 1995: 140; Gough 1996: 14; Trifiletti 1999: 50; Matsaganis et al. 2003: 642; Ferrera 2005: 8). In Italy, as in the other cases, this has been made possible by the persistent strength of the family, which has insulated adult children from risk. This is an especially important phenomenon since Italian youth (and particularly young women) are more likely to enter atypical, unstable employment, and the group as a whole also has a much higher unemployment rate, at 27.9% for those under 25 and 14.7% for those aged 25 to 29, compared to 8.4% for the population as a whole[16]; the combination of these two factors mean that there is a substantial

16 Data for 2010. The relevant figures for France, by comparison, are higher for the total population (at 9.3%) but lower for both under 25s (at 22.5%) and for 25-29s (at 12.1%).

generational division in Italy when it comes to accessing unemployment benefits (Barbier and Fargion 2004, 455; OECD 2012c).

These circumstances at least partially help to explain why Italian children are substantially more likely than children in France (and indeed, in most Western countries) to remain at home later: constraining ourselves to the pre-crisis period, while in 2007 the average French woman moved out when she was 23 and the average French man did so at 24, the corresponding figures for Italy are 29 and 31 (Eurostat 2009: 29). In point of fact, home-leaving ages within Southern Europe have actually tended to increase since the 1970s, which may be connected to the interaction of a cultural tradition of not leaving home before marriage and the post-sexual revolution tendency to delay marriage (Giuliano 2007: 943). Yet in addition to these cultural factors, there are of course financial ones: a 2007 Eurobarometer survey of Italian youth (aged 15-30), for instance, suggests that the principal motivation for remaining at home longer is financial, with just under half (49%) of them responding that this is the case (compared to 30% in France) (Gallup Organization 2007: 72). This is further reinforced by responses suggesting that while approximately 50% of young Italians derive most of their income from their relatives/partners, 0% receive it from unemployment benefits (in France, the relevant numbers are 30% and 6%, respectively) (Gallup Organization 2007: 75). Since only about 10% of Italian men and 23% of Italian women live with a partner (compared to 30% and 43% in France) these numbers suggest an even more striking reliance on relatives in Italy (Eurostat 2009: 32).

The prediction is therefore that this ability to rely on the family affects the attitudes of the young towards the unemployment benefit system, thereby removing a potential source of electoral pressure towards reform. Indeed, evidence that consumption losses associated with unemployment spells are actually lower in Italy and Spain than they are in the UK and Germany suggests that family networks may actually be able to do even more work for the unemployed than comparatively generous welfare states (Bentolila and Ichino 2008). This is of import since youths, dramatically overrepresented among the unemployed and atypically employed, offer a potential pressure point for reform as parties jockey to attract electoral support – as was the case in France (see Silver 1994: 533). While welfare state insiders would typically be expected to be either ambivalent or opposed to the types of reforms in question (given that they already qualify for generous benefits and extension would potentially threaten those benefit levels), the perspective of outsiders on the matter serves as our central focus.

The argument here is that since welfare state outsiders (i.e. individuals without direct access to benefits) are sometimes found within a family unit that ultimately contains someone who does benefit from the current system, the insider/outsider division can come to be viewed in familial terms; in other words, if your parents benefit from a generous system of protection and pass along some of those benefits to you, you will likely be less bothered by your lack of direct access to those protections. This is especially the case if you expect to one day become an insider yourself. In light of the higher ages at which youth leave home in Italy, this mechanism would be expected to be of greater relevance than in France: protected by their families in their current moments of need from entering a free fall, Italian youths are still able to derive a sense of protection from the system (as well as a hope that they will one day be able to benefit directly from it), thereby pre-empting pressure to recalibrate the design of unemployment benefits. (The corollary of this lack of protection outside the family structure is, of course, that remaining home later is actually incentivised by Italian social policy.) With family income derived primarily from those already on the inside, insider benefits (rather than the extension of residual, low-level benefits to youths themselves) take prominence.

What is more, to the extent that youth are perceived to be the ones most prone to falling through the gaps in the unemployment system, popular concern over the issue is likely diminished by the knowledge that most of them can simply rely on their families. Thus, while the first two Southern European characteristics have a more general dampening effect on the demand for and perceived possibility of reform, this latter factor has both a general effect and a more targeted one. Note that this argument, combined with the trend towards Italian youth remaining at home later – the median home-leaving age increased from 25.1 in the early 1980s to 29 by the mid-2000s – helps to make sense of the puzzle illustrated in Figure 1 (Billari et al. 2001: 28; Eurostat 2010).

As a final note, a similar logic also applies, of course, to other groups that disproportionately hold outsider status: most notably women and immigrants. Both groups may be broadly perceived to be undeserving of benefit extension, whether due to the potential access to benefits via family members (particularly for women) or through the potential for cheating by those employed in the informal economy (especially vis-à-vis immigrants). What of the potential for pressure from these welfare outsiders on their own accord?

Taking the groups in turn, insofar as women lacking personally derived access to benefits have spouses with access, their interests shift to align with welfare state insiders; this of course leaves women who do not themselves qualify for direct access and lack a spouse who does – but once youths and immigrants are excluded from this group, the number of restrictions leaves a limited number of women in this category. Using the 2008 European Values Study (EVS) to calculate a rough estimate of the size of this category, for instance, suggests that only about 1.5% of women (excluding retirees as well) fall into this group.

Immigrants and their children, on the other hand, are considerably more numerous and are both disproportionately more likely to be labour market outsiders and to lack benefit access through a family member (unlike with youths and women) (EVS 2008). Yet the fact that so many immigrants lack citizenship, and hence the right to vote, obviously diminishes their potential impact; in other words, these individuals are often triply outsiders – in the labour market, the welfare state, and politics. Furthermore, there are a number of factors that have made immigrants unlikely to create a strong popular movement for reform in Italy: the recent nature of most immigration (with the immigrant population one of the smallest in Europe until the late 2000s) has left the group less established and relatively marginalised; their more disparate origins (when compared with France) give even the largest groups – Romanians, Albanians, and Maghrebi – limited common ground for mobilisation (Istat 2011); and the whiteness of the majority of immigrants (coming from Central and Eastern Europe) prevents the issue from being framed in terms of anti-racism (as happened in France). Overall, then, youths remain the principal group of interest in examining the lack of pressure for reform.

To summarise, the preceding section has suggested that certain characteristics common to Southern European welfare states – namely the prevalence of the informal economy, administrative difficulties, and family support – has, in Italy, undercut potential electoral incentives towards reforms of the sort seen in France. In addition, administrative problems at the municipal level have further complicated reform by making improvements more difficult.

Conclusion

This chapter has explored the contrasting fates of the French and Italian RMI programmes in an attempt to better understand the determinants of benefit extension – specifically via residualisation – within broader conditions of fiscal constraint. After laying out three potential theories that might give us insight into this process, the chapter proceeded to examine the factors surrounding the development of the respective RMI schemes. There it was suggested that theories based on partisanship are unable to explain the divergence: while the French benefit developed primarily out of internal debate and concern regarding *exclusion*, with the RMI enjoying bipartisan support, the implementation of the Italian version was politically contested and largely connected to external factors related to the European Union (as evidenced by the left's failure to reintroduce the programme after regaining office). This contrast helps to explain why, after these factors subsided, the Italian scheme was able to disappear without much fanfare.

In order to explain this absence of internal pressure (or conversely, electoral incentives) in Italy, it was then argued that certain characteristics of the Southern European welfare states, as highlighted by Ferrera (2005), worked to diminish internal pressure for reform. More specifically, the prevalence of the informal economy and central role of the family in the Italian welfare state have mitigated calls for reform by decreasing the perceived precariousness of being unemployed with no access to unemployment benefits. The role of the family in particular is claimed to have had the effect of pacifying pressure from the young, who are disproportionately unable to access benefits. In addition, a lack of administrative capacity on the part of many municipalities has further complicated government attempts at reform and arguably added to public scepticism regarding the feasibility of an RMI-style programme. While conclusively linking these factors to a lack of reform would be rather difficult, given that we are attempting to explain non-events over long periods of time, the next chapter will nevertheless provide some support for the theory using survey data.

Ultimately, we arrive at point where we must theorise about a dog that did not bark. It is obvious that the structure of the Italian welfare state (among others) creates a rather large group of individuals in typical employment who do well by the skewed nature of unemployment benefits. That neither they nor the unions (excepting CGIL) that represent so many of them should press the government to reform the system is no surprise. The lack of popular pressure from the large number of individuals that are excluded from coverage (or who otherwise do not particularly benefit from the current system) is indeed peculiar, and it indicates a general lack of electoral incentives for parties to pursue reform. To explain this, it has been suggested that certain characteristically 'Southern European' attributes have diminished calls for reform. The result of these factors is thus a level of popular discontent with the current system that is lower than might otherwise be expected, which in turn helps us to understand the contrasting outcomes in France and Italy.

There are a few signs of hope for the future, however. Faced with persistent high unemployment (especially among youths) and poverty rates since the start of the Eurozone crisis, some public attention has recently shifted back to the failed project. At the regional level, several regions and autonomous provinces have recently introduced their own variants of the programme. While these smaller-scale programmes are not functional equivalents of RMI discussed above, they do at least seem to point towards some political interest in minimum income schemes.

Most importantly, this culminated at the national level with a signature-collecting campaign for the institution of a minimum income-style programme submitting over 50,000 signatures to the parliament in April 2013. Subsequently, the Grand Coalition government introduced a restricted minimum income-style project in the 2014 Legge di stabilità ([Financial] Stability Legislation), enacted as a limited anti-poverty measure. The programme is to last three years and will be implemented only in a few major metropolitan areas. Yet this temporary, limited measure far from necessarily spells the beginning of a move to permanently institute a minimum income scheme. What the future holds for the project therefore remains quite unclear, especially once the Eurozone Crisis passes. In light of past experiences, public attention may well fade with a return of the economic status quo ante.

3 Public Attitudes towards the Unemployed in Continental, Southern Europe, and Beyond

As we have seen in Chapter 2, comparing attempts at benefit extension for the unemployed (via residualisation) in the French and Italian cases brought a number of key features to the fore: namely, the prevalence of informal work, limited administrative capacity, and the centrality of the family in the Italian welfare state. The obvious next question is whether and to what extent these findings are applicable in a broader setting. This chapter takes a first cut at this question by looking at a set of broadly similar countries, coupling an examination of policy trajectories with a discussion of public opinion.

We begin by laying out developments in six other Continental and Southern European countries: respectively, Austria, Belgium, and Germany; and Greece, Portugal, and Spain. In doing so, we highlight the similarities and differences across policy trajectories in these countries, with a particular focus on whether they mirror their French and Italian counterparts. This qualitative assessment of generalisability will serve to complement the quantitative approach undertaken in the next chapter. A number of considerations highlight the value of providing a cursory overview of additional cases. At a broad level, the goal is clearly to determine the extent to which our two central cases can be taken as indicative of broader trends – but this has different implications for the French and Italian cases.

With France, which was a clear laggard among Continental welfare states in extending benefit coverage for persons not covered by unemployment insurance, we are left wondering about earlier moves to extend benefit coverage. Did other Continental countries undergo similar reforms earlier on, driven by similar factors? Or did the other countries follow entirely different trajectories? With regard to Italy, given our broader focus on benefit extension, the discussion of Italian failure to reform is in a certain sense dissatisfying on its own. How did other Southern European countries, faced with similar status quo pressures, overcome these obstacles to reform? What distinguishes late reformers from early ones, and countries that have extended benefits from those that have not? The case studies will attempt to provide some answers to these questions. However, as we shall see, while the Continental European cases can highlight different policy trajectories in addressing the issues related to benefit standardisation and universalisation, the Southern European cases offer more analytical leverage vis-à-vis generalisation.

After laying out these case studies, we then proceed to the second stage of analysis undertaken in this chapter: an exploration and comparison of the factors influencing public opinion in these countries, presenting results for each of the cases individually (excluding Portugal, for which the survey data we employ are unavailable). The goal here is to begin to incorporate public opinion into our analysis, given its central role in our argument. Of course, examining the countries individually and comparing the results invariably limits the depth of the analysis: it restricts us to including only the potential individual-level determinants of public opinion, in the process preventing us from considering the country-level factors that we argue are also important. The investigation nevertheless provides a first indication of whether our key individual-level factors might have an impact in Continental and Southern European countries, and it serves as a first step towards the multi-level model survey analysis undertaken in the next chapter. In proceeding with the second step of this chapter's analysis, we begin with a discussion of public opinion within Italy and France, and then compare the results with those in other Southern European and Continental countries.

Overall, the current investigation allows us to broadly situate and expand upon the discussion in Chapter 2. Most notably, our findings here suggest that the Southern European cases seem to share very similar challenges in their attempts to extend benefit coverage, while the European Union was a relatively common factor facilitating extension. In addition, our preliminary country-level survey analysis provides some support for the explanatory factors discussed in the previous chapter, though the strongest support coming from the Italian case itself.

Extending the Comparison

Before continuing to the additional country studies, we begin by first discussing why these specific additional cases were selected. The classification of countries within welfare state typographies has been much debated (see, for example, Arts and Gelissen 2001; Scruggs and Allan 2006). Certain cases raise fewer issues than others, however, and it is these countries that we focus our attention upon.

The selection of additional Southern European welfare states – Greece, Portugal, and Spain – is especially straightforward in this regard. These countries are generally included within the same welfare type (e.g. Ferrera 1996b; Bonoli 1997), and the list is relatively exhaustive (leaving aside non-European countries and the highly contested Switzerland). While there has been some subsequent divergence among these countries, discussed in more detail below, the broad similarities remain (see, for example, Karamessini 2008). Researchers have had a rather harder time, by contrast, settling on a definitive list of Continental welfare states (for an overview, see Arts and Gelissen 2001: 149-150). In selecting our additional cases, we addressed this uncertainty by excluding the most hotly debated countries: the Netherlands and Switzerland. After excluding Luxembourg (for its very small size), this left us with our three European cases – Austria, Belgium, and Germany.

In selecting our additional cases we have therefore attempted to avoid the most fundamental issues entailed in welfare state categorisation.[1] In addition, the two sets of selected cases also have the virtue of broadly reflecting a division among healthcare systems, thereby permitting us to use the same additional countries in the second half of the book. We leave that discussion, however, for Chapter 6.

Continental Europe

Turning first to the Continental European cases – Austria, Belgium, and Germany – all introduced general social assistance schemes comparatively early, with France the latecomer among Continental welfare states in this regard. Almost all of the key reforms in Continental Europe occurred prior to the heightened labour market challenges facing France and the Southern European countries when debates around minimum income programmes arose there. Yet the comparison nevertheless brings to light a number of interesting points owing to the three very different trajectories across these countries.

To begin, the Austrian case is marked by an early but fragmented introduction of benefits for unemployed persons who fell outside of the unemployment insurance system. Here minimum income programmes were introduced over the course of the 1970s, with the first scheme created in 1971 and the last introduced in 1978. This points towards a number of caveats inherent in a comparison with French developments. On the whole, this extension of coverage occurred prior to the dramatic expansion of atypical

1 There are of course many remaining important dissimilarities among the cases that complicate comparison, but we attempt to address the most pertinent differences in our discussion below.

employment: indeed, even *Länder* governments in the late 1970s were more likely completing the broader process that began in 1971 than responding to growing non-standard employment. What is more, the central role of federalism in this case adds addition complications, not least because of the various partisan stripes of *Länder* governments introducing the programme.

Yet despite these differences, it is worth pausing to draw out implications of the trajectory of minimum income benefit standardisation in Austria. In particular, the very decentralised Austrian approach to social assistance meant that these benefit schemes remained under the purview of the *Länder* until very recently. As a result, although the programmes together covered the country in its entirety, there has historically been considerable variation in available benefits – a feature Austria held in common with Spain, as discussed below (Moreira 2008: 3). This variation extended not only to benefit levels, but also to a requirement in certain *Länder* that recipients (or their families) pay back the government for benefits they received while on social assistance. The negative effects of these differences were somewhat mitigated by the fact that these regional programmes were relatively marginal to the broader system, with the special unemployment assistance scheme covering the majority of long-term unemployed persons; but the number of persons reliant on social assistance was not negligible, reaching about 2% by the 2000s (Bahle et al. 2011: 54, 57).

Subsequently, and most interestingly for our purposes, the various provincial benefits were replaced in 2010 by the uniform Social Minimum (Bedarfsorientierte Mindestsicherung). This programme, by virtue of being organised at the federal level, established a common minimum across Austria (although the *Länder* are permitted to go above the minimum if they see fit). Since this standard was established with the aim of levelling up the minimum income benefits across the *Länder* to coincide with the more generous systems (such as that of Vienna), the Social Minimum programme should be viewed as a measure intended to extend additional protection to outsiders. Indeed, the reform was part of a broader trend, beginning in 2007, towards increasing flexicurity, with both the Grand Coalition government and the social partners on board (Obinger et al. 2012: 183). While the proposal was not entirely uncontroversial – most notably evoking opposition from the Austrian People's Party, on the basis of argued disincentives for work – it was ultimately passed with broad support. In the Austrian case, then, we find a two-step process, but one which nevertheless points towards an openness to reform that more closely resembles French developments than Italian ones: while minimum income programmes were generally introduced prior to the considerable growth of atypical employment, programme variation across the *Länder* until 2010 made it a partial laggard, with the broadly supported standardisation part of a move towards what Obinger et al. (2012: 185) refer to as Austria's 'smoothed dualization'.

Belgium, by contrast, was comparatively early to introduce a standardised minimum income programme – but given that the so-called Minimex programme (now called the Revenu d'integration sociale) was introduced in 1974, the potential influence of labour market divisions is suspect. Nevertheless, the Belgian case offers up a series of noteworthy observations, primarily connected to the broader trajectory of developments vis-à-vis the relationship between insiders, outsiders, and the unemployment benefit system. First and foremost, the role of this programme is smaller than one might think, since the country has, in a rather singular fashion, greatly circumscribed the role of the scheme. They have done so by enacting limited restrictions on eligibility to unemployment insurance, instead focusing almost exclusively on lowering replacement rates. The result has been comparatively high levels of coverage under standard unemployment benefits and very limited reliance on social assistance (Clegg 2007: 607). Viewed from a certain perspective, one might view this as an atypically outsider-friendly approach to the problems of differential access raised by the growth of non-standard employment.

Yet the end result of this process cannot legitimately be described as very wide access to insider benefits. This is because the government, with the support of the social partners, has pursued a broad decoupling of unemployment insurance benefits from standard Bismarckian factors such as wages and work history, with a focus instead on assumed need (Marx 2003: 237). Unemployment insurance benefits have thus been transformed into a form of social assistance. Consequently, while a general social assistance benefit was adopted quite early and remains unusually marginal, the Belgian case is marked by a very different sort of transformation, whereby the insurance principle has gradually been undermined. Instead of creating a residual scheme to deal with growing numbers of atypical workers, the approach in Belgium has witnessed the undercutting of the primary system for insiders (rather than simple residualisation). As a result, despite displaying the higher propensity to extend benefits to outsiders that we would expect from a Continental welfare state, it differs dramatically from all of our other cases.

Belgium's attempt to balance unemployment insurance coverage against unemployment insurance replacement rates thus raises questions about why their approach has differed so dramatically from that of other

European countries. The explanation here most likely reflects a factor that will come to the fore in our discussion of healthcare reforms: organisational incentives created by benefit systems. In an attempt to explain the very different patterns of reform noted in the Belgian and French case, Clegg (2012) highlights the impact of the unemployment benefit disbursement system's structure on union interests: first, Belgian unions attract both resources and members through their management of the system, and as a result they have a strong interest in maintaining as integrated a system as possible; and second, Belgian unions also have a higher degree of popular legitimacy in their management of the unemployment benefit system, and are therefore in a stronger position than their French counterparts to shape the direction of programme reform. As a result of this atypical development, the Belgian case thus offers some insights into factors that might incline certain governments to maintain or expand broad access to the *primary* unemployment benefit scheme.

The German case, in turn, is characterised by the earliest introduction of a minimum income programme, with the creation of Sozialhilfe in 1962 under the Christian Democratic Union. In Germany, the extension of coverage for the unemployed thus most clearly predates the rise of nonstandard employment, which would not start its dramatic rise for several decades.[2] This situates the German case in an especially different context from that in France, with the programme introduced in the heyday of the welfare state's expansionary age. Yet as with the Austrian case, the programme was considerably reformed in recent years – and it is here that the German case can offer some insights on our broader analysis of benefit standardisation and universalisation.

In particular, although the social assistance programme remained in place over the course of the transformation of Germany's labour market, its role within the broader benefit system was gradually decreased. This occurred, especially over the 1990s, through the introduction of various categorical assistance programmes (for groups ranging from immigrants to the elderly) that reduced the scope of the general social assistance scheme (Bahle et al. 2011: 92). As a result, earlier levels of standardisation were in fact progressively undermined, even though broader access to one benefit or another remained stable.

This situation continued until 2005, when unemployment assistance (an intermediary but still earnings-related benefit) was merged with social

2 The ratio between standard and non-typical work growing from 5:1 in the early 1970s to 3:1 in the mid-1980s, and reaching 2:1 a decade later (Bleses and Seeleib-Kaiser 2004: 33).

assistance as part of the Social Democratic government's Hartz reforms. This led to a partial standardisation of benefits across recipients of unemployment assistance and social assistance, although the number of individuals accessing the latter programme had already dwindled considerably. Most importantly, the reform was part of a move to reinforce the distinction between contributory and income-tested benefits, clearly marking a move towards dualisation (Palier and Thelen 2010: 135). The reach of the new benefit was substantial: after combining the benefits, over 50% of unemployed persons were receiving assistance rather than insurance benefits (Clasen and Clegg 2006: 538). On the whole, then, the German case illustrates the far more standard and clear-cut version of dualisation often highlighted in the literature. Although the minimum income programme was introduced remarkably early on, social assistance has been substantially reconfigured in recent decades, and in such a way as to reinforce the divide between insiders and outsiders. Yet the especially early introduction of the programme also meant that this occurred within a context quite different from that of either France or Italy, as the maintenance of replacement rates was not clearly being balanced against worries about unemployed persons entirely excluded from the unemployment benefit system.

Overall, the Continental cases are marked by both relatively robust coverage rates for the unemployed and the early introduction of minimum income schemes, prior to the dramatic rise of atypical employment in these countries. Nevertheless, the Austrian, Belgian, and German experiences highlight the comparatively early development of these programmes, especially in contrast to Southern Europe. They also direct our attention towards interesting parallel developments relating to outsider access to benefits, as well as the political contexts surrounding them: in Austria, with the late standardisation (in 2010) of benefit levels across the *Länder;* in Belgium, with the gradual transformation (largely driven by unions) of unemployment insurance into a benefit not all that dissimilar from social assistance, with both an expansion of access and a lowering of benefit levels; and in Germany, with the increasingly narrowed scope of the general social assistance programme and its ultimate merging with unemployment assistance (thereby reinforcing the split between insurance and assistance benefits).

Southern Europe

The Southern European countries, by contrast, were all quite late to implement minimum income programmes – if they did so at all. This is not surprising, given that an underdeveloped system of benefits for the unemployed was one of central features of Ferrera's (1996b) original Southern European welfare state categorisation. On the one hand, the cases therefore provide an opportunity to assess the extent to which factors that seem to have impeded reform in Italy also mattered in other contexts. On the other, since Italy remains especially underdeveloped, the comparison provides us with an opportunity to examine the circumstances surrounding successful reforms – though as we will see, these successes were often only partial.

The Greek case is the most similar to the Italian (although ongoing developments suggest that the picture may be moving towards reform). To a certain extent, of course, delays in the expansion of the Greek welfare state can be understood by the relatively late (compared to Italy) experience of dictatorship, which only ended definitively in 1974. Developments in subsequent decades in fact show considerable overlap with the Italian case. Matsaganis (2005), discussing the more or less explicit historical antipathy towards creating a minimum income benefit, points to a number of factors that broadly reflect our discussion of Italy: faith in a 'trickle-down' approach to poverty; budgetary concerns; administrative difficulties determining appropriate beneficiaries; and the fact that social exclusion among the poor remained relatively uncommon. While concerns around administrative difficulties provide a clear parallel with Italy, the relatively limited number of socially excluded poor persons, once unpacked, reveals further similarities. To explain this, Matsaganis (2005) highlights a number of factors that have insulated the poor from social exclusion – factors which could just as easily be used to describe the Italian case: the ability to rely on the family unit; the concentration of unemployment among women and youth (who are often insulated by the male breadwinner of the family); and the prevalence of social exclusion among immigrants and other outsiders who do not have a strong political voice.[3]

This does not mean that there have been no moves to guarantee benefit access for unemployed persons in Greece. Indeed, the programme had intermittent boosters on both the centre-left and centre-right, with the first proposal for a minimum income programme coming in 1998 from an opposition, centre-right member of parliament – though it failed to gather real support from any portion of the political spectrum (Lalioti 2016: 85). The programme was rejected largely on the basis of cost (a particular concern

3 In addition to these shared attributes, Matsaganis (2005) also points to the traditionally very rural nature of poverty in Greece, which facilitated the integration of poor people into their communities.

given the aim of meeting Maastricht criteria), and the policy continued to divide politicians – even on the left – after joining the Eurozone (Matsaganis 2005: 70-71). Crucially, proposals seem to have typically been floated more as pre-election campaigning tactics than anything else, and the programme has lacked broader social and political support, both from trade unions and the left as a whole (Lalioti 2016: 86-87). Instead, subsequent governments have preferred to focus on categorical, narrowly targeted benefits, which avoided many of the potential pitfalls of more broadly available programmes. As Ferrera (2005: 10) points out, concerns that minimum income benefits might serve as 'welfare patronage' in Southern Europe – due to discretion on the part of local authorities – have been a broad point of contention with the scheme.

There are signs, however, that the situation may be changing under the weight of Greek economic troubles. The major development here occurred in 2014, when a minimum income pilot programme was introduced in thirteen municipalities, on the basis of a push for reform from the centre-left PASOK (the Panhellenic Socialist Movement). The reform is best understood as the product of a move by PASOK to attract left-leaning supporters in the context of a deep economic crisis, declining standards of living, and the rise of SYRIZA (the Coalition of the Radical Left) (Lalioti 2016: 85-86). Yet it is too early to tell whether this will ultimately lead to the programme's full implementation or if its fate will resemble that of the Italian RMI. On the one hand, the International Monetary Fund's support for the pilot programme's introduction and the fact that there have been signs that Syriza intends to 'assess the pilot project [...] with a view to extending it nationwide' are positive indications for the future; but the continued fear of Grexit and SYRIZA's derision of the programme in 2014 (while in opposition) as 'crumbs of state charity' leave the future uncertain (quotations from Matsaganis 2015).

In Spain, the broader context has also had much in common with the Italian one, while also sharing with Portugal and Greece the experience of dictatorships well into the 1970s. In addition to the strong role of the family and life-cycle redistribution, there is what Arriba and Moreno (2005: 141) refer to as 'a compelling household micro-solidarity'. On the basis of these shared characteristics, one would expect to find a similar trajectory to that of Italy. Yet between 1989 and 1993, the Spanish regions independently introduced diverse attempts at minimum income schemes, making the country the first among its Southern European peers to implement the programme (Laparra and Aguilar 1996). This began with the Basque government in 1988 (where the programme enjoyed wide support), extended to Catalonia in 1990, and then spread to other regions, arguably as they sought to avoid falling behind their peers in assuming important government competencies; but, paralleling the Austrian case pre-2010, the various regional programmes have quite heterogeneous levels of protection, coverage, and insertion methods (Arriba and Moreno 2005: 176, 187, 189).

How can we understand these developments? In the first place, it is worth noting that (as in Italy) the European Community helped to influence the reform trajectory. The situation here broadly reflects that in Italy, with Spain looking outwards to other European countries, attempting to conform to European norms and strengthen the anti-poverty components of the welfare state (Arriba and Moreno 2005: 150). Yet, as the divergent outcomes in the two cases might suggest, this is but a small part of the story. In reality, accession to the European Union, with the concomitant pressure to meet certain minimum benefit levels, only had limited impact on social policy convergence in Spain – partly due to the large gap in starting points and fiscal difficulties (Threlfall 1997). Instead, regional and local governments were central to this process of benefit extension, with the principles of universal access and equal treatment central to regional welfare legislation. This was especially the case after 1988, when the Ministry of Social Affairs, which was explicitly set-up to develop social policy, embarked on a process of co-ordination with the lower-level governments (Arriba and Moreno 2005: 148, 149).

Yet despite the role of these broader factors, one finds considerable variation in factors driving programme implementation across the regions: some were the result of relatively clear government initiatives; some were the product of pressure from opposition parties; and some came about due to mobilization by trade unions and non-governmental organisations (Arriba and Moreno 2005: 176). Notably, however, these factors highlight that the reforms in general were not the product of explicit popular demand, and policy implementation did not line up with ideological party divides; instead, benefit extension was the result of regional governments asserting their constitutionally derived autonomy by implementing European Union recommendations (Arriba and Moreno 2005: 186-187, 189). The Basque Country, as the first region to introduce the programme, was particularly key in this regard. After introducing the programme in 1989 with broad parliamentary support (alongside that of major union confederations and numerous religious groups), other 'historical nationalities' moved to assert their respective autonomy by following suit (Lalioti 2016: 84).

In this way, then, we find confirmation that partisan politics was less central to these reforms than one might expect, and that popular levels of support for benefit extension were not especially key. At the same time, the contrasting outcomes in Italy and Spain point to the potential role of decentralisation.[4] While the two countries both have asymmetrical decentralised systems with special autonomous regions, sovereigntist sentiment and the level of decentralisation in Spain are nevertheless clearly greater (see, for example, Treisman 2002). This mix of nationalism and jurisdictional competence appears to have been central to Spain overcoming the impediments to benefit extension that have remained predominant in Italy and Greece. Nevertheless, it is important to keep in mind that the decentralised Spanish approach, while producing some headway, has also created limits to the de facto extension of benefits to the unemployed due to extensive regional variation. Indeed, both benefit and coverage levels vary to such an extent that Arriba and Moreno (2005: 176, 178, 187, 189) classify only the Basque Country benefit as an actual minimum income scheme; and although there are a few others that approximate one (in Madrid, Catalonia, and Navarre), they describe most of the programmes as weaker forms of social assistance and categorise several others simply as workfare. The Spanish case must therefore be viewed as at best only a partial success story for minimum income reform in Southern Europe.

Portugal, by contrast, is the exception that proves the rule. It is the only Southern European country with a national, comprehensive minimum income programme, and is therefore of special interest for our purposes. Historically, there had been very limited attention to poverty until 1986, when Portugal joined the European Economic Community (Capucha et al. 2005: 206). Growing unemployment, inequality, and poverty following the 1993 economic crisis was followed by the 1995 election campaign in which both the Socialist Party (along with the Communists) highlighted the importance of anti-poverty and social inclusion measures (Capucha et al. 2005: 235). Yet this was not simply a domestic matter, as here again the European Union played a role, with the European Council's 1992 recommendation to introduce minimum income schemes cited by leftist parties pushing for reform at the time (Capucha et al. 2005: 236). Within this context, the Guaranteed Minimum Income (Rendimento Mínimo Garantido) was introduced in 1996 (following the electoral victory of the Socialists) alongside other active social policies – the so-called 'new generation' of active social policies. These policies modernised the system, prevented

4 Indeed, we discuss decentralisation at length in the second half of the book, as it seems central to the process of healthcare benefit extension.

subsequent financial problems, and moved Portugal towards the European Union's *acquis communautaire* (Matsaganis et al. 2003: 648).

The prominent role of the Socialist Party in Portugal, as well as the Communist Party's support for the programme, suggests a greater role for partisanship than one might expect based on the other cases. What is more, a number of major trade union confederations (alongside several religious organisations) voiced public support and were even incorporated into the drafting of the legislation (Lalioti 2016: 82). Yet, the situation was in fact not entirely dissimilar from that in France. Although the policy was the subject of some debate during the election – specifically with regard to the fears of fraud, dependency, and skyrocketing costs – it was subsequently passed with limited debate in parliament, and became permanent following a one-year experimental phase (Bruto da Costa 2003: 75). Overall, the programme, which includes both a benefit and a social integration contract, came to enjoy broad popularity and even attract the support of formerly critical groups (Lalioti 2016: 82).

That is not to say, however, that the scheme was immune from the concerns present in our other countries. As one might expect from the other Southern European cases, fraud was a particularly sensitive topic, and a controversial report from the Audit Department of the Exchequer in 1999 forced this risk to the fore; as a result, the government re-highlighted the use of anti-fraud measures, and a fraud inspection campaign confirmed that fraud remained relatively uncommon (Capucha et al. 2005: 247). Nevertheless, the report helped to generate some sustained political backlash against the programme, led by the Popular Party's criticisms relating to programme costs, dependency, fraud, and weaknesses around the insertion element (Capucha et al. 2005: 247). Despite these criticisms and the considerable debate it inspired in the 2002 elections, no party overtly proposed to eliminate the programme in the 2002 elections, and the centre-right government that took power after the election ultimately only slightly altered the programme (Bruto da Costa 2003: 94).

So what explains the atypically (for Southern Europe) broad basis of support in Portugal? The European Community played a role in increasing attention to the issue, but this was a common feature across each of our Southern European cases. Instead, it would appear that the couching of the programme within the broader move to reconfigure and modernise the Portuguese welfare state – and especially to move towards an activation-based approach – was central in cementing support for the reform. This came through government discourse in two intricately related ways: first, through a focus on combatting social exclusion, both among adults and children (Lobo and Magalhães 2004: 92); and second, by stressing the centrality and reinforcement of the activation component, for example with the move to rename the programme the Social Insertion Income in 2004 (Matsaganis et al. 2003: 649). The more effective use of the social insertion component of the benefit scheme, including the Horizontes 2000 programme attempt to attract further business interest in insertion, also appears to have done considerable work in this regard (Capucha et al. 2005: 247). As such, programme framing (within the broader context of a reorientation of the welfare state) appears to have been a key factor in helping the Socialist government to overcome the standard Southern European obstacles to reform.

Overall, then, the other Southern European cases generally provide support for the findings of Chapter 2 – albeit with some important caveats. The European Community played at least a tangential role in all cases, while public opinion appears generally to have played a minimal role, with the sole possible exception of the Portuguese case. In Portugal, the active push by the Socialists for a minimum income scheme as part of a broader move towards social inclusion and active social policy, coupled with the party's subsequent election and the programme's staying power, suggest that the policy had some recognisable mass appeal even in Southern Europe. In Spain, by contrast, drives to assert greater autonomy in regions with historic national communities in Spain were central, and the extensive variation among regions in terms of benefit coverage and generosity underscores this point. Finally, the Greek case, with its policy experimentation during the crisis, may be moving towards a national minimum income programme, but it is simply too early to tell.

With regard to impediments of benefit extension, there are clear, parallel refrains across the cases. Notably, these revolve around concerns about fraud (heightened in Southern Europe by the larger informal economies), municipal administrative capacity, and clientelism. In addition, the prominence of familial financial support is also a widely cited factor in the literature. It would appear, then, that although there has been some divergence among the cases, most of the key Southern European characteristics originally highlighted by Ferrera (1996b) remain common. Interestingly, however, there is evidence of an growing divide, suggestive of a reciprocal relationship between public opinion and policy change: namely, numerous researchers have observed that the traditional Southern European familialism is currently on the decline in Portugal and Spain, while it remains more entrenched in Greece and Italy (Naldini and Jurado 2013; Moreno and Marí-Klose 2013; Torres et al. 2013).

Examining Public Opinion

The Central Cases

These six additional case studies have provided some initial indications of policy trajectories in other Continental and Southern European countries. As a further step in assessing the factors highlighted in the previous chapter, we now proceed to examine public opinion, in light of its central role in our broader argument. We do so first by examining France and Italy, in order to establish a baseline of comparison as we move forward, and then more broadly across the majority of our additional cases.

Part of the expected impact of the key factors discussed in the case comparison is the diminishment of popular dissatisfaction with the current benefit system. This prediction, of course, presupposes that there is a difference of public opinion in these two countries. Directly comparing French and Italian survey responses alone would not be particularly informative, however, since they are situated within starkly contrasting systems: while French social transfers reduce the population at risk of poverty by 50%, the equivalent Italian figure is a paltry 16% (well below even the European Union average, at 35%) (Eurostat 2010: 101). As a result, we begin by looking at the Italian responses to the 1999 European Values Study, which took place around the time the Italian RMI experiment began, and then proceed to consider attitudes elsewhere.

Table 3.1 Age and Mean Concern for the Unemployed in Italy

Mean Survey Responses on the European Values Study (1999)		
	Aged 35 and Under	Over 35
To what extent do you feel concerned about the living conditions of unemployed people in your country: 0 to 1, where 1 signifies very much	0.644 *(.009)*	0.676 *(.006)*
N	716	1264

Source: EVS 2011. Own calculations using two tailed t-tests
Standard errors are italicised in parentheses.

Table 3.1 provides an initial indication of the attitudes of Italians towards the unemployed. Respondents were asked to what extent they were concerned about the living conditions of the unemployed, and were given five potential answers ranging from 'not at all' to 'very much' (recoded from 0 to 1 in our analysis). The table presents the mean Italian responses of those 35 years of age and under versus those over 35. As one notes from the descriptive statistics, Italian youth – despite their disproportionate status as welfare state outsiders – are if anything slightly less likely than their older counterparts to be worry about the living conditions of the unemployed, potentially due to their general lack of experience with truly precarious unemployment.[5] This is especially striking since, given the precarious position in the labour market, one would expect youth to be more, not less, concerned about the unemployed.

Table 3.2 Living with Parents and Mean Concern for the Unemployed in Italy

Mean Survey Responses on the European Values Study (1999)		
	Italians aged 35 and under	
	Does not live with a parent	Lives with a parent
To what extent do you feel concerned about the living conditions of unemployed people in your country: 0 to 1, where 1 signifies very much	0.647 *(.014)*	0.644 *(.011)*
N	252	444

Source: EVS 2011. Own calculations using two tailed t-tests
Standard errors are italicised in parentheses.

Table 3.2 then proceeds to separate out the mean attitudes of those youths who live with their parents from those that do not. While at first glance the latter might appear to be slightly more concerned about the unemployed, the difference is marginal and is not statistically significant. Furthermore, when we compare Tables 3.1 and 3.2 it becomes clear that the gap between the attitudes of youths who do not live at home and those over 35 is approximately as large as that between youths on the whole and over-35s. This suggests that there may be something particular about the Italian youths in general, but to further explore whether our variables of interest are of import we must turn to more sophisticated statistical analysis.

5 The difference between the responses is statistically significant ($p<.01$), despite only amounting to a difference of around 0.03 (with a standard deviation of about 0.22 for the entire population).

Table 3.3 Predicting Italian and French Concern for the Living Conditions of the Unemployed

	Italy	France
Independent Variables		
Youth Living in Parental Home	**-.059*****	-.054
	(.016)	*(.033)*
Youth Outside of Parental Home	-.018	**-.052****
	(.019)	*(.020)*
Unemployed	-.071	**.131*****
	(.058)	*(.036)*
Parental Home & Unemployed Interaction	.050	-.012
	(.067)	*(.102)*
Belief in Increasing Municipal Power	.025	**.034***
	(.016)	*(.020)*
Full-time Employment	**-.038****	-.024
	(.017)	*(.022)*
Family Income	-.003	-.001
	(.002)	*(.004)*
Male	-.007	-.022
	(.013)	*(.017)*
Education Level	-.010	**.026****
	(.009)	*(.010)*
Retiree	-.005	**.044***
	(.019)	*(.026)*
Constant	.675	.597
	(.023)	*(.030)*
N	1360	1210
R^2	.033	.042

Note: Cells contain OLS linear regression coefficients with standard errors italicised in parentheses. Coefficients that reach significance (p < .10) are bolded.
* p < .10, ** p < .05, *** p < .01
Source: EVS 2011

Indeed, ordinary least squares (OLS) regression results (presented in Table 3.3) suggest that once the standard controls are included in the analysis, we do in fact see the predicted effect of living with a parent on the attitudes of youths.[6] Our key explanatory variable is *youth living in the parental home* (defined as being 35 or under and living with at least one

6 Note that the results, both here and below, are not notably impacted by the linear modelling, as ordered probit analysis produces similar findings. Given that, results from the linear regression analyses are presented here for ease of interpretation.

parent).[7] A variable for *youth living outside of the parental home* is included in the analysis as well, to test for the possibility that what may really matter is being young (with the reference group being non-youths).[8] We also include *unemployment* and a variable measuring a belief in *municipal administrative capacity*, constructed using a question asking whether 'more power to local authorities' is a good thing (with three possible responses – 'bad thing' (coded 0), 'don't mind' (coded 0.5), and 'good thing' (coded 1)). Building on models used by authors such as Blekesaune and Quadagno (2003), Jæger (2006), and Van Oorschot (2006), other standard variables included are: *full-time employment* (defined as working over 30 hours a week); *part-time employment*; *self-employment*; *family income* (with brackets of low (0), medium (0.5), and high (1)); *gender; education levels* (with brackets of lower (0), middle (0.5), and upper (1)); and being *retired*.

Looking first at Italian public opinion, results support our expectations and suggest that living with a parent has the predicted impact on the attitudes of youths. Findings suggest that living in the parental home is the major factor at work, tied to statistically significant decreases of just over 0.06 (out of a total range of 0 to 1). Whether through a lack of experience with true precariousness or due to indirect access to welfare state insider perks, residing with one's parents is associated with noticeably lower levels of concern for the unemployed in Italy.

The only other variables in the model that achieve significance are related to employment status (in keeping with the results of Burgoon and Dekker (2010)). Both full-time employment and being self-employed are associated with decreases in concern for the unemployed, with a statistically significant negative impact of about 0.04 and 0.05, respectively. While the former makes intuitive sense (given the group's greater access to benefits), the latter is somewhat unexpected. This may reflect the attitudinal dispositions prevalent among the sort of persons who start their own business, especially given that the category includes individuals who have employees. Regardless, there appear to be two clear routes to lowered concern for the unemployed: through employment status (i.e. being self-employed or holding a full-time job) and being a young person living in the parental home.

7 Since the design of the relevant survey question does not allow one to distinguish adult children living in their parent's home from those who have brought their parent into their own home, a cut-off age of 35 (given a median home-leaving age of about 30) was chosen to prevent the likelihood of the latter possibility affecting the results.

8 Combined with retirees, it completes the controls for age (with three brackets, 15-35, 36-64, and 64+).

Turning to analyse French attitudes, more of the standard variables reach significance, with both unemployment and education associated with statistically significant increases in concern for the unemployed. Belief in municipal administrative capacity has a similar effect. Yet in this instance, living with one's parents does not reach statistical significance (with a p-value of 0.100). What is more, being a young person *outside* of the parental home appears to be associated with lower levels of concern for the unemployed. What explains this? Rather than there being something special about this particular group of youths, we would argue that it is a function of the distribution of youth living arrangements across the countries: in France, as one would expect, a much larger proportion of youth in the sample live outside the parental home (at 77%) than in the Italian case (at 39%).[9] As a result, in the French case the 'youth outside of the parental home' category largely stands in for 'youth'. Conversely, the small number of observations within the category of 'youth living with parents' at least partially explains why the variable only nears significance in France; although the coefficient is about the same as in the Italian model, the standard error is over twice as large.[10]

Within Italy and France, then, this first cut at analysing public opinion suggests that only the former reflects our expectations. Clearly we need to be able to include national-level factors, such as poverty reduction and the size of the informal economy, in the analysis, but the results are nevertheless suggestive. In Italy, while different conceptions of local administrative capacity do not appear significant, youth do seem to be less concerned for the unemployed than their older compatriots. Given that these youths in particular are both more likely to hold atypical work and are disproportionately ill served by the current system, this result is rather counter-intuitive. Once we include controls in the analysis, living with a parent appears to at least partially explain their counterintuitive responses (as per our prediction). Whether these findings reflect country-specific patterns in our broader set of cases will be the subject of the next section.

Exporting the Model

In our first step towards investigating public opinion more broadly, we begin by applying the same national-level model to an additional two Southern

9 In the Spanish and Greek samples, in turn, approximately 52%, and 42% of young people lived outside of the parental home, respectively.

10 Indeed, the same is true in the German case, discussed below.

Table 3.4 Predictors of Concern for the Living Conditions of the Unemployed in Southern Europe

	Spain	Greece
Independent Variables		
Youth Living in Parental Home	-.036	**-.042****
	(.023)	*(.019)*
Youth Outside of Parental Home	-.018	**-.055*****
	(.021)	*(.021)*
Unemployed	.022	-.056
	(.039)	*(.092)*
Parental Home & Unemployed Interaction	-.041	.060
	(.059)	*(.101)*
Belief in Increasing Municipal Power	.015	**.093*****
	(.018)	*(.016)*
Full-time Employment	-.007	-.003
	(.019)	*(.018)*
Family Income	.002	-.001
	(.004)	*(.004)*
Male	-.001	-.011
	(.017)	*(.017)*
Education Level	**.023***	-.021
	(.012)	*(.013)*
Retiree	.019	.020
	(.026)	*(.037)*
Constant	.598	.669
	(.026)	*(.039)*
N	714	905
R^2	.013	.040

Note: Cells contain OLS linear regression coefficients with standard errors italicised in parentheses. Coefficients that reach significance (p < .10) are bolded.
* p < .10, ** p < .05, *** p < .01
Source: EVS 2011

European[11] (Spain and Greece) and three Christian Democratic (Austria, Belgium, and Germany) welfare states. The insurance principle is paramount in all of these cases, but the Southern European states obviously share a greater number of features with Italy; these countries have generally higher home-leaving ages, larger informal economies, and greater administrative

11 As mentioned above, missing data on Portugal unfortunately prevents us from including it here, which is especially unfortunate given its position as the only Southern European welfare state with a nationally available minimum income scheme. The next chapter will, however, reincorporate the Portuguese case into the analysis.

difficulties, as well as a poorer record of poverty reduction via social transfers (with all three countries around 16%) (Eurostat 2010: 101). As such, one would generally expect a similar mechanism to be playing out in these instances.

That being said, we should of course recall here that in terms of minimum income (RMI) schemes, Italy has more in common with Greece than Spain. Yet, as we discussed above, the scope of the difference is not quite as stark as one might initially think, given that only a few regions have programmes that even approximate an RMI-style benefit (see Arriba and Moreno 2005: 178).

With that in mind, Table 3.4 presents the results of the analysis on both Spain and Greece. In Spain, only one variable reaches significance: level of education, which is associated with increased concern for the unemployed. At least part of this general lack of findings may reflect issues with the Spanish data. About a third of Spanish respondents did not provide any indication of their income, and the result a sample size that is much smaller: with just over 700 observations, Spain generally has around 600 fewer observations (and at minimum around 200 fewer) when compared to the other cases. While excluding the income variable leads living at home to reach statistical significance, without an alternative income variable it is difficult to determine whether the effect is robust.

In the Greek case, in turn, being young in and of itself seems to decrease concern for the unemployed, as living in or out of the parental home have coefficients that are statistically indistinguishable. In line with our predictions, however, belief in local authorities reaches significance in this instance and has a sizeable increase in concern; a belief that increasing the power of local authorities is a good thing is associated with an increased concern for the unemployed of about 0.19 (out of a total range of 1).

Across the Continental welfare states, by contrast, we find rather more variation (see Table 3.5). Most of the control variables reach statistical significance in one country or another, with unemployment and education the more standard across the models. With regard to our central explanatory values, belief in increasing municipal power does not appear to matter in any of the countries, which is not surprising given the different manner in which this question might well be interpreted in federal systems. As for the parental home variables, the Austrian results provide the clearest suggestion that the effect might matter outside of Southern Europe, with the 'youth in the parental home' reaching statistical significance and the 'youth outside of the parental home' remaining insignificant. In Belgium, by contrast, the difference between the two youth groups is marginal and not statistically distinguishable, while in Germany, being a young person *outside* of the parental home is correlated with lower levels of concern for

Table 3.5 Predictors of Concern for the Living Conditions of the Unemployed in Continental Europe

	Austria	Belgium	Germany
Independent Variables			
Youth Living in Parental Home	**-0.110*****	**-0.0628****	-0.044
	(0.0300)	*(0.0294)*	*(0.050)*
Youth Outside of Parental Home	-0.0301	**-0.0572*****	**-0.044****
	(0.0220)	*(0.0164)*	*(0.019)*
Unemployed	**0.105***	**0.128*****	**0.070****
	(0.0584)	*(0.0288)*	*(0.031)*
Parental Home & Unemployed Interaction	0.00610	-0.0170	-0.013
	(0.153)	(0.0857)	*(0.069)*
Belief in Increasing Municipal Power	0.0320	0.00961	-0.022
	(0.0196)	*(0.0177)*	*(0.019)*
Full-time Employment	**-0.0412***	-0.0265	0.007
	(0.0220)	*(0.0186)*	*(0.023)*
Family Income	0.000801	**-0.00820****	0.004
	(0.00352)	*(0.00324)*	*(0.005)*
Male	0.0140	0.00661	**-0.041****
	(0.0177)	*(0.0148)*	*(0.017)*
Education Level	**0.0317****	0.0162	**0.052*****
	(0.0131)	*(0.0106)*	*(0.013)*
Retiree	0.0381	0.0114	0.041
	(0.0269)	*(0.0232)*	*(0.025)*
Constant	0.483***	0.560***	0.493***
	(0.0306)	(0.0302)	(0.035)
N	1104	1386	1343
R^2	0.054	0.052	0.042

Note: Cells contain OLS linear regression coefficients with standard errors italicised in parentheses. Coefficients that reach significance (p < .10) are bolded.
* p < .10, ** p < .05, *** p < .01
Source: EVS 2011

the unemployed. This result is most likely driven by a similar dynamic to that discussed in France, as the proportion of youth in the sample living outside the parental home nears 90%. Here again, we would therefore suggest that the 'youth outside of the parental home' is simply standing in for 'youth' in the German case, and that the results do not suggest something particular about this group vis-à-vis home leaving.

Taken together, these country-specific analyses provide an initial indication that the factors discussed in the French-Italian comparison may matter more broadly, both in Italy and elsewhere. Without controlling for contextual variation across countries, however, it is impossible for us to properly assess the relationships at play. We must therefore move to a broader comparison and incorporate the impact of the national-level factors on attitudes – a task which we take up in detail in the next chapter.

Conclusion

Overall, this chapter has offered a first cut at analysing the extent to which the findings from Chapter 2 might apply in other contexts. In doing so, we have proceeded in two steps: first, by examining policy trajectories in a series of other Continental (Austria, Belgium, and Germany) and Southern European (Greece, Portugal, and Spain) welfare states; and second, by briefly analysing country-level public opinion in both our core cases and the additional countries. Here we summarise our findings before turning, in the next chapter, to a more thorough statistical assessment of generalisability with regard to both opinion and policy.

Turning first to policy trajectories, we find, as expected, that the most striking divergence is between the Continental and Southern European cases. Beginning with the Continental countries, the discussion confirms that although the countries share much in common, France's laggard status positions it as somewhat of an outlier. Indeed, the other countries had all introduced minimum income schemes by the time atypical employment began to really take off. Nevertheless, the additional Continental case studies highlighted three very different policy trajectories vis-à-vis outsider access to benefits, thereby offering insights on our central questions about benefit standardisation and universalisation. Specifically, we contrasted Austria's 'smoothed dualisation', Belgium's (largely union-driven) expansion of access to a gradually weakened unemployment insurance system, and Germany's more traditional dualisation path.

The Southern European comparison, by contrast, was more directly applicable to the question of generalisability, with clear connections between the cases. Similar impediments to reform were found to exist in all of the cases, despite some variation in outcomes: the Greek case most closely resembles the Italian, with an experiment implemented only very recently (in 2014), and its fate still in question; Spain saw some successful reforms, with minimum income schemes (or close approximates) in several regions, but a high degree of variation in the coverage, benefit generosity, and programme type across the regions; while Portugal is the only clear success story, with its nationally available minimum income programme in place since 1997. While the problems highlighted in the Italian case seem to be reflected in each of the other Southern European countries, Portuguese exceptionalism was at least partly driven by the Socialist government's success in yoking activation to welfare state modernisation and making the minimum income scheme a central plank of this broader reform platform. The combined focus on social exclusion and activation requirements appear to have done considerable work in generating broad support for the programme and making it viable in the long term.

Finally, results of the country-level survey analysis provided some preliminary indications that the mechanisms discussed in Chapter 2 may well shape public attitudes. The clearest support came from the Italian context, where being a young person in the parental home is associated with a substantial decrease in concern for the unemployed. Analysis of the survey data from other countries provided more mixed results, but this is to be expected if poverty reduction levels and other national-level factors matter vis-à-vis concern for the unemployed. The next chapter will undertake this task, alongside other approaches to assessing the determinants of attitudinal and policy change, as we continue to examine the conclusions from the French-Italian comparison.

4 Southern European Characteristics in the Broader Context

Continuing our assessment of the conclusions drawn from the French and Italian comparison, this chapter will provide a statistical assessment of the generalisability of the findings on unemployment coverage. This analysis will be carried out in two stages, with the ultimate intention of conceptually linking (albeit not directly) the results of the survey analysis with actual policy changes. The first step will explore the factors influencing public opinion, including the effects of different national-level variables on individual preferences using multi-level modelling. The goal here, building on the previous chapter, is to analyse demand-side variation on the issue of benefit extension, both at the individual and national level. The second step will shift our attention towards actual outcomes, employing two approaches to deal with different types of changes: time-series analysis will be used to examine the national-level determinants of incremental changes in coverage levels; while duration analysis will allow us to move beyond the typical approach and directly address policy change. As we will note, focusing on the likelihood of reform itself helps us to better understand the timing of dramatic increases (or lack thereof) in coverage extension of benefit access via the introduction of national, broadly available social assistance programmes.

Before proceeding with this investigation, the chapter will begin by briefly setting out the variables to be included in the analysis; this discussion will include, where appropriate, arguments for the use of non-ideal data when better options are not available. The subsequent section of the chapter will then proceed to present the results of the statistical investigation, laying out each type of analysis in turn. These results will then be followed up with a brief summary and some conclusions, including references to the limitations of the findings and directions for future research.

To preview the findings, this chapter will suggest that the variables set out in Chapter 2 have more generalisable effects. The results of the multi-level model survey analysis point towards the broader applicability of most of the factors discussed in the French-Italian comparison. This is an important first step in the analysis, since attitudes shape the electoral incentives for parties to pursue reform. The time-series analysis of incremental changes in unemployment insurance coverage and recipiency ratios provides less clear results, but the findings of the duration analysis, which directly addresses the introduction of residualising policies, are more robust. Both the size of the informal economy and later home-leaving ages appear to have a substantial, negative impact on the probability of revolutionary social policy reforms being introduced.

Taken together, the findings presented in this chapter suggest that the conclusions presented in Chapter 2 are likely generalisable to other cases, with our key variables negatively impacting both attitudes (vis-à-vis concern for the unemployed) and benefit extension via residualisation. Implicit in this argument is the point that the size of the informal economy and late home leaving among young adults are impacting policy changes at least partially *through* their effects on attitudes (by shaping electoral incentives). In the absence of panel data, of course, we are unable to assess this directly – but the consistency of findings across various approaches provides support for our argument and suggests that the limitations are data based rather than theoretical.

The Models

This section will lay out the variables to be employed throughout the rest of the chapter as we attempt to test the generalisability of the variables highlighted in the case studies. We will begin by laying out the dependent variables to be used, and then proceed to the explanatory ones specific to each of the types of analysis. The section will then conclude by outlining the additional variables used in the analysis, listing the standard variables in the literature that will be included.

Dependent Variables

Dealing first with the public opinion data, the variable used in Chapter 3 remains at the centre of our analysis: concern for the living conditions of the unemployed. The idea here is that, controlling for (inter alia) the extent of poverty reduction in a given system, popular concern for the unemployed should indicate support for benefit extension and, more generally, concern for welfare state outsiders. The survey question used in this analysis is taken from the 1999 European Values Study (EVS) (2011), with answers ranging from 'not at all' to 'very much'.[1] This European data is used to allow us to

1 There are, of course, some potential limitations to using these sorts of survey responses, particularly since our question is in the middle of a battery of similar ones, which may introduce

further build upon the analysis already carried out in the previous chapter, but as a consequence the number of countries included in the analysis is rather limited.

For the time-series analysis, although we are able to incorporate a broader range of countries, obtaining data that deal directly with our outcomes of interest is more complicated. Difficulties isolating policy change through statistics alone makes the task of discovering a single perfect measure of access to unemployment benefits rather complex. One of the standard measures in the literature on welfare states, spending levels, obviously serves as a rather poor indicator of changes in coverage levels. As Allan and Scruggs (2004) point out, even if we look directly at spending on unemployment benefits, it is unlikely to directly correlate with the extent to which welfare states protect citizens vis-à-vis the market. Increases in the number of welfare recipients may not be apparent in aggregate social expenditure levels if they coincide with welfare cuts; furthermore, in cases where the cost of welfare service delivery increases over time due to exogenous factors, providing a stationary level of service provision would actually require

As such, rather than using spending levels, we employ more direct measures of coverage. Yet since an ideal measure of coverage data is not available, two distinct dependent variables are used in the time-series analysis. The first of these variables is *unemployment insurance coverage levels*, gauged as a proportion of the labour force insured for unemployment, taken from Scruggs (2004). The data here cover sixteen countries, typically from 1960 up to the early 2000s (though the exact dates vary depending on the country).[2] Unfortunately, for our purposes the measure suffers from some serious limitations, as it fails to incorporate all of the aspects of benefit coverage that we are interested in conceptually; most notably, since the measure looks only at unemployment insurance, it cannot capture the difference between countries where citizens have access to unemployment assistance and those where they do not. It is therefore unable to distinguish between countries with residualised systems and countries with no benefits for those who cannot access the primary system. Furthermore, it lacks observations

some non-random response error (see Green and Citrin 1994) . Furthermore, cultural norms around deference, politeness, etc., may also lead respondents to give responses that may or may not reflect their true opinion on an issue (e.g. Javeline 1999). Yet despite these limitations, the question is a relatively standard one and should serve as a broadly reasonable measure of concern for the unemployed.

2 These are: Australia, Austria, Belgium, Canada, Denmark, Finland, France, Germany, Ireland, Italy, the Netherlands, New Zealand, Norway, Sweden, the United Kingdom, and the United States.

for any Southern European welfare states apart from Italy, and even there it is only available for the 1960s and 1970s.[3]

Due to these limitations, a second, unpublished Organisation for Economic Co-operation and Development (OECD) measure – *recipiency ratios* – is used as a complementary measure.[4] This variable presents the proportion of income-replacement benefit recipients out of the total number of people who are technically unemployed. As a result, it provides a measure of the proportion of *unemployed* welfare state outsiders that avoids the aforementioned conceptual difficulties with Scruggs' measure. While using this measure removes a substantial number of the country-year observations available in the alternative measure,[5] it does contain data on more Southern European countries (specifically Spain and Portugal, though it does not contain any data whatsoever on Italy). Yet due to the measure's focus on the currently unemployed, it is still unable to tell us how many individuals would lack access to unemployment benefits if they were to lose their jobs. In light of these drawbacks, this data will therefore be used alongside the Scruggs measure in an effort to compensate for both of their shortcomings.

Finally, there is the dependent variable used in the duration analysis: *the existence of a national social assistance programme* – in particular one aimed not simply at specific categories of potential recipients (e.g. the elderly, war veterans, etc.). Since both of the above coverage measures are incapable of fully capturing the changes in coverage levels as expressed in the qualitative chapters, a binary variable was created to indicate the presence (coded 1) or absence (coded 0) of a universally available benefit programme for the unemployed (i.e. a residualised system). In this way, we are able to distinguish reforms that expand coverage through residualisation from those that simply extend access to unemployment insurance. This measure was constructed on the basis of qualitative information about the various countries, derived principally from *The Last Safety Net: A Handbook of Minimum Income Protection in Europe* (Bahle et al. 2011) and the *Social*

3 Note that the Southern European countries have both the largest informal economies and the highest median age at which children leave home. While the rest of the countries demonstrate no real pattern in this regard, these countries are exceptions – making it particularly unfortunate that we are unable to include all of the Mediterranean countries in a single model looking at coverage level.

4 This data was obtained via a personal communication with David Grubb at the OECD.

5 Nevertheless, aside from the loss of Austria, Belgium, and Italy and the addition of Portugal and Spain, the included countries remain the same as in the unemployment insurance coverage levels data.

Security Programs throughout the World database.[6] The resulting dataset spans the 1960 to 2010 period and includes a total of eighteen countries.[7] The measure was then used to indicate the length of time taken for a universally available, national benefit programme to be introduced. This binary distinction does of course mean that some nuance is lost, such that the introduction of one-off municipal or regional programmes is not reflected in the data, but it more accurately allows us to assess the changes that are of interest to us. The variable thus illuminates large-scale policy changes that might otherwise go unnoticed using other measures.

Explanatory Variables

Two variables serve as the primary focus of our analysis and will be used in all three iterations of our analysis: (1) *the size of the informal economy* and (2) *the median age at which youth leave home*. Within the survey analysis, a variable indicating whether the respondent is a young adult (35 and under)[8] living in their parental home is included as well,[9] as is a variable measuring a belief in municipal administrative capacity, constructed using a survey question asking whether 'more power to local authorities' is a good thing (with three possible responses – 'bad thing' (coded 0), 'don't mind' (coded 0.5), and 'good thing' (coded 1). To recap, the size of the informal economy is expected to negatively impact coverage by decreasing popular concern about the lack of welfare state access to labour market outsiders, while late home leaving by youths has a duel effect: on the individual level, young outsiders in the parental home will be less pro-reform thanks to their less precarious life; and on the national level, knowledge that young outsiders are protected by the family in the absence of welfare state provision will decrease popular concern towards the need for extensive benefits and high coverage levels. Greater faith among citizens in municipal administrative capacity, in turn, is expected to increase the belief that local authorities can

6 See US Social Security Administration 2012.

7 These are: Australia, Austria, Belgium, Canada, Denmark, Finland, France, Germany, Greece, Ireland, Italy, the Netherlands, New Zealand, Portugal, Spain, Sweden, the United Kingdom and the United States. Due to the nature of duration analysis, however, certain countries were necessarily dropped from the final analysis.

8 Since the design of the relevant survey question does not allow one to distinguish adult children living in their parent's home from adult children who have brought their parent into their own home, a cut-off of age 35 was chosen to prevent the likelihood of the latter possibility affecting the results.

9 A variable for those youths who live outside of the parental home is included in the analysis as well, to test for the possibility that what may really matter is simply being young.

Figure 4.1 Informal Economy Size Comparison (1980s and 2000s)

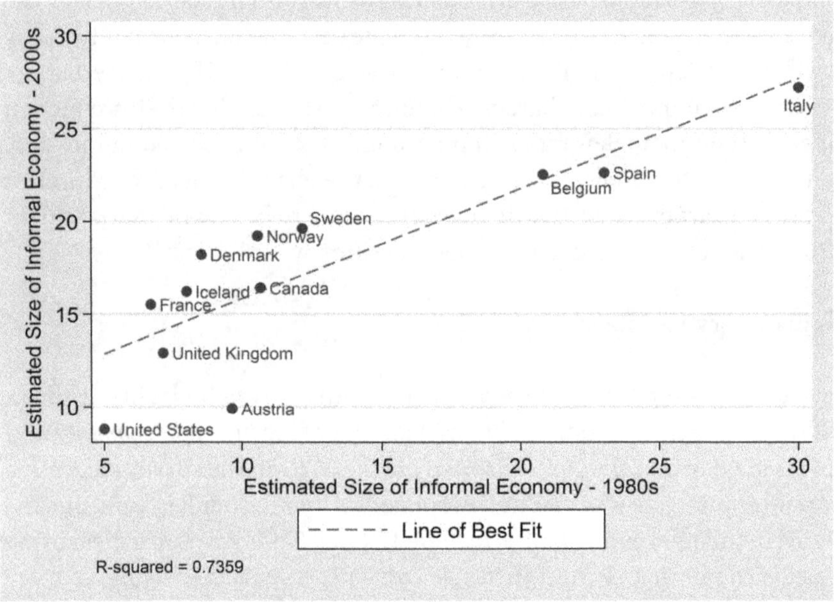

be entrusted with overseeing benefit distribution. The section will begin by describing the datasets that were used in the case of the two national-level variables, and then outline how the non-longitudinal data has been used for our time-series analysis.

In the case of the informal economy, its very nature obviously makes its size difficult to estimate. For our purposes we use the 2010 database prepared by Schneider, Buehn, and Montenegro for a World Bank study, which includes data for 162 countries from 1999 to 2007. Since the time period is not long enough for our longitudinal purpose (data covering a longer time period is unfortunately unavailable),[10] the mean value was taken for the 1999 to 2006 period (2007 is excluded due to data limitations). The estimation uses a Multiple Indicators Multiple Causes model (a type of structural equations model) on a broader scale than other comparable studies; the advantage of this approach is that it avoids basing the estimation on any one particular predictor of the size of the informal economy (such as currency demand or electricity usage) (Schneider et al. 2010: 10).

While using an average from this limited period is clearly not ideal, access to the limited earlier data that does exist suggests that this approach

10 This problem is obviously avoided in the case of the survey data analysis.

does not notably distort relative differences among countries. To examine the reasonableness of this approach, Figure 4.1 presents the growth of the informal sector in a sample of OECD countries, with earlier data taken from a number of sources compiled in Schneider and Hofreither (1986: 21). The data here are presented as suggestive, since there are a two particular limitations to longitudinal comparisons in this instance: first, the 1980 data are calculated as a percentage of gross national product (GNP), conflicting with the gross domestic product (GDP) calculation for 2000; second, although the figures are – as usual – estimates,[11] the values were calculated using the (less sophisticated) currency-demand approach, which suggests that they are unlikely to be as accurate as recent measures.

Despite these drawbacks, however, examining the countries in descending order of the eventual size of their informal economy, we note that almost all of the countries (save for the largest three) have experienced considerable growth of their informal sector. Italy, Spain, and Belgium, with strikingly large informal economies in 1980, appear to have hit an upper limit, with the former two even decreasing slightly. Yet despite this, the overall ordering of countries in 2000 is generally predictable from the size of the informal economy in 1980, with only a few exceptions for countries on the lower end. Overall, this suggests that the most recent estimates can be relatively reasonably projected backward.

Nevertheless, projecting more minute differences among the countries back through time would be problematic, as it would require excessive faith in the over-time consistency within countries. Instead, the informal economy measure for the longitudinal analyses was constructed by dividing the countries into terciles on the basis of their position in the rank ordering, with low-, average-, and high-value countries grouped together (respectively coded 1, 2, and 3).[12] This approach allows us to deal with the data limitations credibly while also getting at the effects of the informal economy.

An analogous approach was taken with regard to home-leaving ages. Measuring the age at which youth leave the parental home requires some nuance, since in some instances young people leave the nest only to return to it (or indeed, never leave at all). The standard current approach, which we follow here, is to employ the *median age of home leaving*, calculated as the age at which half of all youth no longer live with their parents (Iacovou 2011: 2). Here the bulk of the data are derived from Eurostat (2010), which

11 In cases where the estimates indicated ranges of potential values, the mean value was used.

12 By contrast, the variable was left as is for the survey analysis, with their specific values taken for 1999.

Figure 4.2 Leaving Home Age Comparison (1980s and 2000s)

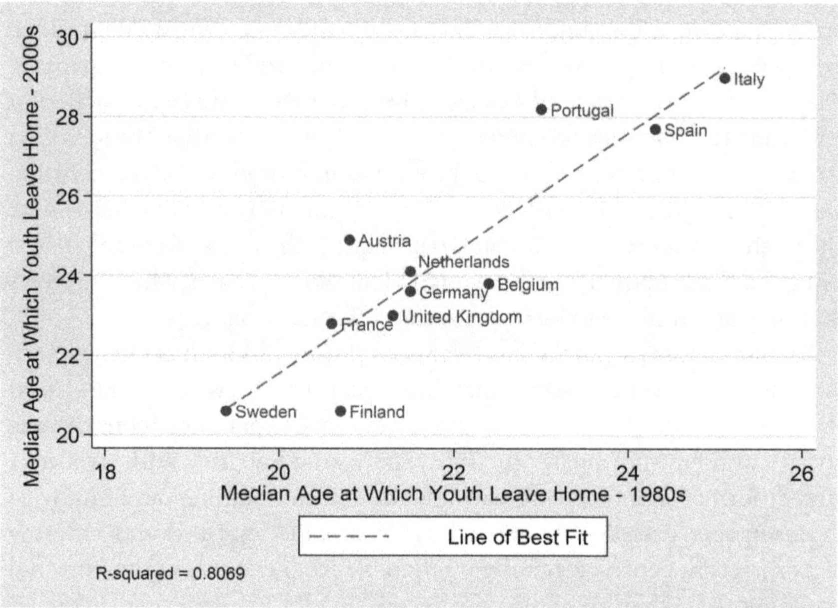

includes all of our European countries. Additional data were then added for the non-European countries for which comparable data exists,[13] bringing the total number of cases to eighteen. Unfortunately, a lack of longitudinal data on this measure – with data coming from the 2000s[14] – raises the same issues here that we faced with the measure of informal economy size.

This lead us to take the same approach employed above to ensure validity (see Figure 4.2), using the limited data available from an earlier period (taken from Billari et al. 2001). Comparing data for home leaving in the 1980s with home leaving in the 2000s, one notes that there is only a very limited amount of shifting around: youth in countries that left home relatively early in the past continue to leave early, while countries in which they left later in life continue to be found at the upper end of the spectrum. There are some outliers, with Portugal in particular experiencing a notably greater increase than one would have predicted, but overall the order of countries remains

13 These are: for Australia: *ABS Censuses of Population and Housing* (2009); for Canada: Statistics Canada, *Censuses of Population* (2001); for New Zealand: *Family and Household Projections 2001(base)-2021* (2004); and for the United States: U.S. Census Bureau, *Current Population Survey, Annual Social and Economic Supplements, March* (2007).

14 In most instances, the data refer to 2007, though for Canada and New Zealand only data from 2001 were available.

consistent. As was the case with the size of the informal economy, it would appear that while countries have generally experienced an upward trend in the median age at which youth leave home, a similar pattern persists. This leads us to use the same categorisation employed for the measure of the informal economy, dividing the countries into low-, average-, and high-value groups (coded 1, 2, and 3, respectively).[15]

Overall, this tercile approach to addressing longitudinal data limitations clearly has both benefits and drawbacks. On the one hand, in addition to allowing us to carry out analysis that would otherwise be impossible, it helps to mitigate issues related to the rather high collinearity between median home-leaving ages and the size of the informal economy.[16] On the other hand, the tercile approach in the time series and duration analysis poses its own complication: it obliges us to use time-invariant categorisations in trying to explain changes over time, thereby limiting our ability to draw strong conclusions from the analysis. Nevertheless, it remains the best available option in light of the available data, and given that home-leaving ages and the size of the informal economy exhibit general stability over time, the tercile measure serves as an indicative interval variable. While data availability prevents us from assessing the impact of gradual changes in these values, we are still able to assess the broad impact of low, medium, or high levels of the variables.

Standard Variables

The final additional variables included in the models reflect the controls and other explanatory variables typically pointed to in the literature. The multi-level model survey analysis builds on the models used by authors such as Arts and Gelissen (2001), Blekesaune and Quadagno (2003), Jæger (2006), and Van Oorschot (2006), as well as that constructed in Chapter 3. Variables include: (1) *unemployment*; (2) *full-time employment* (defined as working over 30 hours a week or being self-employed); (3) *family income* (in deciles); (4) *gender*; (5) *education levels* (with brackets of lower, middle, and upper); and

15 Note that, once again, precise values (rather than terciles) will be used in the survey analysis, as we can be rather more confident in their accuracy given the availability of data from either the exact year (in the case of the informal economy) or within several years (in the case of home leaving).

16 The correlation between the values of the fifteen countries included in our time series is just under 0.14, with six of the countries in the same category for both variables. This is quite a considerable drop from the correlation between the specific values in the broader sample, at approximately 0.64.

(6) *being retired*. In light of findings by authors such as Boeri et al. (2001b), Bonoli and Haüsermann (2009), and Taylor-Gooby (2011b), we expect these standard variables to be highly important. At the national level, controls are also added for: (7) *poverty reduction*, measured as difference between pre-transfer and post-transfer poverty rates (own calculation using Eurostat data (2012)); (8) *the structure of inequality*, using the 90/10 ratio (see Lupu and Pontusson 2011)[17]; (9) *change in migrant stock* (see Soroka et al. 2016)[18]; (10) the *mean unemployment rates* over the past three years (to indicate the general labour market conditions); and (11) *change in GDP per capita* (with the latter two taken from the OECD (2012b; 2012d)). Since we expect that our mechanisms of interest are likely impacted by the prevalence of the insurance principle (rather than means testing or universalism) in a given system, we also include (12) an *insurance principle dummy* variable for Corporatist and Southern European welfare states (see Esping-Andersen 1990; 1999; Ferrera 1996b; 2000; Naldini 2003).[19] While most of these variables are standard, poverty reduction is added in to control for the effect of different levels of social transfers on concern for the unemployed.

The longitudinal models, in turn, take as their foundation the work of (to name but a few) Hicks (1999), Huber and Stephens (2001), Swank (2001), Allan and Scruggs (2004), and Soroka et al. (2006). Although the variables are typically applied in regressions looking at welfare state expenditure, generosity, or decommodification, they remain relevant insofar as all three of these issues are tied up with coverage levels. Presented in the order in which they are listed in the regression results, these standard variables are: (1) *the previous year's coverage levels* (depending on the dependent variable), which is included to take into account the effects of potentially cumbersome welfare states or, conversely, institutional inertia; a variety of lagged economic factors – namely, (2) *GDP per capita*, (3) *inflation*, and (4) *unemployment* – to capture changes in the number of unemployed persons; (5) *the percentage of the labour force that is female*, with increases in the size of the female workforce hypothesised to increase social service provision by changing popular attitudes towards the value of social services (see Huber and Stephens 2001: 56); (6) *an interaction effect for left government and union*

17 Data from LIS (2013) for the closest available year to 1999 (ultimately ranging from 1998 to 2001).

18 Data from United Nations 2009.

19 This may be the case since the institutional structures that tend to be associated with the insurance principle (e.g. a multitude of occupation-based unemployment schemes) may inculcate different attitudes towards other potential benefit recipients – both those who qualify for access and those who do not.

density; and *change in migrant stock* (see Soroka et al. 2006). Save for left government (derived from Armingeon et al. 2011), change in migrant stock (taken from United Nations 2009), and the lagged versions of coverage levels (with their sources discussed above), each of these variables is taken from the OECD (2012b; 2012c; 2012d).[20] In most cases, the variables are lagged by a year to take into account the circumstances with which governments were concerned at the time of devising the next year's budget.[21]

Findings

Turning now to the empirical analysis, this section will present the results of the survey analysis (via multi-level models), time-series regressions, and duration analysis. While the survey analysis will be carried out on a subset of European countries using EVS data from 1999, the time-series and duration analysis are performed on a sample of OECD countries over varying segments during the 1960 to 2010 period. Due to data limitations, the countries included in the samples vary somewhat across the different types of analysis, and are specified in each instance. The multi-level modelling is carried out using generalised least squares (GLS) random-effects regressions (using country clusters),[22] while the time-series analysis is carried out using ordinary least squares (OLS) linear regressions with panel-corrected standard errors. The findings are presented below in the following three sections, using survey, time-series, and duration analysis to examine benefits for the unemployed. The discussion of the results from these various models will be centred upon the ways in which the factors pointed to in Chapter 2 may impact both attitudes and policy changes. Of central concern is the possibility that decreased concern for the unemployed may decrease the likelihood that a country will extend benefits.

20 For the duration analysis, however, GDP data is taken from the Conference Board Total Economy Database (2015) to provide us with additional data from the 1960s (see http://www.conference-board.org/data/economydatabase/).

21 The only exception is unemployment levels, where the *change* (rather than lagged value) is taken since increases in unemployment may, depending upon the nature of the benefits, directly impact coverage and/or recipiency.

22 Although the dependent variable is ordinal, which at first glance would suggest that a mixed effects ordered logistic regression might be more appropriate, our interest in interaction effects means that such an approach would create further more difficulties (see, for example, Norton et al. 2004 and Williams 2009 for a discussion of further complications). Nevertheless, the mixed effects ordered logistic approach does return the same pattern of statistical significance.

With that in mind, we begin by turning to the results of the survey analysis.

Understanding Attitudes

In this section we explore the demand side of the equation, attempting to determine what individual- and national-level factors shape individual concern for the unemployed – and by extension, popular interest in the extension of benefits for the unemployed. While it is true that concern for the wellbeing of unemployed persons does not necessarily equate to mass pressure for benefit extension, without it we would expect political discourse on the issue likely to be quite muted. Thus, by exploring the variables impeding such concern we attain some insight into factors that ultimately (though indirectly) help to shape the possibility of reform itself.

In carrying out this analysis, we construct the multi-level models using data from almost 12,000 respondents across twelve European countries.[23] Model 1 includes only the key explanatory variables, Model 2 introduces individual-level controls, and Model 3 adds national-level controls as a robustness check. Table 4.1 presents this analysis. Despite the significance of many of the standard variables and theories in the literature, for our purposes, the most interesting results pertain to youth in the parental home, support for municipal power, median home-leaving age, and the size of the informal economy. While the limited number of country clusters limits our ability to draw strong conclusions about the country-level effects, the analysis nevertheless provides a solid starting point for the remainder of the investigation, which focuses exclusively on these factors.

Key results at the individual level are consistent across the models. Both being a young person inside the parental home and out of it have statistically significant impacts, with only a insignificant difference between the coefficients. Yet for young unemployed persons living at home, we find a notably lower level of concern for the unemployed than is exhibited by other unemployed persons. A belief in increasing municipal power, in turn, consistently has the predicted positive impact.

23 These are: Austria, Belgium, Finland, France, Germany, Greece, Ireland, Italy, the Netherlands, Spain, and the United Kingdom. The total number of observations per country ultimately included in the regression analysis ranges from 563 (for the United Kingdom) to 1386 (for Belgium), with an overall average per country of 979.

Table 4.1 Concern for the Living Conditions of the Unemployed – Multi-level Model Analysis

	Model 1	Model 2	Model 3
Independent Variables			
Youth Living in Parental Home	**-0.063*****	**-0.054*****	**-0.054*****
	(0.008)	*(0.008)*	*(0.008)*
Youth Outside of Parental Home	**-0.058*****	**-0.050*****	**-0.049*****
	(0.005)	*(0.006)*	*(0.006)*
Unemployed	**0.091*****	**0.084*****	**0.085*****
	(0.010)	*(0.011)*	*(0.011)*
Parental Home & Unemployed Interaction	-0.036	**-0.044***	**-0.044***
	(0.024)	*(0.024)*	*(0.024)*
Increase	**0.025*****	**0.032*****	**0.033*****
Municipal Power	*(0.005)*	*(0.005)*	*(0.005)*
Poverty Reduction	-0.441	**-.501*****	**-0.478*****
	(0.364)	*(.051)*	*(0.052)*
Median Age of	-0.193	**-0.219*****	**-0.210*****
Home Leaving	*(0.167)*	*(0.024)*	*(0.002)*
Home Leaving & Poverty Reduction	0.020	**0.023*****	**0.022*****
Interaction	*(0.018)*	*(0.002)*	*(0.002)*
Size of the Informal	0.059	**0.066*****	**0.065*****
Economy	*(0.056)*	*(0.008)*	*(0.008)*
Informal Economy & Poverty Reduction	-0.005	**-0.006*****	**-0.006*****
Interaction	*(0.005)*	*(0.0006)*	*(0.001)*
Full-time Employment	---	**-0.026*****	**-0.025*****
		(0.007)	*(0.007)*
Part-time Employment	---	-0.010	-0.009
		(0.009)	*(0.009)*
Self-Employment	---	**-0.024****	**-0.022****
		(0.010)	*(0.011)*
Family Income	---	-0.006	-0.005
		(0.006)	*(0.006)*
Male	---	**-0.008***	**-0.009***
		(0.005)	*(0.005)*
Education Level	---	0.010	0.010
		(0.006)	*(0.006)*
Retiree	---	**0.017****	**0.019****
		(0.007)	*(0.007)*
Mean Unemployment	---	---	**0.003****
(1997-1999)			*(0.001)*
Δ GDP	---	---	-1.91e-08
			(1.24e-07)
	---	---	

	Model 1	**Model 2**	**Model 3**
Independent Variables			
Constant	4.656	5.236***	4.953***
	(3.391)	*(0.472)*	*(0.482)*
Number of Observations	11745	11745	11745
Number of Groups	12	12	12

Note: Cells contain GLS random-effects regression coefficients with standard errors italicized in parentheses. Coefficients that reach significance (p < .10) are bolded.
* p < .10, ** p < .05, *** p < .01
Source: EVS 2011

At the national level, our central variables attain statistical significance once standard individual-level controls are included in the analysis. Higher home-leaving ages are associated with decreased concern for the unemployed, as suggested by the paired comparison – although (as anticipated) this effect is moderated in countries that already reduce poverty fairly well. Mean unemployment also reaches statistical significance, and has the positive impact predicted by Pfeifer (2009).

By contrast, the size of the informal economy appears at first glance to be correlated with *greater* concern for the unemployed (rather than having the predicted negative effect). Yet this result is driven entirely by Spain: dropping Spanish data removes the significance of the informal economy entirely. All other variables of interest remain unaffected, whether through the removal of Spanish data or data from any other specific country. Furthermore, these findings are not simply the result of correlations with important individual-level factors: neither the median home-leaving age nor the size of the informal economy is particularly correlated with other individual-level variables associated with greater concern for the unemployed.[24]

On the whole, these results provide support for the findings of the previous chapters. At the individual level, advocating the extension of municipal power is correlated with increased concern. While we found a similarly decreased level of concern for the unemployed among youth both in and out of the parental home,[25] unemployment does not appear to effect youth

24 Within our sample, the only correlations that surpass 0.1 are between: median home leaving and living in the parental home (0.24); the size of the informal economy and education levels (0.15); and the size of the informal economy and living in the parental home (0.21).

25 This generally low level of concern among youth may reflect the fact that, outside of Southern Europe, there is an especially high proportion of post-secondary students living in their parental homes.

in the parental home the way it affects others. These youth exhibit a notably lower level of concern for the unemployed (of which they are a part) than one would expect.

What is more, late home-leaving ages are associated with a general decrease in concern for the unemployed within the broader population. As expected, however, welfare states that substantially reduce poverty appear to reinforce themselves via public opinion and/or diminish popular attention paid to the neediness of unemployed youth. The apparent unimportance of the informal economy, by contrast, suggests that the variable may be less important internationally than one would expect based on the French-Italian comparison. Yet we hesitate to draw strong conclusions here, given the small number of cases and the high correlation among our national-level variables: poverty reduction, the size of the informal economy, and median home-leaving age are all correlated at rates between 0.71 and 0.86. This complicates our ability to assess generalisability, but results nevertheless provide a good indication that most findings from the French-Italian comparison may be exportable to other contexts.

Thus far, however, we have focused on the impact of these variables on attitudes, which obviously begs the question of whether they are actually associated with distinct outcomes regarding welfare state coverage. In order to deal with this issue, we must turn to examine actual changes in outcomes.

Understanding Changes in Coverage Levels (Part One)

We now turn to our first attempt at analysing outcomes, using the standard approach of employing time-series analysis to examine gradual changes to coverage levels (which provide a proxy for the proportion of welfare state outsiders). The analysis is carried out via linear regression (with panel-corrected standard errors) on our two datasets. As discussed above, in light of issues with the data on access to unemployment benefits, we examine both of the aforementioned coverage-level measures listed. As such, Table 4.2 examines unemployment insurance coverage (i.e. the proportion of workers with access to the principal system) while Table 3 looks at income replacement for the unemployed (i.e. the proportion of the unemployed with access to either the principal or residual system). In each case, the full models are once again built stepwise, moving from Model 1, the null model (with only our key explanatory variables), to Model 2, which adds the standard economic controls, and finally to Model 3, which includes all of our variables. As mentioned above, the countries included in the two datasets

Table 4.2 Time-Series Analysis – Unemployment Insurance Coverage Levels

	Model 1	Model 2	Model 3
Independent Variables			
DV $_{t-1}$	**-0.080***** *(0.006)*	**-0.084***** *(0.007)*	**-0.094***** *(0.007)*
Size of Informal Economy (Tercile)	-0.110 *(0.076)*	**-0.145**** *(0.074)*	**-0.347***** *(0.081)*
Median Age Youth Leave Home (Tercile)	**-0.643***** *(0.138)*	**-0.761***** *(0.133)*	**-0.941***** *(0.182)*
GDP $_{t}$	---	-0.0000001 *(0.0000001)*	9.32e-08 *(1.40e-07)*
Inflation $_{t}$	---	**-0.041**** *(0.018)*	**-0.113***** *(0.022)*
Δ Unemployment	---	**-0.482***** *(0.095)*	**-0.493***** *(0.096)*
Female Workforce $_{t-1}$	---	---	**-0.122***** *(0.017)*
Union Density $_{t-1}$	---	---	**0.025***** *(0.008)*
Left Government $_{t-1}$	---	---	0.001 *(0.005)*
Left & Union Interaction $_{t-1}$	---	---	-0.00003 *(0.00009)*
Δ Immigration	---	---	0.413 *(0.555)*
Constant	7.875*** (0.532)	8.783*** (0.611)	14.22 (1.218)
N	423	423	423
Number of Panels	15	15	15
R^2	0.056	0.068	0.077

Note: Cells contain OLS linear regression coefficients with panel-corrected standard errors italicised in parentheses. Coefficients that reach significance (p < .10) are bolded.
* $p < 0.10$, ** $p < 0.05$, *** $p < 0.01$

differ somewhat, while the overall number of country-year observations is somewhat higher with the unemployment insurance coverage data (423 versus 291).[26]

On the question of factors affecting unemployment insurance coverage, the results from Model 3 suggest a number of significant standard variables: namely, inflation, change in unemployment, the lagged size of the female

26 See above discussion of the datasets for the list of countries in each.

Table 4.3 Time-Series Analysis – Unemployment Benefit Recipiency Ratios

	Model 1	Model 2	Model 3
Independent Variables			
DV $_{t-1}$	**-0.037***	**-0.048****	**-0.074*****
	(0.020)	(0.022)	*(0.028)*
Size of Informal Economy (Tercile)	**0.938***	0.549	-0.999
	(0.561)	(0.548)	*(0.952)*
Median Age Youth Leave Home (Tercile)	-0.341	-0.519	1.713
	(0.844)	(0.839)	(1.270)
GDP $_t$	---	**-0.0000007*****	**-5.37e-07****
		(0.0000002)	*(2.55e-07)*
Inflation $_t$	---	0.166	0.201
		(0.165)	*(0.163)*
Δ Unemployment	---	**-1.106****	**-1.110*****
		(0.452)	*(0.457)*
Female Workforce $_{t-1}$	---	---	**0.228***
			(0.131)
Union Density $_{t-1}$	---	---	**0.091***
			(0.049)
Left Government $_{t-1}$	---	---	0.017
			(0.024)
Left & Union Interaction $_{t-1}$	---	---	-0.001
			(0.001)
Δ Immigration	---	---	-0.795
			(1.187)
Constant	3.165*	4.815+	-7.394
	(1.580)	(2.824)	(5.843)
N	291	291	291
Number of Panels	14	14	14
R^2	0.022	0.061	0.084

Note: Cells contain OLS linear regression coefficients with panel-corrected standard errors italicised in parentheses. Coefficients that reach significance (p < .10) are bolded.
* $p < 0.10$, ** $p < 0.05$, *** $p < 0.01$

labour force, and lagged trade union density.[27] In addition, the lagged values for the dependent variable are statistically significant, as expected. More importantly, both the size of the informal economy and the age at which youth leave home appear to have significant, negative effects on coverage

27 Note that the effect of female labour market participation is in the opposite direction one might expect. This may reflect that unemployment insurance, with its often-rigid qualification requirements, was historically a relative bastion of male breadwinners, such that as women have increasingly entered the labour market (often on a part-time or short-term contract basis), coverage levels decreased.

levels. Note that median home-leaving ages are significant regardless of the controls included or excluded from the model, while the informal economy attains statistical significance once economic factors are included. Removing Italy from the sample, however, leads all of these latter factors, save for the size of the female labour force, to lose their significance – most likely because, after dropping Italian data, there is no Southern European case left in the analysis.

To compensate for the limitations of this measure, we then turn to Table 4.3, which examines factors impacting the proportion of income-replacement recipients. Note that, as mentioned above, although this measure lacks data on Italy, it does include the Spanish and Portuguese cases. Comparing these results to those from the coverage analysis, the lagged dependent variable and changes in unemployment retain significance, as do both union density and female labour force participation.[28] The only other variable to reach significance is GDP per capita, which is correlated with decreased coverage. Neither the size of the informal economy nor the median age at which youth leave home, however, reach statistical significance in this instance. It is worth noting that this finding arises despite, not because of, Portugal and Spain, which have both high home-leaving ages and the two lowest recipiency rates. At least with regard to recipiency ratios, the expected impact of home leaving may simply be a Southern European phenomenon.

Taking these results in tandem, however, it is clear that there are severe limits to what time-series analysis can tell us about changes in the availability of benefits for the unemployed. As referenced above, the time-series analysis approach raises a number of issues: these results fail to include together the Southern European welfare states that are likely to be most similar to Italy; and each of the coverage-level measures suffers from additional problems, both conceptually and due to a limited number of observations for certain key countries. Perhaps most importantly, the time-series analysis as a whole points more towards the determinants of gradual changes in coverage than policy changes necessarily. This poses an especially large problem since our analysis in Chapter 2 was concerned with the introduction of new benefit regimes.

As such, careful analysis of policy change requires another approach to parse out what factors actually lead to major increases in unemployment coverage levels.

28 Similar results arose when the regressions are run with centre and right-wing parties included instead.

Understanding Changes in Coverage Levels (Part Two)

In order to deal with the shortcomings of the time-series analysis, we proceed instead to directly analyse social policy changes themselves, using duration analysis to examine the likelihood of a country implementing a nationally available social assistance programme (i.e. residualising its system). The data here cover the period from 1960 onward, such that any country that developed a broadly available social assistance programme before then is excluded from the analysis. The result is the inclusion of thirteen (primarily Corporatist or Southern European) countries[29] – three of which (Portugal, Spain, and Greece) were not democracies for the entire period; this complicates the analysis since we would obviously expect dictators to relate differently to public opinion than democratically elected politicians, but in order to avoid equating (for example) the early 1960s with the late 1970s, we use 1960 as the starting point. In any event, neither including a 'democracy' dummy variable nor excluding the non-democratic years alters the findings.

Figure 4.3 Countries without a National Social Assistance Programme

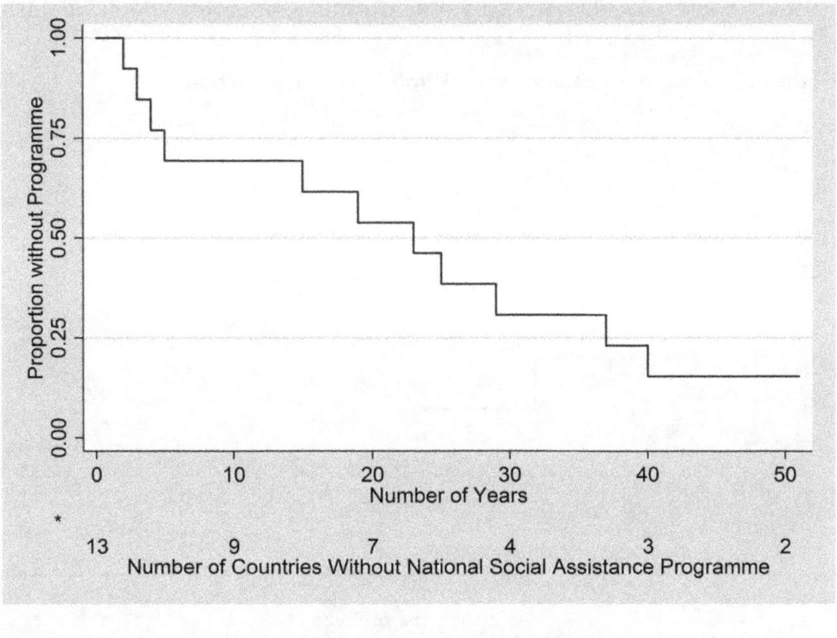

29 These are: Austria, Belgium, Finland, France, Germany, Greece, Italy, the Netherlands, Portugal, Spain, Sweden, and the United States.

Figure 4.3 presents a visual representation of the introduction of these programmes across these countries. Starting from 1960, the graph illustrates the number of countries that lack national social assistance programmes in any given year, with countries dropping out as they introduce the scheme. As the figure suggests, the introduction of these programmes occurred with rapid frequency in the first few years of the 1960s, picked up again (though more slowly) in the mid-1970s, and stopped entirely by 2000. Note that this means that while some countries adopted the programme during the period of welfare state expansion, numerous others introduced it during the period of broader retrenchment. In the end, two countries (Italy and Greece) fail to develop a commensurate programme.

As a first indication of the potential relevance of our variables of interest, Figure 4.4 then presents the pattern of programme introduction in countries that fall below and above the average home-leaving ages and informal economy sizes (not controlling for other factors). Both graphs in Figure 4.4 suggest that countries falling below the mean levels were much quicker to develop the programmes than their above-average level counterparts. Not only did the process begin notably earlier in these cases – with that first surge of early 1960s development evidently occurring only in countries with below average home-leaving ages and informal economies – but it was also

Figure 4.4 Median Home Leaving and Programme Introduction

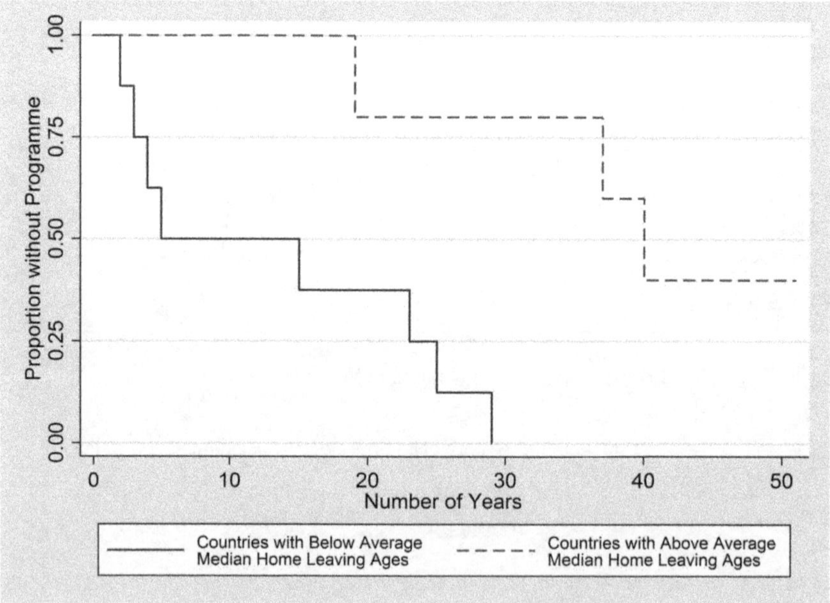

entirely completed across these cases in under thirty years. In the above average-level countries, by contrast, the process was much more sporadic and ultimately remains incomplete.

It is of course quite likely, however, that above average home-leaving ages or larger-than-average informal economies is associated with other characteristics such as a less-developed economy; as a result, it is difficult to discern from the graphs alone whether the variables actually have any impact in and of themselves. While the above results are only indicative, performing duration analysis allows us to include other potentially relevant factors in the examination. The results largely confirm the apparent relationship between these two variables and the extension of benefit access via these programmes (see Table 4.4). While we have a total of thirteen countries in the sample, data limitations lead that number to drop to twelve in Models 2 and 3 (through the loss of the Netherlands).[30] The relatively small number of cases and collinearity issues limit the number of variables that can reasonably be included in the full model – so we instead construct a basic model (using only variables of interest), a basic model with political variables, and a full model that incorporates economic controls.

Model 1, which features only the informal economy and home-leaving variables, suggests that both of our variables of interest attain significance with the predicted direction of the effect. Here we note that moving from the below-average to the above-average group (i.e. a two-point increase) in terms of home leaving is associated with just over a 110% decrease in the likelihood that their country will introduce the benefit scheme. Making the same move across the groupings of informal economy sizes, in turn, is associated with about a 128% decrease.

Model 2 then includes political variables in the analysis. The impact of both the informal economy and the median age at which youth leave home fully achieve significance, with an even stronger negative impact on the likelihood of introducing the programme. In addition, the size of the female workforce perhaps surprisingly (though in keeping with the results of the time-series unemployment insurance coverage model above) decreases the likelihood of programme introduction. Government partisanship fails to achieve significance, though this may possibly be because leftist parties have had a different relationship to reform in the period of welfare state expansion versus the period of welfare state retrenchment (see Pierson 1994).

30 Note, however, that the results of the Model 1 do not change notably when run only with the cases included in Models 2 and 3.

Table 4.4 Duration Analysis – Benefits for the Unemployed

	Model 1: Basic Model	Model 2: Basic Model with Political Variables	Model 3: Full Model
Independent Variables			
Size of Informal Economy (Tercile)	**0.359*** *(0.058)*	**0.285**** *(0.049)*	0.087* *(0.082)*
Median Age at which Youth Leave Home (Tercile)	**0.443*** *(0.075)*	**0.215**** *(0.024)*	0.059* *(0.070)*
Female Workforce	---	**0.772*** *(0.053)*	**0.591**** *(0.047)*
Union Density	---	1.140 *(0.164)*	---
Left Government	---	1.053 *(0.460)*	---
Left & Union Interaction	---	0.998 *(0.366)*	---
GDP	---	---	1.000 *(0.593)*
Unemployment	---	---	**0.330*** *(0.057)*
N	13	12	12

Note: Cells contain survival analysis hazard ratios with p-values italicised in parentheses. Hazard ratios that reach significance ($p < .10$) are bolded.
* $p < 0.10$, ** $p < 0.05$, *** $p < 0.01$

Model 3, however, which adds the economic variables to our already significant ones, returns a similar pattern of results.[31] What is more, the size of the apparent effect increases substantially. With regard to the median home-leaving age, moving from the below average group to the above average one is associated with a 188% decrease in the likelihood of programme introduction in any given year. An analogous shift in the size of the informal economy, in turn, is associated with a 182% decrease in likelihood. Of the controls, the size of the female labour force retains a similar effect to that found in Model 2, while a single point increase in the unemployment rate appears to decrease the likelihood of programme introduction by just over 67%.[32]

31 Note that including left government and union density does not noticeably impact the results.

32 Overall, the findings from the duration analysis do not appear to be driven by any one particular country, though the model is unable to run when certain countries are excluded.

Summing Up

Drawing the above findings together, there are a number of overall observations we would make. First, unemployment rates either appear to matter in all of the models. In the time-series analysis, higher unemployment rates are associated with both decreased unemployment insurance coverage and decreased recipiency ratios. Furthermore, judging by the results of the duration analysis, each percentage point increase in unemployment is responsible for a substantial decrease in the likelihood of programme introduction.

What logic underpins this finding? In the case of the time-series results, the explanation likely relays certain non-political implications of increased unemployment on insurance coverage/recipiency rates. In the former instance, increased unemployment may lead fewer individuals to qualify for insurance coverage, or may be indicative of bleak labour market conditions that push more individuals to take more precarious jobs. In the latter instance, increases in the number of unemployed individuals may indicate difficult labour market conditions in which individuals are likely to become long-term unemployed (potentially losing their access to benefits). Alternatively, they may also signify that precarious labourers, with their weaker job protection and (in some instances) decreased access to benefits, are the workers who are disproportionately 'shed'. The duration analysis results, by contrast, suggest a more political explanation: countries with higher average unemployment are less likely to residualise their system of benefits for the unemployed and extend access (through implementing a broadly available social assistance benefit), possibly because the costs of doing so would necessarily be higher. This appears to be the case despite the results of the multi-level model survey analysis, which suggested that mean unemployment rates are associated with slightly higher concern for the unemployed. Irrespective of the explanations we adopt, however, the impact of unemployment is evidently rather robust.

Of our key variables of interest, the size of the informal economy and the age at which youth leave the parental home both reached significance repeatedly, although the former did so less frequently.[33] In the case of the informal economy, the findings are as we would expect, although in the

33 Note that increased faith in municipal power also has the predicted positive impact in the attitudinal analysis. As was mentioned above, however, extending this variable from Southern European to other countries potentially complicates the exact import of this finding since it may be standing in for attitudes towards devolution in some countries.

case of the public opinion analysis the results are not robust to the exclusion of the Spanish case. The time-series analysis, in turn, suggests that a larger informal economy is associated with lower insurance coverage levels, but these results appear to be driven principally by the Italian case. The most consistent results, however, came from examining programme introduction directly via duration analysis, with larger informal economies associated with a sizeable decrease in the likelihood of reform introduction.

Similarly, the findings suggest that the age at which youth leave the parental home appears to be of broad import. In terms of attitudes, later home leaving is associated with decreased concern for the unemployed more generally, while living with one's parents while being unemployed appears to have the same effect at the individual level. The results of the time-series analysis are less robust, but the relationship in the duration analysis model is as predicted. Taken together with the results of the multi-level model survey analysis, the results of this chapter are consistent with our overall argument that later home leaving may lead to decreased concern for the unemployed more broadly, which in turn may result in less pressure on governments to expand coverage via residualisation.

Overall, the findings presented in this section suggest that the size of the informal economy, the age at which youth leave home, and unemployment rates are the factors that consistently appear to impact attitudes towards the unemployed and the introduction of a (non-categorical) social assistance programme. This suggests that although the factors vary somewhat in their impact on incremental changes across different measures of coverage, when it comes to attitudes and the – arguably connected – more sweeping (i.e. third order) changes, the findings of the qualitative analysis can be generalised.

Conclusion

In sum, this chapter has further developed our investigation of the generalisability of the findings in Chapter 2 regarding the extension of benefits for the unemployed through residualisation. Specifically, this has meant paying special attention to the size of the informal economy and late home leaving among young adults, employing three types of quantitative analysis (multi-level model survey analysis, time-series, and duration analysis) to explore three different aspects of benefit extension/welfare state residualisation (respectively, public opinion, incremental changes in coverage, and residualisation itself). It began by giving a brief overview of the variables to be included in the analysis, and then proceeded to present the results of the analysis. The findings of the multi-level model survey analysis were presented first, and the results suggested the general applicability of most of the factors discussed in the French-Italian comparison. In an attempt to examine the possible connection between the impact of these variables on attitudes and actual outcomes, this was then followed by the time-series analysis. Here we looked at incremental changes in unemployment insurance coverage and recipiency ratios, though the approach yielded relatively little of interest.

By contrast, examining the determinants of policy change directly was far more fruitful. This was accomplished using duration analysis to more precisely examine our subject of interest: the factors driving the introduction of a national social assistance programme. Note that it is in this way that we attempt to overcome a common problem in quantitative analysis: namely, the use of simplified dependent variables (based on available time-series data) that may not actually reflect policy changes. The results of the investigation suggest that both the size of the informal economy and the median age at which youth leave home likely matter more generally. The findings of this chapter thus suggest that many of our earlier findings may be generalised to at least the broader OECD context, with our variables of interest negatively impacting both attitudes (vis-à-vis concern for the unemployed) and benefit extension through policy reform (shaped by the electoral incentives implicit in those attitudes).

Taken as a whole, the general pattern we are highlighting in this chapter has at its core an interest-preferences-policy connection. Policy structures both what citizens need and what they view to be the state's proper realm of responsibilities; and while we may think of the different coverage levels as a tangible manifestation of culture, that 'culture' is itself impacted by the effects of policy and broader institutional settings on popular attitudes. With home leaving, policy both effects the possibilities for youth to leave their parental home while at the same time decreasing general demand for policies (such as increases in benefit coverage) that would assist youth who cannot (or choose not to) rely on their parents; the result contributes to institutional inertia by decreasing demand for change and removing electoral incentives for parties to pursue reform. The size of the informal economy exhibits a similar impact, being both shaped by and shaping government policy – in this instance through public preferences formed under conditions of either higher or lower probabilities that (so-called) unemployed persons are in need of state aid (and/or that such social assistance programmes can adequately assess who actually needs assistance). The resultant preferences then condition the apparent impact of partisanship, as they allow/require leftist parties to seek out reform.

5 Bismarck, Beveridge, and Making the Transition

As was the case with unemployment benefits, a basic distinction can be drawn between insurance-based and universalist healthcare systems. In the first instance, access to healthcare is derived from occupational status, with the frequent implication that an individual's benefits and contributions vary depending on occupation. Even more importantly, however, labour market outsiders (e.g. the unemployed, the informally employed, or caregiving spouseless women with atypical employment patterns) can end up falling through gaps in the system. Universalist healthcare systems, on the other hand, base access to healthcare not on occupational status but on citizenship or residency. Such systems therefore privilege equality of access and care across individuals and geographic regions, although the extent to which they achieve these goals clearly varies.

In drawing out a comparison of France and Italy, this chapter will present outcomes that contrast with the trajectory highlighted in Chapter 2. As has already been pointed out, with regard to benefits for the unemployed, France gradually filled the many gaps in the insurance system by building up benefit coverage via universally available means-tested benefits (engaging in residualisation, most dramatically from 1989 onwards); in Italy, by contrast, the insurance approach remains paramount and large coverage gaps persist. An alternative process arose in healthcare, however. Both countries built up semi-public insurance-based systems in the post-war period and were faced with coverage gaps and variations in benefit levels. Yet Italy made a complete transition to a Beveridgean system in 1978 (taking the universalisation route), while France opted to maintain and extend its Bismarckian system (most notably, yet again, via residualisation). In both the realm of healthcare and unemployment in France, therefore, one notes a greater focus on working within the current broader framework (what Hall refers to as 'second order' changes), but in Italy, paradigmatic (i.e. 'third order') changes in healthcare coexisted alongside a general failure to reform benefits for the unemployed (1993: 278-279). The Italian case in particular raises important questions, given the trend towards greater segmentation and coverage gaps in other social policy areas. Before examining what factors led to divergent outcomes across our two policy fields, however, we must investigate how to best explain the French and Italian divergence in healthcare.

This chapter begins with a brief presentation of background information on the two healthcare systems, laying out the historical trajectories in France and Italy, and then turns its primary focus to explaining the pursuit of different approaches to coverage extension in the two countries. This contrast is framed principally by reference to the 1999 French Couverture Maladie Universelle (CMU) and the 1978 Italian Servizio Sanitario Nazionale (SSN). After making a case for the importance of the distinction between the types of reforms pursued in France and Italy, the chapter will proceed to examine how the dramatic institutional change in Italy can best be understood. The broader Italian context will then be compared to that of France, with the ultimate aim of understanding the divergent approaches to dealing with the welfare state outsiders. This analysis includes a combination of secondary sources and insights derived from interviews with party and union officials, as well as supplementary archival research.

Through an examination of healthcare system evolution, this chapter will attempt to address another aspect of the evolution of welfare state dualisation, examining the determinants of residualisation versus universalisation in an effort to deal with coverage gaps under conditions of relative fiscal constraint. Although in this case the Italian reform occurs in a period that might generally be thought of as more expansionary vis-à-vis the welfare state, in reality fiscal and economic difficulties were already dominant in Italy, with the SSN introduced within the framework of austerity. While atypical labour was still relatively marginal at that point, there was nevertheless a sizeable group of citizens without access to the healthcare system.

Two aspects of this approach distinguish the present investigation from previous studies looking at the determinants of healthcare reform. First, the welfare state insider/outsider framework is employed in order to gain insights regarding universalist versus residualist attempts to correct for gaps in coverage. This is particularly fruitful because variations in benefit access and coverage have important likely knock-on effects, related to both health-status and monetary burdens. Second, this analysis is carried out with the ultimate goal of contrasting developments in two infrequently compared domains (i.e. healthcare and benefits for the unemployed), which permits us to draw out important and frequently overlooked similarities. In the end, this chapter will once again suggest an impact of structural factors on party and popular preferences (particularly on the leftist end of the political spectrum). As before, this analysis will be couched in a discussion of how different systems have managed, impacted, and/or accommodated those preferences.

More specifically, the argument highlights the ways in which institutions have affected preferences, which in turn have shaped electoral incentives and therefore affected policies – leading to the altering or complete restructuring of institutions; as a result, some institutions are more prone to change than others. In Italy, the failure to more substantially reform the healthcare system after the Second World War left certain constitutional principles and political aspirations unrealised (similar to the case with social assistance). In the 1970s, however, a broader movement for welfare state reform coincided with the fiscal crises of the insurance funds to open a window for change, and the pro-reform Italian Communist Party (PCI) was able to capitalise on the situation. In terms of pro-reform public opinion, popular movements, and the invocation of republican principles, here we see some parallels to the case of the French RMI. Yet in this instance organisational incentives added another layer to the story: specifically, the clientelistic aspects of the health insurance system provided the PCI with an additional incentive to push for dramatic healthcare reform, as it allowed the party to undermine the network of clientelism of the Christian Democrats (DC).[1] Once the PCI's influence in government peaked, a massive overhaul of the system was enacted.

The story of French healthcare reform also has some parallels with the case of the French RMI – but without the added organisational incentives for left-wing parties. Compared with the Italian case, the French semi-public health insurance system enjoyed greater popular legitimacy, made state intervention more politically feasible, and gave unions pro-status quo incentives. Furthermore, earlier reforms of the system, coupled with the absence of rampant clientelistic networks, also affected the policy preferences on the left, particularly within the French Communist Party (though in any event its political influence upon entering government in 1981 was not comparable to that of the PCI in the late 1970s). The end result of these factors was the residualisation of the French healthcare system and the universalisation of the Italian one.

Contextualising the Cases

While grouping healthcare systems into specific types can be somewhat complex (cf. Ferrera 1995; Wendt et al. 2009; Freeman and Frisina 2010; Toth 2010), the French and Italian healthcare systems in the immediate post-war

1 Undermining the DC's clientelistic networks improved the PCI's electoral competitiveness, while developing its own clientelistic resources facilitated the maintenance and expansion of the PCI's support base.

decades can broadly be defined as relying on the insurance principle rather than universalism. Both systems preserved the privileges of groups that had previously enjoyed generous benefits (under already existing fragmented schemes), with the funds divided along occupational lines – thereby entailing variations of coverage and contributions. While both countries maintained a fragmented insurance model that allowed previously well-protected groups to jealously guard their benefits, the management of the funds in France saw a far greater role for workers' representatives than that of Italy. Subsequent reforms saw the Italian healthcare system shift over to a universalist NHS in 1978, while a little over 20 years later the French eventually created a residual means-tested system and standardised benefit packages for most covered persons.

France

The current healthcare framework in France was introduced in the months immediately following the Second World War, with the creation of the modern French social security system (which includes healthcare) via a law (the Ordonnance du 4 octobre 1945) that created a unified social security programme (the *régime general*).[2] This new social insurance scheme, developed over the next two years, marked a transition away from targeted medical assistance benefits, a centralisation of some of the already existing occupational schemes, and an extension and reform of the previous system (Rochaix and Wilsford 2005: 99). The law made attachment to the social insurance scheme obligatory for most categories of workers (whether French citizens or residents), laying out the framework for the healthcare system (France 1945).

Emboldened by the political weakness of the centre-right at the time, the left was able to push through the reform during the Liberation period when parliament was unable to overturn executive decisions; the more radical aspects (such as the establishment of a single fund for all citizens), however, were undermined quite quickly thereafter, as the return to parliamentary normalcy opened up space for opposition from doctors associations, Catholic forces, and those workers with access to better quality benefits (Immergut 1990: 400). The eventual compromise reached by 1947 would

2 This replaced the initial French social insurance healthcare scheme, which had been introduced over the course of 1928-1930 and made health insurance compulsory for all employees. A paragon of fragmentation, this new system would consist of 793 separate funds by the end of 1932 (Korpi 1995: 641-642).

therefore see the implementation of a less radical reform and the entrenchment of certain already existing privileges, which would come to shape the subsequent period greatly; most notably, this occurred through the variety of insurance providers, the system of partial reimbursement, and, relatedly, the continued relevance of insurance mutuals through complementary coverage (Evans 2005: 281; Steffen 2010: 360).

Structurally, rather than having the state or private companies run the scheme, the actors involved agreed to exclude the state from direct management of the system and create a corporatist, semi-public system with the central role given to employees' representatives and employers' associations (Catrice-Lorey and Steffen 2006: 168). While union dominance of the system was the norm for the first two decades (with 75% of seats going to unions), parity was restored in 1967, leading to significant contestation between unions and employers (as well as among unions) (Steffen 2010: 361). The exclusion of the state from the insurance funds, in turn, was the product of general agreement, reflecting both a distrust of the central government and the importance broadly assigned to intermediate institutions (Palier 2002: 4). Nevertheless, the state would increasingly assert its ultimate control over subsequent decades, with final authority resting with the state (Rochaix and Wilsford 2005: 101).

Here, as with unemployment insurance, the hope was that through the expansion of the occupations covered under social insurance, eventually the entire population would have healthcare coverage. This was achieved not only through the *régime général*, which covered about two-thirds of all workers, but also through 122 additional occupational schemes (known collectively as the *régimes spéciaux et particuliers*), covering occupational groups that initially refused to join the *régime général* (about a fifth of the working population), and nineteen independent schemes, largely for the self-employed and agricultural workers (Bonoli and Palier 1996: 243-244). The extension of health insurance was gradual, with schemes slowly added for groups such as students (1948), soldiers (1949), farmers (1961), and self-employed non-agricultural workers (1966).

This process was further developed in 1974, when individuals who did not fall into any of the already existing occupational schemes were provided access to health insurance benefits, so long as they paid the necessary contributions. For those who could not afford to pay, a request could be made to have their *département* make the contributions for them. In reality, however, coverage problems persisted, as the availability and conditions of this exemption varied greatly across *départements* (Sandier et al. 2004: 7). More generally, the fragmented system also had the effect of failing to provide uniform benefits across groups, with some occupational schemes providing better health benefits than others (Sandier et al. 2004: 8).

The most dramatic shift away from this system involved two developments under Jospin's centre-left government (though the ideas had originally been floated by Juppé's previous, centre-right government)[3]: the introduction of a residual health insurance scheme, the Couverture Maladie Universelle (CMU) in 1999[4]; and the 2001 standardisation of the benefit packages provided by the three main insurance funds. The CMU sought both to extend healthcare to those not covered and provide free complementary health insurance to those who would otherwise be unable to afford it. Under this scheme, all residents of France who pass a means test are eligible to access benefits from the programme, with the regime co-financed by the state, the insurance funds, and the complementary health insurance providers. To that end, it created the CMU to 'guarantee everyone healthcare treatment by a health insurance regime, and to those with the lowest income a right to complementary coverage and an exemption from upfront payment' (France 1999). Given that access is means-tested, however, it is important to note that the programme did not mark a transition to a Beveridgean universal system (despite the use of the term *universelle* in its name) but rather the extension of the Bismarckian system via the introduction of an additional scheme (Barbier and Théret 2003: 144; Steffen 2010: 380). At the same time, of course, delinking coverage from work obviously introduced a shift away from classical Bismarckianism (Bouget 1998: 166).

Furthermore, benefit standardisation across the three main insurance funds (the Régime général (which includes CMU recipients), Mutualité sociale agricole, and Caisse Nationale d'Assurance Maladie et Maternité des Travailleurs non-Salariés des Professions non Agricoles) had the effect of standardising health insurance coverage and benefits for approximately

3 During his time as prime minister, Juppé had made an issue of the equity issues intrinsic to the Bismarckian model, complaining that 'There are currently nineteen different regimes – the source of inequalities, complications, and additional costs. The universal regime will initiate a right to the same benefits for all, under the condition of regular French residency. It will permit the coordination of contributions of every insured person. It will be created gradually; it will not involve the creation of a "single regime" because it will remain compatible with a occupation-based organisation of funds; but it will permit a drastic simplification of the relations between regimes and the conditions of qualification; it will bring with it the guarantee that all will be covered by health insurance – that, in a word, every French person will be well cared for' (Juppé 1995).

4 Although this was a relatively expensive initiative at 9 billion francs, the state redirected funds that had previously been assigned to local authorities to provide healthcare to the poor, thereby lowering the effective cost of the programme to about 2 billion francs (Levy 2001: 276).

95% of the population (Sandier et al. 2004: 36). In addition to extending coverage (both primary and complementary) to those unable to afford it, the Jospin government was therefore also responsible for standardising the benefits received by the vast majority of the population. Note, however, that all of these reforms occurred within the health insurance framework.

Italy

In the immediate post-war period, there was initially a sense that healthcare should be completely reformed by the state.[5] This position was reflected in both the D'Aragona Commission's report and the new constitution, with the latter proclaiming that 'The Republic safeguards health as a basic right of the individual and in the interests of the collectivity, and guarantees free treatment for the poor' (Italy 1947; Spence 1996: 61). Yet despite these assertions, drastic changes were blocked by a weak Italian economy, political polarisation, and a confluence of actors opposing reform, resembling those that prevented more radical reform in France: employer's associations, sections of the Church, medical associations, and occupational groups with generous benefits under the previous corporatist system (Ferrera 1993: 234).

Under these circumstances, successive governments opted to retain a more traditional system of health insurance funds (with more fragmented control than that found in the French system of semi-public funds under divided worker and employer association control) and were hesitant to regulate and standardise their benefit packages. At the same time, health insurance coverage slowly extended to previously excluded occupations, particularly over the course of the 1950s and 1960s, with new mutuals (having their own contribution, benefit rules, and administrative structures) usually formed 'under strict DC control' (Ferrera 1986: 456; Ferrera 1996a: 55). The eventual result was the proliferation of funds, which also served as a clientelistic network, as well as the near complete coverage of the Italian population (Piperno 1983: 157). Indeed, by 1977 only about 3% of the population, many of whom were unemployed, had no coverage (OECD 2012b). At the same time, certain public elements of the system were simultaneously

5 The previous system, developed under fascism, had made healthcare (unsurprisingly) a corporate affair, with health insurance constituting a part of collective agreements, paid for by employers and employees (without any contributions from the state). The result was a complex system of benefits characterised by enormous variation, with many groups of workers having no access to benefits whatsoever (particularly in the field of agriculture). While the different insurance funds were eventually brought under a single administrative body in 1943, this did little to deal with the vast disparities in provision that continued to exist (Spence 1996: 60-61).

developed alongside the insurance system, particularly with the creation of public hospitals and the increasingly autonomous state administration in charge of certain public health issues (Maino 2001: 74).

The limitations of this system were many, however, and despite the fact that atypical employment had not yet begun its dramatic uptick, variation in both access and benefit generosity tracked the labour market position. Some of these issues resulted from the nature of health insurance systems more broadly and some from specifically Italian peculiarities: benefits were dependent on labour market status rather than citizenship; there was a high level of organisational fragmentation among the funds, with over bureaucratisation and variable coverage among insurance funds; there was striking North-South regional variation (in terms of access to doctors, hospitals, etc.); the funds consistently flirted with bankruptcy, leading the state to step in repeatedly to save them; and there was a decided lack of emphasis on preventative medicine (Ferrera 1995: 278-279). Yet despite all of this, opposition from doctors, the health insurance funds, and those insured individuals with particularly high-quality benefits combined together with the difficulty of actually reforming the entire system to draw out the reform process considerably (Maynard 1975: 158-159; France and Taroni 2005: 172).

This would all change with the 1978 creation of a National Health System (Servizio Sanitario Nazionale (SSN)) (created by Law 833/1978), which enacted a thorough reform of the system, shifting from a health insurance system to one of universal healthcare. This position was highlighted in the principles delineated in the law, echoing the Italian constitution and declaring that 'The Republic safeguards health as a fundamental right of the individual and a concern of the collectivity through the national health service. The protection of physical and psychological health must take place in obedience to the dignity and liberty of the individual' (Italy 1978). In practice this reform entailed eliminating the vast array of insurance funds, standardising benefits, extending benefits to uncovered citizens, and reconceptualising healthcare as a right of citizens rather than workers (Brown 1984: 80; Ferrera 1995: 279). The original intent for this new system was to include both aspects of full universality (free and equal use for all citizens, regardless of income, location, or employment status) and democratic control (through the involvement of political parties) (Donatini et al. 2001: 14). The latter aspect in particular had considerable negative repercussions: assigning administrative positions to parties on the basis of their electoral strength had the predictable effect of placing many unqualified individuals in managing positions and creating considerable friction between those individuals and career administrators (Ferrera 1995: 281-282).

Beveridge versus Bismarck

While the primary goal of this chapter is to explain the divergent approaches to benefit extension in the French and Italian healthcare systems, the developments highlighted above lead us to first address a separate issue: namely, is the distinction between a Bismarckian health insurance system and a Beveridgean universalist one meaningful for our larger purpose?

While the gulf between the two approaches is not quite as great as one might expect, the difference is nevertheless a meaningful one. The creation of the Italian SSN clearly affected the degree to which benefits were available, extending coverage to the 3.5 million Italian citizens – and eventually even non-citizens – who had previously fallen outside of the system. Similarly, it removed the individual basis for health insurance, taking the focus away from contribution records and thereby providing for far more equal access across groups (Freeman 2000: 37). Those individuals with poor employment records (disproportionately women) or who fell outside of the traditional labour market (i.e. labour market outsiders) thereby received a notable improvement in their access to health services; what is more, this occurred in a manner incommensurate with simply developing health assistance benefits for those who cannot access regular coverage, since in general they provide lower-quality benefits (Guillén 2002: 50-51).

As a result, this approach to reform effectively erased the welfare state insider/outsider distinction. Although the demands insiders and outsiders place on the system reflect other dimensions (in particular health status and age), the key point here is that individual access to care becomes regularised regardless of employment history. What is more, the creation of the SSN standardised benefit packages across all occupational groups (and even for those outside of the labour market), further contributing to equality of access and care. Taken together, these changes have the potential to mitigate – though of course not erase – differences in health status and level the total out-of-pocket payments individuals are required to pay out. The central role given to equity under universalist healthcare systems is therefore not just interesting from a theoretical perspective, as it has real-life ramifications as well.

Of course, none of this is to suggest that the universal nature of the Italian healthcare system results in better health outcomes writ large than those in France. First, the Italian system undoubtedly has its shortcomings. The SSN has certainly struggled to provide standardised care across the regions (see Saraceno and Negri 1994: 21) and has notably demonstrated a few peculiarities even vis-à-vis other universal healthcare systems. The funding of the SSN, for instance, took quite a few years to approximate that of other countries with universal healthcare: even though the financing of the system itself was immediately shifted to the central government, the move away from occupation-based contributions to general taxation in Italy was a slow one (with all of the implications for progressivity in tax/contribution collection that implies). Indeed, there is some debate about whether the Italian healthcare system should be grouped in precisely the same healthcare typology as the Northern European variants (cf. Moran 2000: 147; Palier 2004b: 28; Toth 2010: 340), and Ferrera went so far as to label it a system of 'conditional universalism' (1995: 281). Nevertheless, the shift away from an insurance model is quite evident.

Second, the French system, despite maintaining its insurance-based system, has also moved towards greater coverage and equity through residualisation as well as some standardisation. In the former case, this occurred through the aforementioned introduction of the CMU (which extended benefits to those falling outside of the system) in 1999. In the latter, it was carried out most notably through the 2001 benefit standardisation that resulted in adherents to the three principal insurance funds (together covering approximately 95% of the population) having access to the same healthcare benefits. Although this (incomplete) standardisation does leave occupationally derived differences for those individuals in the remaining 5% of the population (including such disparate groups as miners, clergy, railway workers, and artists), they have become the exception rather than the rule.[6] Yet despite these improvements, the system at the very least retains a distinction between those insiders with access to the principal system and those outsiders who access the residualist one.[7][8]

6 The acceptability of such differences seems to derive partially from questions of choice ('they had the choice to integrate into the system during the creation of the generalized social security, and they didn't want to'), partially from divisions among workers and employers ('we don't agree with [...] acting in solidarity with "employer" regimes'), and partially from differences in contribution levels ('they don't make the same contributions anyways'), as Force Ouvrière confederal secretary Patrick Privat stated to me in an interview (Privat 2012).

7 Aside from questions of access, France too suffers from issues surrounding variation in the quality of care along both geographic and income-based lines continue to be a problem (cf. Rodwin and Le Pen 2004: 2261).

8 By way of one final caveat, it should also be noted that the differences between the two systems do not map easily onto either quality of care or levels of public satisfaction with the systems. Despite the persistent inequities of the French system, it has sometimes been pointed to as a model of care – ranked, for instance, first overall by the World Health Organization (just ahead of second-place Italy) in the late 1990s (2000: 153). Public satisfaction with the two healthcare systems, on the other hand, is far more divergent. The French are considerably more satisfied with their system than their Italian counterparts and, indeed, expert rankings tend not

Instead, the main differences of interest here relate to the nature of the healthcare systems themselves, with regard to both institutions and philosophies. In the former instance, France's insurance system is still highly fragmented institutionally, providing a means-tested scheme for would-be outsiders. In the latter instance, the French system assigns the insurance principle and complementary residualism prominence over universalism. For our purposes, the relevant juxtaposition is driven primarily by the French focus on benefit extension via residualising reform within the existing broader framework in the field of healthcare coverage, as well as the considerable time lag in these developments (with the principal reforms occurring just over two decades after the Italian reform). The stark contrast with the Italian reforms, both in healthcare coverage (where the system was completely recreated via universalisation) and in the field of benefit coverage for the unemployed (where governments largely failed to act) makes this divergence particularly interesting. Our ultimate emphasis, of course, remains on different approaches to addressing gaps in welfare state coverage, with changes in healthcare programmes serving as one example of how these processes might play out. As such, even if one believes that the French and Italian systems are functional equivalents, the different reform paths to the current systems remain of theoretical interest.

Explaining Healthcare Reform

Having acknowledged the significance of the divergent trajectories in France and Italy, we now turn to our principal question: how can one explain the contrasting decisions to extend coverage (and standardise benefits) through universalisation in Italy and residualisation in France? Drawing on the literature studying the introduction of universal healthcare, one notes a number of (often complementary) theories that may explain the extension of healthcare benefits through universalisation. These theories will be reviewed with the aim of both laying out existing work and drawing out the implications that are potentially related to insider/outsider divides.

to reflect citizen satisfaction with the healthcare systems in their respective systems (Blendon et al. 2001) – though of course most citizens lack comparative experiential knowledge of different health systems, and attitudes may reflect various other factors (e.g. media coverage, political discourse, etc.). Either way, the key point here is that these sorts of institutional differences are not necessarily reflected in either public satisfaction or quality of care.

Theory 1: Left-wing Strength

First, there are arguments stemming from Power Resource theory, suggesting that a strong working class, organised through labour unions and left-wing parties, leads to more egalitarian outcomes. Given that this theory implies a concern with welfare state outsiders on the part of left-wing actors, this approach is obviously similar to the Egalitarian Left theory discussed with regard to benefits for the unemployed. In trying to explain social policy outcomes, Korpi, for instance, stresses the importance of the distribution of power between workers and employers; this is evident in the extent to which the labour force is unionised, the vote share of leftist parties, and their presence in government (measured both over time and within a given government) (1980: 307). In one application of this framework to healthcare reforms specifically, Navarro argues that universality will be pursued by the working class in order to strengthen broad class solidarity (and similarly will be opposed by the capitalist class to maintain class fragmentation), with: 'the different types of funding and organization of health services [...] explained primarily by the degree to which the differing class aims in the health sector [...] have been achieved through the realization of class power relations' (1989: 891-892). Note that there are two relevant theoretical implications to the Power Resource approach. First, the theory implies that public opinion within the working class is inherently pro-reform – that workers generally prefer universalist systems. Second, the argument that leftist parties and organisations will reach out to welfare state outsiders rather than turning in upon themselves and trying to protect traditional insider supporters/members (or, alternatively, organisational strength derived from the existing institutional arrangement). It therefore provides an interesting addition to the theories discussed in Chapter 2.

Indeed, the strength of left-wing parties is a rather consistent variable in explanations of major healthcare reform in Italy, for instance (e.g. Robb 1986: 622; Vicarelli 1995: 129; Spence 1996: 63-64; France and Taroni 2005: 173; Toth 2010: 329), so one of the principle aims in this chapter must be to examine the role played by the French left.

Theory 2: Interest Group Weakness

Another oft-stressed factor in discussions of divergent developments across different healthcare systems (including with regard to the gradual universalisation of benefits funds (see Wilsford 1994: 258-275; Freeman 2000: 26; Guillén 2002: 58-59)) is the impact of interest groups, in particular doctors' associations and insurance funds. In this instance, positive public attitudes towards the insurance funds and doctors' associations, as well as the absence of schisms within the groups, are seen to augment their ability to counteract reformist forces. Additionally, we can expect the impact of these groups on healthcare policies to be mediated through institutional arrangements that either facilitate or thwart the potential influence they can exert, affecting the type of interest groups formed and the strategies their leaders employ (Immergut 1992: 3). Rather than suggesting any particular stance by welfare state insiders/outsiders or parties, this theory highlights the potential role of interest groups and institutional arrangements on the balance of pressures for and against reform – specifically through the strengthening of a countervailing force. This chapter will therefore explore the difference between the relevant French and Italian lobbies as well as their institutional settings in order to assess the extent to which these factors might help us understand the differing outcomes.

Theory 3: Political Decentralisation

Decentralisation may also matter through the shaping of demand for reform and the encouragement of experimentation at lower levels of government. Examining the contrasting outcomes in Canadian and American healthcare developments, for example, Maioni suggests that the federal and parliamentary aspects of the Canadian political system facilitated provincial experimentation, the formation of a new pro-reform party, and the eventual creation of a universal healthcare system (under a Liberal minority government relying on the support of the New Democratic Party); in the United States, by contrast, the weakness of the executive in the legislative arena and party discipline, as well the institutionally driven tendency for the Democratic Party to move towards the centre (with a broad coalition of support incorporating both typical proponents of reform (e.g. labour unions) and opponents of it), has persistently prevented change (1997: 424-425). Indeed, the development of regional governments is another relatively common theme in the literature on institutional impact, with the process associated with structural reorganisation and a changing context for party strategy in both Spain and Italy (Ferrera 1989: 116; Guillén 2002: 58). Broadly speaking, decentralisation may shape popular demand for government provision of healthcare by creating a lower level of government with greater perceived administrative capacity, or it may increase demand for a universal healthcare by showing (through policy experimentation) that such programmes are indeed feasible. Despite the fact that neither country has a federal system, a consideration of the role of decentralisation in France and Italy will therefore be included as well.

With these hypotheses serving as our working framework, let us now turn to a closer examination of benefit extension and standardisation in Italy and then France. Given that the above theories are themselves often drawn from analyses that include the Italian case (and in a few instances the French case as well), our primary purposes in this chapter will be to (1) sketch out the Italian process of universalisation and (2) investigate whether and to what extent those same factors were present in the French case. The goal here is to refocus historical analysis on the aspects of the already existing theories that might tell us something about the extension of benefits to welfare state outsiders more generally, giving us insights into the choice to pursue that goal either through residualisation or universalisation. Overall then, the next two sections will attempt to draw attention to the instances in which the comparison either casts doubt on or reinforces the existing theories, always with an eye to ultimately exploring varying, across-domain approaches to gaps in welfare state coverage.

Italian Advancements

As was mentioned above, while the principles underlying the 1978 reform could be found in the constitution itself, it took over three decades for the system to be implemented.[9] The universalisation of healthcare in Italy was thus subject to considerable delay, and given that the constitution also laid out a right to social assistance, it was in no sense a foregone conclusion. While the decision not to implement universal healthcare immediately upon the ratification of the constitution can largely be understood in terms of financial difficulties, a number of other, more political factors also played a role: most notably political polarisation and opposition from Confindustria (the Italian employers' confederation), doctors, Catholic associations, and the occupational groups that stood to have their privileged position in the previous system eroded (Ferrera 1993: 234; Vicarelli 1995: 127-128). Yet

9 It is worth noting that the perception of the SSN's creation as primarily an overdue realisation of constitutional principles was common among those left-wing party and union representatives with whom I spoke (Fantozzi 2012; Touadi 2012; Treves 2012; Zipponi 2012). As the director of the Labour Division of Italia dei Valori put it, 'these cornerstones of the Republican constitution were not easy to put into effect, since in many cases there were counter tendencies, such as [...] the belief that healthcare must be run as a business, with a market, competitiveness, and competition – making it no longer a case of solidarity but of the market' (Zipponi 2012).

the delays to reform long outlasted the centrality of fiscal limitations, as the latter would gradually decrease with the Italian boom that began in 1950. As a result, in order to understand the universalisation of healthcare in Italy we must investigate what potentially relevant factors changed over the course of those years.

To begin with, one notes that the SSN reform was preceded by mass mobilisation in favour of reform. One of the most critical steps towards reform was the spread of the movement for change, with the 1970s in particular marking the growth of popular movements pressing for welfare reform, including in the field of healthcare (Paci 1989: 90). In this way, one notes the importance of public opinion recurring yet again, with the apparent shift in preferences towards reform creating electoral incentives for parties to restructure the system. Insofar as the working class and its related movements were heavily incorporated into this movement, this growth in public pressure also conforms with the theory highlighting *Left-wing Strength* and contrasts with the broadly status quo preferences that seem to dominate attitudes around unemployment benefits. The leftist union CGIL (Confederazione Generale Italiana del Lavoro) in particular had been pressing for the creation of an SSN since 1956, with their Executive Committee claiming that

> the moment to realise the institution of a modern national health service has arrived [...] It is urgent and indispensible to resolve as quickly as possible this barrier to human and societal progress for the entire nation, in the interests of the huge mass of workers and their families. (CGIL 1956: 462)

Note that this early framing, put forth in an era that was nominally still one of welfare state expansion, constructs the issue as one of broad societal progress and interests, without resorting to referencing distinctions among groups in terms of access and benefit generosity.

Yet this movement, framed by one CGIL director as a 'battle by trade unions and the working class to prevail over the insurers', was joined not only by rising left-wing parties but also by large contingents of doctors hoping to reform a system they argued was ill-functioning (Vicarelli 1995: 128; Treves 2012). Countering the 'free choice' arguments of the major medical union (FNOM), for instance, the national secretary of another medical union (ANAAO) argued that 'free choice must comprise the freedom of citizens to participate in the organisation of healthcare and the power to decide the criteria of this organisation' (Testai 1971). Coinciding with the expectations of the *Interest Group Weakness* hypothesis, this break in the anti-reform front helped facilitate change: professional opposition to reform was less powerful than it might otherwise have been (and had been in the past), as doctors themselves were divided on the issues (Freeman 2000: 26). Recall that medical associations played a role in blocking more radical reform in the immediate post-war period not only in Italy but in France as well.

Further supporting the Interest Group Weakness theory, pressures to fundamentally refashion the system were exacerbated by the recurring crises of the insurance mutuals. With their continual return to the brink of bankruptcy, the funds appeared increasingly incapable of keeping the system afloat on their own, challenging their credibility and sway over public opinion (Spence 1996: 63). This then culminated in the 1974 assignment of hospital debt to the public sphere, after the insurance funds failed to deal with rising costs, which in turn resulted in increasing calls for reform in the media (Brown 1984: 77; Vicarelli 1995: 129). 'It's increasingly urgent that we fully attain a new healthcare system, carry out the things that remain to be done, [and] eradicate the "sickness industry"', read an article in *La Stampa* discussing the recently enacted reform; 'INAM', the main insurance fund in Italy, 'spends more by itself than the entire British NHS', declared *L'Unità* in an article entitled 'How Much Does Not Reforming Healthcare Cost?' (Scarpa 1974; De Vito and Giliberto 1975). The result was the arrival of a critical juncture, as decisions about how the system could be stabilised were pushed to the fore, during a period of particularly low public support for the insurance funds. This later factor also had the added effect of diminishing the potential force of countervailing pressures from the funds.

Pro-reform popular movements, schisms within the medical community, and popular concern over the crisis of the insurance funds occurred alongside an additional key institutional development: regionalisation. Although the *Political Decentralisation* hypothesis does not apply perfectly since Italian regionalisation did not introduce a proper federal system, the creation of the Italian regional governments in 1970 (another longstanding unfulfilled promise from the constitution) nevertheless contributed to the pro-reform environment. In particular, the newly created regional governments broadly acted as an additional pro-reform force (Ferrera 1986: 458). The stance of the regions on the issue was largely guaranteed by the jurisdictional promises set out in the constitution, which assigned the regional governments numerous responsibilities over healthcare; yet perhaps even more importantly, the creation of the regions also made possible the delegation of control to a lower level of government – one less tainted by a lack of public respect than the central government (Guillén 2002: 58; France and Taroni 2005: 172-173).

Popular scepticism towards government competency was thereby at least partially muted (recall the role of concerns about administrative capacity discussed in Chapter 2), and the new regional governments provided an additional pressure group for reform that had been lacking in the 1940s.

Yet while these factors created an atmosphere generally favourable towards reform, the most direct cause of healthcare reform was the electoral strengthening of the left, which resulted in the 'historic compromise' (*compromesso storico*) with the government relying on support from the PCI) government that would shortly thereafter create the SSN (Robb 1986: 622; Immergut 1992: 240). The support for Power Resource theory here is obvious, with the PCI a working-class party with considerable connections to the labour movement, most notably through its connections with the CGIL. The party was well positioned ideologically to deal with public concerns about decreasing the role of the market and effecting egalitarian and universal access to healthcare. Indeed, implementing an SSN-style system had been a pet project since the early 1960s, though even with the introduction of the first proposal in 1962 they were arguing that 'a favourable outcome required that public opinion follow and sustain this struggle' (Brown 1984: 77; L'Unità 1962). This position, in turn, was complemented by the pro-reform stance of the Italian Socialist Party (Partito Socialista Italiano, PSI) (Ferrera 1986: 454).

Note that reform was viewed not only as a popular measure to seek, but also as contributing to the grander project – which is to say that it was attractive for both vote-seeking and ideological reasons; the PCI considered the complete refashioning of the healthcare system central to both workers' health and 'the broader transformation of the organisation of society' (Collettivo dell'Istituto Superiore di Sanità 1971: 39). Furthermore, given that the health insurance funds constituted one of numerous clientelistic networks from which the DC distributed posts and derived political power (see Ferrera 1996a), the PCI also had a more practical interest in redesigning healthcare. In this way, the eventual SSN reform can be seen to reflect more than just a desire for benefit extension. Indeed, the party had been waiting for years for circumstances to align and thereby make such a transformation possible. As the plan's architect, Giovanni Berlinguer, stated at a 1963 conference pushing for the reform,

> [W]hat are the realistic time frames for the transition from a mutualistic system to a national health service? It is not oversimplification but rather realism to affirm that they depend essentially on the relationships among political and even electoral forces, between those who want reform and those who impede it. (L'Unità 1963: 13)

Evidently these conditions would not arise until the mid-1970s, when the PCI's surge in electoral strength – coupled with the refusal of other parties, especially the PSI, to continue to join governing coalitions that excluded the PCI – made its continued exclusion from government appear increasingly difficult to maintain.

The (temporary) cross-party consensus that arose during the 'historic compromise', in turn, also helped to overcome the instability of parliamentary majorities in the Italian system (similar to that which the French had experienced under the Fourth Republic) (see Immergut 1992: 240). The contrast with the immediate post-war period is striking, as the PCI had not been in government since the May 1947 crisis. By the time of the 'historic compromise', however, the party was not only strong enough to demand the reform in exchange for its support (Ferrera 1989), but also held enough seats to help pass the legislation without requiring the government to rely on a plethora of smaller parties. Couched within a broader strategy of trading exclusion from cabinet posts for both legitimisation and policy influence, the PCI hoped to finally enact, through the 'policy of austerity', long-sought structural changes while simultaneously consenting to deflationary measures (D'Alimonte 1999: 148). The goal here was to use the broader crisis as an occasion for progressive transformation, with, as then PCI national secretary Enrico Berlinguer explained, objectives such as: moving beyond consumerism; achieving full equality and liberation for women; carving out a role for worker and citizen participation in firms, the economy, and the state; and, more broadly, 'proposing ways of life and relationships among individuals and states that are more integral, social, [and] human' (Berlinguer 1977: 26). Unsurprisingly for the period, the framing remains far more society-wide than insider/outsider based despite the variations in access. The only partial exception here is the reference to women, with gender at least partially of import due to women's disproportionate status as labour market outsiders.

The scope and extent of these policy goals arose in circumstances best summed up by the then DC prime minister Giulio Andreotti's famous statement in 1978 that 'without the approval of the Communist Party, the Italian parliament could not even send out Christmas cards' (quoted in Ruscoe 1982: 4). While the SSN reform legislation had initially been both pushed for and largely drafted by the left, the DC and its partners, fearful of provoking and subsequently losing a referendum on the issue (as had already happened with divorce), allowed the reform to pass without substantial revision (Robb 1986: 622). The importance of the PCI in this process – and the political instability that led to their inclusion in government – is highlighted by the fact that once its support was no longer relied upon by the government, consensus around the reform collapsed (Spence 1996: 63-64).

Yet despite the central role of the party, to characterise the overhaul as simply a product of the PCI would be an exaggeration. For one thing, there is evidence to suggest that the PCI was generally pro-insider in its approach to welfare state reform, with a preference for the insurance principle over targeting (Ferrera et al. 2012). Indeed, even in the remaining Communist circles the importance of other key factors would appear to be uncontroversial. The national director of the Work, Welfare, and Citizenship Policies section of the Communist Refoundation Party (Partito della Rifondazione Comunista, one of the remaining unreformed fragments of the old PCI), for example, stated that the creation of the SSN 'saw the convergence of different political and non-political forces, of which the PCI was an example [...] [of] those who committed themselves to this reform' (Fantozzi 2012). The temporary increase in the PCI's political power was combined not only with the systemic financial crises of the old model, but also with regionalisation and a broad movement for reform; indeed, the latter was comprised of not only the public but also the regional governments and certain medical associations. In this way, the adoption of the SSN broadly corresponds with Kingdon's theory of policy windows (Kingdon 1984). The contrast with the circumstances surrounding the creation of the previous healthcare system in the immediate post-war period is stark: with a stronger economy, a surging PCI, new regional governments hoping to realise their constitutionally assigned power, and financially troubled insurance funds, the forces favouring the maintenance of the mutualistic system had slowly seen their position weakened.

Under these circumstances, reform of some sort appears to have been almost overdetermined – but why did the Italian government pursue universalisation rather than residualisation? At first glance, it might appear that a less transformative reform of the health insurance system would not have been enough to deal with mounting political and popular pressure for reform. The nature of the insurance funds meant that variations in access to healthcare would have persisted regardless of whether the system could be made to function properly and without recurring government assistance. Even a 1973 attempt by the government to introduce a two-tiered system met with complaints about variation in access, particularly from politicians on the left – with one former PCI Deputy, for example, arguing that the proposal 'calls for a pyramid-shaped healthcare system: at the lowest level the national service, at the apex the clinics for the rich' (Scarpa 1973). While we cannot map back onto this critique a concern for labour market insiders and outsiders (rather, the concern is obviously class based), it is clear that at base it is a critique of a divide between welfare state insiders and outsiders.

This desire to use healthcare reform as a means for more transformative reform – one that had long been a 'pet project' of the PCI – can also be understood along less ideological and more pragmatic lines. As was mentioned above, the erstwhile health insurance system served as a valuable clientelistic resource of the DC. The pursuit of reform through residualisation would have done little to undermine that network, and even if the PCI could have used its enhanced power at the time to attain clientelistic spoils for itself, it could not trust the DC to keep its word when the PCI's support waned. By contrast, the broadly supported 'democratic' element of the new system – ostensibly designed to promote democratic representation – promised to consistently provide parties of all stripes with clientelistic spoils to distribute as they continued to build up their party machines (Ferrera 1996a, 54-55). For the PCI (and even the PSI), then, the DC's strong ties to the old system meant that anything short of a complete overhaul would leave the party's greater influence intact. Combined with ideological preferences, this meant that the form that benefit extension took was actually a central issue on the left, especially for the PCI. The means used to achieve benefit extension mattered as much as the end, with universalisation far more preferable than residualisation.

Elsewhere on the political spectrum, other factors conspired against residual reform as well. For the more technocratically inclined, knowledge of rising costs and the general poor functioning of the system in the past helped to drive would-be centrist and centre-right reformers away from proposing such changes, and there was also a certain appeal to central budgetary control and cost containment (Brown 1984: 78-79).[10] Yet the DC had other reasons to alter its position with regard to healthcare reform: although they were the dominant party and were most likely to favour a non-transformative reform of the old system (in light of its ties to both the insurance funds and the Church hospitals), to the extent that a more revolutionary reform was inevitable, carrying it out under DC tutelage actually allowed them to guarantee their own share of the spoils (Brown 1984: 79). As such, the party's earlier proposals for only moderate tinkering were eventually replaced in the early 1970s by calls for a national health service (albeit without the nationalisation of either medicine or physicians),

10 Here the British NHS was clearly an inspiration for parties across the spectrum, providing a model for both equality of access and cost-containment – though for obvious reasons the left focused more on the former and the right on the latter (Spence 1996: 63).

though they were rather timid in pursuing reform on their own (De Miguel 1977: 386).[11] The rising fortunes of the PCI then pushed the DC towards accepting even more dramatic reform.

By way of one final consideration, given the central role of the PCI in this story, one is perhaps left questioning how (and to what extent) the SSN survived the end of the 'historic compromise' in 1979. In particular, support for a universalist healthcare system began to dissipate over the course of the 1980s as the shortcomings of the system – in combination with sky-rocketing expenditures (especially on pharmaceutical drugs) and an inability to discipline regions for overspending – became apparent (Ferrera 1995: 280).[12] Anti-SSN fervour eventually reached its apex in the 1994 elections, when abandoning the universal nature of the healthcare system was a significant campaign issue, with division falling along coalition lines; indeed, the first Berlusconi government (1994/1995) planned to privatise the health system, but the government collapsed before it had an opportunity to do so (Spence 1996: 48). More generally, however, reforms have taken a less revolutionary tack, tapering certain aspects of the system's universalism via regulations on prescriptions, the increasing use of co-payments (for specialist care, diagnostic tests, and pharmaceutical drugs), and the phasing out of coverage for certain types of care (e.g. dental).[13] Lacking recurrent crisis of the healthcare system and a popular movement for reform, institutional inertia has therefore prevailed: the complete overturning of the system entailed high fiscal and political costs of reform with low potential payoff – especially in light of the fragile governing coalitions and opposition by regional governments (France and Taroni 2005: 175).

Summing up, the post-war reform of the healthcare system was particularly unsatisfactory for the Italian left, as it failed to base healthcare access on citizenship or grant greater worker input through the structure of health insurance administration, while at the same time also providing the DC with important clientelistic resources. This led to early clamouring

11 That persistent delay of such reforms was attributed to the same sorts of delays that plagued the immediate post-war period: economic difficulties and opposition from certain employers' associations, pharmaceutical companies, medical associations, and segments of the Church (De Miguel 1977: 389).

12 The popularity of the system would soon be dealt a further blow with revelations of the vast corruption at work up to the Tangentopoli scandal.

13 While initially controversial, the use of co-payments would slowly become more normalised, over time gaining broad political support. As a Partito Democratico deputy – one who described the universalism of the healthcare system as 'indispensable' – would later put it, 'perhaps we exaggerated in the past [by making access to] services completely free' (Touadi 2012).

for transformative reform, which would restructure the founding principle of the system from insurance-based to universalistic. The 1970s then saw a culmination of circumstances that substantially augmented pressures for change: mass mobilisation for reform suggested that public opinion supported the reconfiguration of the system, shifting the potential electoral costs for parties interested in maintaining the status quo; recurring crises of the insurance funds challenged the system's sustainability, both on a technical level and in the eyes of the public; the newly created regional governments increased calls for reform, both through the desire of these governments to increase their own powers and through bringing into being a level of government less tainted by corruption in the public's eyes; and, most importantly, the surge in electoral strength of the PCI dramatically augmented their influence and put the universalising reform on the immediate agenda. The end result was benefit extension and standardisation through the creation of a universal healthcare system.

Staying the Course in France

What, if anything, do these considerations tell us about the preference for a residualising rather than universalising approach to healthcare extension and standardisation in the French case? Turning first to *Left-wing Strength* hypothesis, it should be noted that the preferences on the left in France were formed under circumstances quite different from those in Italy. In particular, by giving unions a central role in the management of the system, the post-Second World War re-organisation of health insurance in France had the effect of placating potential demands from labour for a universal healthcare system.

Whereas an Italian union would be the first organisation to lay out a proposal for the complete transformation of healthcare in Italy, its French equivalents were silent on the issue – instead acting as protectors of the *acquis sociaux*. This likely reflects both the pro-status quo preferences of their membership and the incentives inherent in the social insurance system, which provides unions not only with administrative posts but also power and influence derived from their role in the health insurance funds (Palier 2002: 8). While the centrality of organised labour's role may have diminished after the 1967 reform that re-established parity, French unions ultimately remain far more integrated into the system than their counterparts had been Italy. In this case, then, the developments reflect much more accurately the expectations of the insiders/outsider perspective.

This institutionalised position has led even to a certain unease regarding the residualisation implicit in the extension of coverage via the CMU, with an apparent preference for the primary system – and universalisation of that benefit scheme – instead. As the former national secretary Jean-Christophe Le Duigou of the Confédération générale du travail (CGT) relates,

> If there are people who cannot pay their contributions, the system should cover them [...] The CMU is better than nothing, but in my opinion it was necessary to reflect more deeply upon the idea of giving the Caisse nationale de l'assurance maladie [National Sickness Insurance Fund] the capacity to truly cover excluded individuals [...] You might find this a bit demanding, but we think it's necessary to defend the principles [of the system] without voting in programmes that fall short of these principles [...] We insist on constantly reaffirming that the contributory and solidarity [principles] must go hand in hand. (Le Duigou 2012)

Given the strong predicted role of leftist unions in the push for universal healthcare (see Navarro 1989: 891), this organisational incentive made them considerably more opposed to a revolutionary reform of the system – though they were equally opposed to residualisation as well. As was the case with regard to benefits for the unemployed, although they express concern for excluded individuals, proposals to deal with the issue are often framed in terms of assisting individuals in their quest to find non-precarious jobs (Le Duigou 2012). At the same time, the major leftist unions, the Force Ouvrière (FO) and the CGT, have also been quite sceptical of state involvement in healthcare – with, as FO secretary general Jean-Claude Mailly's would later argue, 'increasing state control seen as a prelude to privatisation' (2008: 113). Organisational incentives around maintaining union support and sources of power (highlighted by research in other welfare domains (e.g. Davidsson and Emmenegger 2013)) combined with low and declining union membership levels (both generally and compared with Italy)[14] to weaken the role they might otherwise have played.

What, then, of the French Communist Party (Parti Communiste Français (PCF))? The pro-status quo institutional incentives experienced by the unions did not apply to the PCF, and given their long-awaited re-entry into French government (the first since the French May 1947 crisis) via a

14 While the gap between French and Italian union density was only five percentage points in 1960 (at 19.6% and 24.7%, respectively), by 1990 it had grown to almost 30 points (at 9.9% and 38.8%, respectively) (OECD 2012c).

coalition under Mitterrand, why was there no similar pressures for reform? The most obvious response is that despite occurring around the same time as the Italian 'historic compromise', the situations were not comparable in that the two Communist Parties had quite distinct levels of power. In France, the PCF was finally included in government not because of worries over destabilisation, but because the Socialist Party (Parti Socialiste, PS) had surged past them right into power, bringing the PCF along as coalition partners. This corresponded with a significant drop in the PCF's electoral support (which had previously been roughly on par with that of the PS) that clearly positioned them as the junior partner, with just a fraction of the seats. This contrasts starkly with the situation in Italy, where the PCI was closing in on the DC, receiving just over 34% of the votes cast in 1976 (not far from the DC's 38.7%).

Above and beyond this point, however, the position of the PCF towards universalistic healthcare systems simply was and is not the same as that held by the PCI. It is worth noting that within the PCF it appears that the French healthcare system (as well as the other social insurance institutions) is conceived of as 'original', falling outside of any Beveridge/Bismarck dichotomy. The editor-in-chief of the PCF's *La Revue Économie et Politique* put it thusly:

> It is neither the state nor business accords that define the level of coverage. It is precisely, in fact, universal [...] a bit like the British system, but [...] financed by the productive wealth of corporations [...] It is not an individual who decides, nor is it the state that decides for individuals. It is a different model, piloted by the workers themselves. (Rauch 2012)

At the same time, however, he also argued that the leftist principles of the system (including 'universalist ambitions') seen to have been incorporated into the system by the PCF in the immediate post-war period, have been 'a progression of attacks that have led to the current situation wherein universalism is less and less the general framework, with a corresponding rise in individual insurance' (Rauch 2012). This understanding led the PCF to oppose the CMU as insufficient, 'a bad solution to a real problem', arguing instead, just as the CGIL did, for universalism via the integration of excluded individuals into the current system; the recurring theme here was to 'create the conditions necessary for excluded individuals to have salaried jobs that permit them [to access the main funds]' (Rauch 2012).

Moreover, my interview subjects at the PCF also argued that universally extending access to the principal system was financially feasible, so long as declining wages (and concomitantly decreased contributions) were reversed through a broader economic shift away from speculation and towards production (Morin 2011; Rauch 2012).[15] Here again the solution to coverage issues and the welfare state dualisation that has resulted from labour market dualisation is situated in the reversal of labour market dualisation itself. Yet even with this undermining of social security, gradual rather than dramatic changes can be viewed as sufficient since the system is seen to have the appropriate leftist principles at its base. Here again, the nature of the post-war health insurance system appears to have conditioned preferences – in this case thanks to greater worker input into the management of the system and an absence of clientelism. As such, potential left-wing pressure for universal healthcare was tapered by the structure of the institutions. If there was any working-class pressure for total reform, it certainly was not reflected in the preferences of even the more radical of its representative organisations.

The Interest Group Weakness theory, in turn, highlights additional effects of the post-war reorganisation of the French health insurance system. In the first instance, what might be conceived of as the insurance lobby (leaving aside the issue of complementary coverage providers) was transformed from the pre-war hodgepodge of insurance mutuals into the co-managers of the semi-public insurance system itself. Given that these co-managers – the social partners – are representatives of labour and employer associations, the creation of the semi-public system had the effect of granting the fund managers much greater legitimacy in the eyes of the public. The influence of doctors' associations, in turn, was stronger under the Fourth Republic (with its many veto points) than it has been under the Fifth; regardless of this diminution of influence, however, their opposition to reform has had little to do with the question of NHS-style healthcare, which has not been a real subject of political debate (see Godt 1987: 467; Immergut 1990: 401). To ascribe explanatory power to the influence of lobby groups would therefore be problematic in this instance, pointing us towards other factors instead.

With regard to the *Political Decentralisation* hypothesis, the French example provides support for this theory through the combination of an absence of federalism and the lack of an NHS-style system. While France has experienced some moderate decentralisation, particularly since the 1986 introduction of regional elections and the corresponding downloading of certain administrative and political competencies, this process has been slower and much more limited than in Italy. Even leaving aside the total

15 Both Morin and Rauch were employed, at the time of their respective interviews, as editor-in-chief of the PCF's *La Revue Économie et Politique*.

lack of federalism, the opportunities for legislative experimentation – a central factor to reform in the Canadian case, for example – are restricted to specific issues and for a set period of time, with the legislation either cancelled or expanded to the national level at that point (Schrijver 2006: 207). In the field of healthcare competencies, downloading has been limited to the 1996 creation of 'regional hospital agencies' (*agences régionales de l'hospitalisation*), charged with improving resource allocation to hospitals (Catrice-Lorey and Steffen 2006: 175). French healthcare itself thus remains quite centralised compared with other health insurance systems, such as the German and Dutch variants (Hassenteufel and Palier 2007: 576). Overall then, the French case has been characterised by both limited decentralisation (generally and with regard to healthcare competencies) and a lack of notable region-driven pressure, all of which is consistent with the *Political Decentralisation* hypothesis.

Most fundamentally, we would suggest that the explanation of the lack of paradigmatic change (and a universal system more generally) in France lies in the institutional organisation of the French health insurance system. Here one can point to four relevant factors in particular, already alluded to above. First, there is the greater institutionalised role assigned to unions in the post-war system, which, with its central role for union representatives, gave it a substantial incentive to maintain the system. Coverage extension through residualisation would undermine this position, so the preferred course of action was effectively increasing the number of labour market and welfare state insiders, ideally to the point where the insider/outsider distinction no longer exists.

Second, the extended role for the social partners (i.e. employer and employee representatives) in the management of the system helped provide the system – and what one might conceive of as the pro-status quo 'insurance lobby' (i.e. the social partners) – with greater popular legitimacy. This provides a significant contrast to the Italian case, where the role for worker representatives was far less entrenched. With its more substantial post-war reorganisation, the deep involvement of the unions in French health insurance management helped to at least partially realise the new conceptions of citizenship rights that became popular (especially on the left) in the wake of the mass sacrifices of the Second World War. In Italy, by contrast, despite constitutional declarations to the contrary, these new citizenship rights went largely unfulfilled in healthcare until the creation of the SSN.

A direct comparison of the largest health insurance boards in these two countries serves to illustrate this point. In France, the board of directors of

CNAMTS (Caisse nationale de l'assurance maladie des travailleurs salariés), which covers about 80% of the population, has traditionally been composed of an equal number of worker and employer representatives, together constituting almost 80% of the board. The situation was quite different with the largest health insurance fund in Italy, INAM (Istituto Nazionale per l'Assicurazione contro le Malattie), which covered just over half of insured individuals by the mid-1970s: although just under a third of the board seats were assigned to union representatives and just over half to employer and employee representatives combined, in reality the DC maintained strict control over (and close connections with) the insurance boards (Maynard 1975: 159; Ferrera 1986: 456; Sandier et al. 2004: 24; Rochaix and Wilsford 2005: 101). What is more, as Ferrera argues, INAM acted as one of the 'most significant fiefdoms of political patronage for the Christian Democrats', further deteriorating the sense that the social partners were central to the system (Ferrera 1996a: 56). The actual role and significance of worker representatives in France was thus much less suspect than it was in Italy – a factor which then shaped public opinion and, as a result, party platforms.

Third and relatedly, the absence in France of an Italian-style system of political patronage fiefdoms altered the preferences of left-leaning voters and politicians, who did not view the health insurance system as a source of political power for the centre-right. Here again, as in Chapter 2, one notes the apparent relevance of particularly Southern European characteristics. The contrasting designs in the two countries therefore afforded the respective systems either more or less popular legitimacy, particularly in the eyes of leftist unions, voters, and parties.

Lastly, in addition to the popular legitimacy aspect, the stronger semi-public characteristics of the French health insurance also legitimised greater state intervention to keep the already existing system afloat. The 2003 Douste-Blazy Law provides a perfect example of this: faced with mounting deficits, the government increased contributions and user fees, and even transferred the debt to a special fund (Caisse d'Amortissement de la Dette Sociale (Fund for the Redemption of the Social Debt)) financed by additional contributions (Sorum 2005: 239-240). In Italy, by contrast, the assumption of insurance fund debt in the mid-1970s resulted in a considerable political and popular backlash. Lack of support for the state propping up the system suggests that any such change would almost certainly have been politically unfeasible in the long term if not accompanied by a major structural overhaul – making universalisation much more likely than residualisation.

By diminishing potential left-wing union, party, and popular pressure for reform, these factors help to explain not only the lack of a universalist restructuring of the French healthcare system, but also the over two decade delay in extending benefits to uncovered individuals and standardising benefits for the majority of users. While the CMU, as a residualist, non-transformative reform, was obviously a simpler approach to extending coverage than the SSN, the broader social insurance framework in France altered the preferences of left-wing actors by requiring that extension occur alongside the preservation of already existing insider privileges (whether for members, voters, or organisations themselves). Although this delay was also likely affected by the more limited nature of the coverage problem in France[16] (at the time of the CMU's introduction in 1999, an estimated 150,000 individuals were without coverage, as opposed to the approximately 1,700,000 without coverage in Italy prior to the SSN's creation in 1978), there was also the additional issue of the 6 million people in France without complementary coverage (Barbier and Théret 2003: 144; OECD 2012b). Furthermore, while the coverage rates in Italy tended to lag behind the French rates by about two percentage points over the course of the 1970s (up until the introduction of the SSN), French coverage levels prior to 1978 were not wholly different from Italian ones (OECD 2012b).

Overall, this chapter has highlighted the use of residualisation in France as a means to extend coverage to welfare state outsiders, though this was nevertheless paralleled by some benefit standardisation (a process that is still not fully complete). In light of the generally popular and comparatively well-functioning semi-public insurance funds, the 1999 means-tested CMU reform under Jospin expanded coverage in a more timid manner than the one pursued in Italy, opting to add a regime (for those without coverage) to the occupationally divided system. This measure was then followed in 2001 with benefit standardisation for 95% of covered persons. As a side benefit, tinkering with the broader insurance model also helped the government bypass opposition from the social partners, thereby making the reform much more politically feasible. Ultimately, then, one notes the use of less revolutionary reforms in France to achieve similar (though, as stressed above, certainly not identical) improvements to the healthcare system.

16 The CGT's former national secretary, Le Duigou, for instance, highlighted the relative lack of a problem by contrasting it to the situation in the labour market: '[in healthcare] there are not, overall, the inequalities that one finds in wages – by contrast, there is a small minority of the population that does not fall within the public system and for whom there was the need to create a right, the CMU' (Le Duigou 2012).

Conclusion

This chapter has outlined the major developments in the French and Italian healthcare systems in order to explain the divergent trajectories of benefit extension and standardisation in the cases. Both countries opted for health insurance rather than universalist systems in the immediate aftermath of the Second World War, and both were faced with gaps in coverage that were slowly filled in a piecemeal fashion (though with greater state guidance in France). While French governments were typically more willing and able to intervene than the Italian ones, variations across insurance funds persisted in both countries and were extended in a piecemeal fashion. Yet Italy would change course entirely in 1978, eliminating the old system and creating the SSN – a development that is of particular interest since it contrasts so starkly with the Italian failure to reform in the field of benefits for the unemployed.

In explaining the different reforms pursued in French and Italian healthcare, this chapter has used a combination of secondary sources, interview data, and archival research to ultimately make a similar argument to that found in previous chapters: one in which structural factors have affected pressures towards reorganisation. Most notably in this instance, the greater role for workers' representatives in the French insurance funds granted the system a greater degree of legitimacy on the left, thereby making greater state intervention possible and giving unions pro-status quo institutional incentives. The power given to workers' representatives in the management of the funds marked the realisation of certain post-Second World War citizenship ideals, which in turn helped bring the PCF on board as well.

The Italian system, by contrast, failed to bring those on the left-leaning citizens and politicians fully into the fold and left certain citizenship ideals (as represented in both the D'Aragona Commission's report and the Italian constitution) unfulfilled. It is doubtful that these points alone would have been enough to spur reform, given that they are also broadly reflected in the case of benefits for the unemployed. A number of additional features, not shared in the case of minimum income benefits, must therefore be highlighted. To begin, the fact that the health insurance funds served as important clientelistic resources for the DC further contributed to leftist opposition to the system and support for transformative reform, though for more pragmatic and less ideological reasons; in this way, one can once again note the import of the characteristics associated with Southern European states. At a more proximate level, the spread of popular movements for reform in the 1970s then suggested a broader shift in public opinion, coinciding with the fiscal crises of the insurance funds and a push by the regions for control over healthcare. Taken together, these factors created the circumstances under which the PCI would press for and achieve the 1978 SSN reform during the period of its greatest influence. Thus, institutions were key here for two reasons: first, the structure of relevant institutions appears to have led the public to be far more pro-reform than was the case vis-à-vis unemployment reform, thereby incentivising pro-reform positions on the part of vote-seeking parties; and second, the PCI in particular derived organisation-related incentives from the institutional context – which is of special interest because the PCI was the key political actor pushing for reform. The overall result was dramatic, paradigmatic ('third order') institutional change ushering in universal coverage and the mass standardisation of benefits.

In France, by contrast, the extension of benefits to welfare state outsider would need to wait just over an extra two decades to occur, and would happen through residualisation – undoubtedly a more timid (and in the case of benefit standardisation, incomplete) 'second order' approach to the issue. The delay can partially be understood as a product of the absence of the above listed pressures for reform from both the public and leftist parties/unions (in each instance structured by the institutional differences highlighted above). It is in part likely also the result of the less serious nature of these problems in France, with the creation of the CMU extending coverage to far fewer previously uncovered individuals than had been the case with the SSN. The French residualist approach to unemployment reform highlighted in Chapter 2 was thus paralleled by a residualist healthcare reform, though in the case of healthcare France was the late developer rather than the early one.

The variation across both the French and Italian cases and the two policy fields are undoubtedly clear at this point, and Chapter 8 will examine how the outcomes in the two policy domains might be understood within a common framework. To preview the conclusions, it will be suggested that the left's relationship to reforms addressing welfare state dualisation is a variable one, since fiscal and/or political limitations prevent the extension of generous benefits to all. More precisely, this variation has been conditioned by institutional arrangements that structure party preferences directly (by creating certain organisational incentives) and indirectly (through public opinion). We will argue that these sorts of considerations respectively impact the choice between universalising and residualising reforms, and the choice between reform and inaction. This heterogeneity across countries and policy domains also means that attempts to uncover a single relationship between the left and welfare state reform are inherently problematic. Even where the left appears to have played a crucial role in addressing welfare state dualisation, institutions matter at least as much as ideology.

Before proceeding to this discussion, however, we must first turn to consider the generalisability of these findings.

6 Healthcare Reform and Public Opinion in Continental and Southern Europe

The comparison of healthcare benefit extension and standardisation in France and Italy has provided us with testable hypotheses, and in this chapter we begin exploring how well they travel. Our assessment of generalisability employs the same framework taken with regard to benefits for the unemployed, combining a discussion of policy trajectories with public opinion as initial steps towards carrying out broader statistical analysis in the next chapter. That said, country-specific analyses of public opinion can necessarily only play a limited role in this instance, given that our key explanatory variables are national-level factors.

The chapter begins by briefly discussing developments in healthcare coverage and equity in the same six additional Continental and Southern European cases: Austria, Belgium, Germany, Greece, Spain, and Portugal. In this case, the former set of cases represent the social health insurance systems, whilst the latter have (quasi-) universalist healthcare regimes. As in Chapter 3, our goal is twofold: first, to illustrate the extent to which the French and Italian cases are typical, deviant, or simply different within their respective welfare state families; and second, to assess whether determinants similar to those highlighted in the French-Italian comparison appear to play a role in these other countries as well. To preview our conclusions, France and Italy do appear to provide relatively standard illustrations of the reform trajectories within their groups. The Continental cases share the piecemeal extension of benefit access that one would expect, despite considerable variation in the timing and means by which those falling outside of the insurance system were given protection. The Southern European cases also share the expected pattern of coverage extension, though benefit standardisation varies considerably. Indeed, the key factors discussed in the French-Italian comparison appear to have largely been responsible for these differences.

We then proceed to present descriptive statistics of country-level survey data, first from France and Italy, and then from our other Continental and Southern European cases. In particular, this discussion centres around two components of public opinion: attitudes towards government responsibility to provide access to healthcare; and beliefs about the need for dramatic reform of the system. We limit ourselves here to a discussion of survey responses since country-level regression analysis would not allow us to include any of our key variables. Instead, the discussion is treated as a first step in building to the multi-level model analysis with which the next chapter begins. The results of this initial inquiry provide the basis for understanding attitudes about public opinion: while social health insurance systems are associated with slightly lower assigned roles of government responsibility, this is likely because the comparison between attitudes in health insurance and universalised healthcare systems take different structures as their referents; and the lower preferences for transformation reflect the lack of relative lack of crises in these systems at the time of surveying.

Taking these findings together, we are able to better contextualise the French and Italian cases and find general support for our previous analysis. The case studies are particularly valuable in this regard, while the discussion of survey responses sets the stage for more sophisticated analysis.

Extending the Comparison

We begin with a word on case selection. As briefly mentioned in Chapter 6, the classification of healthcare systems poses some particular challenges that go beyond the placement of individual countries in particular groupings (see Wendt et al. 2009). Part of the issue here is that limited attention has been paid to how healthcare systems may or may not reflect the standard welfare state regime clusters in which they are found (Bambra 2005). Above and beyond this point, the question of which criteria are central to classification would appear notably less settled: Esping-Andersen's (1990) classification has made far less of a mark vis-à-vis healthcare programmes, and as Freeman and Frisina (2010: 169-170) illustrate, authors give centre stage to a wide variety of key factors in their categorisations.

Despite these difficulties, our general focus on benefit coverage and standardisation allows us to sidestep the more complex categorisation issues and makes our choice of additional cases much less controversial than it might otherwise be. Just as the distinction between France and Italy is far clearer in this regard than it would be if we wanted to incorporate Northern European systems for comparison or contrast, our broader sets of cases – despite meaningful differences within each grouping – plainly form two separate clusters. This is the case whether we side with authors who divide healthcare systems into NHS, social insurance, and liberal/private variants (e.g. OECD 1987; Palier 2004b; Burau and Blank 2006) or with those who suggest the addition of a Southern European variant to the typology (e.g. Ferrera 1995; Moran 2000; Toth 2010).

We therefore continue with the same set of additional Continental (Austria, Belgium, and Germany) and Southern European (Greece, Portugal, and Spain) cases that were used in Chapter 3. Each case study begins with a brief description of the post-war system and its structure, and then proceeds to discuss the extension of coverage and benefit standardisation from that baseline. As we shall see, only the Greek case differs notably from its typological colleagues – and in that one the shared broader circumstances and false start at transformational reform make it a valuable inclusion in the discussion.

Continental Europe

In line with our discussion of French reforms in the previous chapter, the Continental European cases share a common trajectory, with benefit extension first through piecemeal occupational and other categorical additions and, eventually, via residual, means-tested measures. The timing of these developments nevertheless reveals some interesting patterns, and Table 6.1 lists healthcare coverage rates across our Continental cases (including France) from the start of each decade since 1960.[1] Tracking coverage levels over the years illustrates not only temporal variation in the extension of coverage to erstwhile welfare state outsiders, but also the prevalence of regression. We reference these developments within the discussions of each case.

Table 6.1 Total Healthcare Coverage as a % of the Population – Continental Europe

	1960	1970	1980	1990	2000	2010
Continental Europe						
France	76%	95.6%	99.1%	99.4%	99.9%	99.9%
Austria	78%	91%	99%	99%	99%	99.3%
Belgium	58%	97.8%	99%	97.3%	99%	99%
Germany	85.2%	89.2%	92.3%	88.8%	99.8%	100%

Source: OECD 2012b

1 Missing coverage data from the OECD unfortunately prevent a precise pinning down of the exact trajectory of French coverage extension in the 1960s; but what is clear is that by 1970 the categorical extensions referenced in the previous chapters had, combined, brought most of the population into one scheme or another.

The current Austrian health insurance system took its form in 1955 with the passing of the General Social Security Act (ASVG). Insurance coverage was subsequently expanded in the typical piecemeal fashion, rising from 78% in 1960 to 91% by 1970, and reaching 99% by 1980. The earlier extensions were most notably achieved through the addition of occupational benefit schemes for farmers and public servants (Hofmarcher 2013: 20, 88). This was not a steady upward trajectory, however, as coverage rates in Austria dipped over the course of the 2000s, dropping to 97% in 2002 before slowly rebounding over the remainder of the decade.

Structurally, Austrian healthcare reflects the country's federalist system, with schemes divided along regional and occupational lines. The former is the larger of the two categories, and is primarily composed of individuals insured under the ASVG (employees, benefit recipients, freelancers, and apprentices). Together, the nine regional schemes cover about 80% of the population, providing standardised benefits for the majority of the population (Hofmarcher 2013: 89). The vast majority of the remaining residents are covered by special schemes available for particular occupational groups (e.g. farmers, civil servants), and it is here that benefit standardisation notably breaks down. While these funds must meet the standards of coverage set by the ASVG, beyond that common core there is considerable diversity in supplementary coverage (Hofmarcher 2013: 52, 89). As such, benefit standardisation remains incomplete, with the core benefits reaching a smaller proportion of the population than is the case in France.[2]

Trends in coverage levels also reflect those in France: by 1980, when legislation extended access to freelancers and the self-employed, coverage was near complete, leaving only marginal room for extension. The Austrian system nevertheless differed in how it dealt with persons falling outside of the insurance schemes. Namely, for individuals of limited means without access to the Austrian insurance system, healthcare provision was in fact integrated into the social assistance programmes created in the 1970s. Although this moved the outsider's route to access outside of the insurance framework, it mitigated the sorts of issues that affected similarly positioned persons in France.

Yet just as was the case with benefits for the unemployed, recent developments point to problems with this previous model, especially with regard to the delivery of benefits for these individuals. In particular, the 2010

2 In addition, some regional variation in service provision persists and there is evidence of a two-tiered system, with private insurance holders, for example, often able to jump queues entirely (Hofmarcher 2013: 249-250).

introduction of the Social Minimum (Bedarfsorientierte Mindestsicherung) already discussed in Chapter 3 served as an important step forward for those on social assistance: with the introduction of the programme, recipients across the *Länder* were guaranteed access to standard insurance coverage via the ASVG. Recall from our discussion of Austrian social assistance that this was part of a move, on the part of both the Grand Coalition government and the social partners, towards reinforcing flexicurity in the Austrian welfare state (Obinger et al. 2012: 183). The reform also addressed concerns that social assistance recipients were subject to stigmatisation under the pre-2010 system, as they had previously been forced to rely on a separate voucher system (Austria 2014: 80). In addition, this move towards integration followed a 2008 reform limiting the total percentage of costs that one must pay on prescription drugs, thereby mitigating de facto restrictions on access (Hofmarcher 2013: 216). These changes suggest meaningful improvements for those without standard access to the social health insurance system, despite the fact that this process began considerably earlier than it had in France.

Indeed, Belgium was even quicker to extend coverage to those outside the system – a point which should be relatively unsurprising in light of Table 6.1, which highlights the dramatic coverage increase in the 1960s.

Health insurance became mandatory for most of the Belgian population in 1945, with the scheme part of the broader social security system; by the time access was extended to the self-employed in 1963, it came to cover about two-thirds of the population (Maarse and Paulus 2003: 591). What is most noteworthy, though, is that while this process of piecemeal extension continued over the course of the 1960s, it culminated in 1969 with the extension to individuals who were not already covered (Gerkens and Merkur 2010: 21). As a result, coverage rose from 72% in the previous year to 99%, putting it well ahead of any of our other cases. Today the system includes one public and six private health insurance fund associations that together cover over 99% of the population, with the remaining population generally consisting of persons who have yet to pay their social security contributions (Gerkens and Merkur 2010: 15-16, 220). Changes in the size of this latter group explains subsequent fluctuations in coverage rates, which experienced dips in the early 1970s as well as the period stretching from the late 1980s to early 1990s.

In terms of benefit standardisation, while the insurance principle is still central – with coverage via either employment history or, for dependents, relationship to the insured – there are relatively few benefit schemes: the vast majority of persons (about 88%) are covered by the general scheme, while about 10% are within the self-employed scheme (Gerkens and Merkur 2010: 87). Nevertheless, the significance of this distinction was until the 2000s fairly large, as members of the scheme for the self-employed were only protected against major risks. Members of the general scheme, by contrast, also had coverage for minor risks – a category which includes things like minor surgeries, physician visits, out-patient medication, and dental care. The so-called 'Purple Government' (consisting of both social democratic and liberal parties) decided in 2004, however, to eliminate this variation, phasing in the reform from 2006 to 2008 (Nys 2010: 39-40). Yet given that there was some hesitancy about this reform on the part of representatives of the self-employed (due to concerns about the ability of poorer members to pay increased contribution rates), the issues at play in this case were clearly distinct from those in France (Le Soir 2007).

More importantly for our purposes is another 'Purple Government' initiative, this time relating to the 'preferential reimbursement' scheme that reduces co-payment rates for certain groups. The aim here was to ensure de facto access to care, and both the initial programme and subsequent reforms were clearly conceptualised along these lines. Originally introduced in 1963 for groups deemed to typically be more in need, the list was very exclusive, including only widows, disabled persons, pensioners, and orphans. In the wake of the *General Report on Poverty* (King Baudouin Foundation 1995) problematising this exclusivity and pushing for a means test instead, the list was extended twice: first in 1997, to add coverage for additional specific at-risk groups, including social assistance recipients and long-term unemployed persons over 50; and second in 2007, with the creation of the OMNIO system, to include all economically vulnerable persons who pass a means test (Van de Geuchte et al. 2007: 38-39). This latter reform was felt necessary since the 1997 reform had for budgetary reasons excluded various groups (such as the working poor), in the process introducing perverse incentives to remain out of the labour market (Van de Geuchte et al. 2007: 39; Maresso et al. 2015: 18). Despite the early 1969 extension of access to the general scheme, this broader push for extension, coupled with a level of health system legitimacy that more closely resembles that of France than pre-reform Italy, allows us to observe some meaningful parallels with the French case.

Germany, reflecting its trajectory regarding benefits for the unemployed, is yet another early extender. Their social health insurance system was created extremely early, in 1883, with the goal of both protecting workers and (as a corollary) combatting socialism, and its coverage was extended considerably in subsequent decades (Hassenteufel 1996: 462). The quasi-public system, which makes membership in a scheme mandatory for all individuals earning more than a set amount, persisted through the various shifts in political systems (save for under the German Democratic Republic). By 1925 just over 50% of the population was a member of a statutory insurance fund, and by reunification that value had hit 88% in the West German population[3] (Busse and Reisberg 2004: 16, 57). Particularly over the course of the 1970s, various non-occupational groups (such as students and the disabled) were incorporated into the system. This process eventually culminated in 2004 with the inclusion of social assistance recipients, who had previously relied on social assistance itself to directly pay healthcare costs (Busse and Reisberg 2004: 17, 24; Busse and Blümel 2014: 118). Taken together, these reforms created a system that covered not only citizens and residents but also foreign workers.

Benefit standardisation is reasonably high, but the existence of private schemes alongside the social health insurance system introduces some important differences. Those on private schemes amount to about 10% of the population, mainly consisting of the self-employed, civil servants and their dependents, and those with incomes above a threshold level; since these benefit schemes are only obliged to maintain a minimum standard of coverage, this leads to considerable variation in covered add-ons (Altenstetter and Busse 2005: 126; Busse and Blümel 2014: 121).[4]

With regard to coverage, until recently about 0.2% of the population still lacked prepaid coverage, with the group primarily consisting of self-employed persons who failed to pay the necessary contributions into either a statutory or private fund (Busse and Reisberg 2004: 57). While the number of uninsured persons was relatively low, it had in fact increased considerably over the previous decade; as a consequence, there was broad agreement among the major parties that the problem should be addressed, despite some debate about the details of the solution (Busse and Blümel 2014: 249). Importantly, however, the push to remedy this situation related more to moral hazard rather than benefit extension, since uninsured individuals were in fact still permitted to access healthcare via social assistance whenever they became ill. This was seen as especially problematic since uncovered individuals did not in fact tend to be particularly poor. The eventual 2009 reform under the centre-right coalition ultimately permitted those who

3 This number excludes those with private insurance or on sector-specific government schemes.

4 In addition, a small proportion of the population, including military personnel and police officers, are covered by sector-specific governmental schemes (Busse and Blümel 2014: 115).

had previously held social health insurance to re-enter the programme, while those who had not were required to opt for private insurance instead (Busse and Blümel 2014: 122, 249).

Overall, we note that our Continental European cases share certain broad commonalities. We see this both in terms of general coverage levels and the details as to how individuals who would typically fall outside of the principal insurance system were included, although the form and timing of the latter varies. Yet there is nevertheless considerable variation in what coverage actually looked like. In the case of Austria and Germany, those on social assistance were until recently provided healthcare access directly via their assistance schemes. While this system was more effective at ensuring coverage than the French approach prior to the Couverture Maladie Universelle (CMU), it also created room for stigmatisation and concerns about quality of care. Belgian governments, in turn, acted very early on to extend access to the insurance system even for those on social assistance. Even so, Belgian debates around preferential reimbursement in the 1990s and 2000s highlight additional parallels to the French case with regard to de facto barriers to care.

Southern Europe

As we have already discussed, a (near) universalistic approach to healthcare is one of the original characteristic features of Southern European welfare states. Italy, Greece, Spain, and Portugal all have constitutions declaring access to health on the basis of citizenship, and they have each attempted, albeit with varying degrees of success, to put that declaration into practice (Ferrera 1996b: 22). What is more, all of these countries dramatically reformed their healthcare systems over the course of about a single decade, which, in all but the Italian case, followed recent democratisation. Given the parallels with Italy, in this section we focus on the causes, successes, and failures of these universalising reforms, both in terms of benefit coverage and standardisation.

Table 6.2 highlights the changes in coverage these reforms entailed, with the shifts generally more dramatic than those seen in the Continental cases. This is particularly the case with Portugal, where coverage levels rose from 66% to 100% in 1978, and Greece, where they increased from 88% to 100% in 1984. Italy, on the other hand, had a more gradual rate of extension that was eventually capped off with universalisation, while Spain, for rather particular reasons we discuss below, continues to have coverage levels just under 100%. Even setting aside this variation, some important differences clearly persist among these cases, especially with regard to the Greek case – but they nonetheless share much in common.

Table 6.2 Total Healthcare Coverage as a % of the Population – Southern Europe

	1960	1970	1980	1990	2000	2010
Southern Europe						
Italy	87%	93%	100%	100%	100%	100%
Greece	44*	55	88	100	100	100**
Portugal	18	40	100	100	100	100
Spain	54	61	83	98.1***	98.9****	99.2

Source: OECD 2012b
* Data from 1961
** Data from 2008
*** Data from 1989
**** Data from 2001

In Greece, compulsory social (including medical) insurance coverage was extended from public to private sector workers in 1932 with the creation of the 'Social Insurance Foundation' (Matsaganis 2005: 34). Coverage levels were still quite low, however, leading to the introduction of a number of additional funds for professional groups over the remainder of the 1930s, followed by a major extension of coverage to the rural population in 1961 (Mossialos and Alin 2005: 422-423). By the 1980s there were a full 80 different occupational funds, with varying contribution levels and benefits, and a huge urban-rural split in terms of access to care (Guillén 2002: 55-56). The result was a system that was widely viewed as inadequate and in need of reform, creating a broadly pro-reform atmosphere rather reminiscent of that in Italy (Davaki and Mossialos 2005: 156).

Within this context, the National Health System was created in 1983 under the newly elected Socialist government. It was hoped that the reform would help to increase coordination and uniformity, but its effectiveness was severely undermined by elite opposition; in particular, the most vocal opponents came from the ranks of private practice physicians, insurance funds, and the trade unions and members associated with the more generous schemes (Guillén 2002: 56-57; Davaki and Mossialos 2005: 158). Indeed, this situation even led even some high-ranking members of the governing party to oppose the standardisation of benefit generosity (Mossialos and Alin 2005: 424). Together, these actors were able to substantially limit the scope of reform, especially in the absence of a solid pro-reform coalition. The result was a provision only for voluntary (rather than mandatory) unification of the insurance funds – a unification that has yet to occur over 20 years later (Nikolentzos and Mays 2008: 169).

As a result, while the reform was effective at extending benefit coverage, it left much to be desired in terms of benefit standardisation. The universal coverage provided by the system is still tied to the old occupational schemes, with only those outside of any occupational grouping – amounting to about 5% of the population – relying on the system directly (Ferrera 1996b: 24; Mossialos and Alin 2005: 427). This implies vast differences in benefit generosity across occupational groups. Arguably even worse, however, is the fact that many of the groups with the most generous access actually pay less in contributions than average citizens (Nikolentzos and Mays 2008: 167). The result is a system which resembles a hybrid of social health insurance and universalist schemes, with Toth (2010: 330) going so far as to conclude that 'the Greek national health service is such in name only'.

In a certain sense, then, it is clear that the Greek and Italian reform trajectories diverge substantially, especially within the universe of Southern European cases. This divergence raises further questions, since both countries seem to have shared key commonalities in the run-up to reform: most notably leftist party strength and a broad pro-reform context in which the existing healthcare system was viewed as inadequate. The most obvious difference, referenced above and already pointed to as an important explanation in the previous chapter, is the influence of lobby group strength. Opposition groups were powerful enough not only to sow disaccord within parliament more generally, but also within the leftist government. The role of particular insider groups – specific trade unions (and their membership) with access to more generous benefit schemes – is quite noteworthy in this regard, highlighting the relevance of the welfare state insider-outsider framework for healthcare, even prior to the dramatic rise in atypical employment. In addition, it is worth noting that some authors (Mossialos and Alin 2005: 424), in attempting to explain the reform's failures, point to additional factors reflecting those discussed in our analysis of access to benefits for the unemployed: namely, weak administrative capacity and clientelism.[5]

The Portuguese case lies closer to the Italian one in terms of eventual outcomes, despite the continuation of some standardisation issues even

5 Economic constraints arguably also played a role in limited the implementation of reform (Mossialos and Alin 2005: 424).

there. In Portugal, the preceding healthcare system was established in 1935 and took the form of a compulsory social insurance system. In reality, however, health services were only available on a very limited basis due to severe underdevelopment (Capucha et al. 2005: 207). In the years preceding the fall of the Salazar regime in 1974, the extent of public sector control over health services expanded rapidly, and the government pre-emptively began to shift financing away from contributions and towards tax revenue (Guillén 2002: 53). There were clear signals, then, of a move towards reform, and the introduction of a National Health System was the subject of serious discussion for several years (Guillén 2002: 54).

In the end, the speed of Portuguese reform would be considerably quicker than in the Greek or Spanish cases, with the National Health Service created shortly thereafter in 1979.[6] The 1976 election had returned a plurality for the Socialist Party, but after entering into a Grand Coalition, the government fell two years later. Consequently, the legislation was in fact passed under an 'Independent' government appointed by the president and headed by a centre-right politician. The reform led to a dramatic increase in coverage – from 66% to 100% of the population – and notable improvements in health outcomes across a variety of indicators, despite the fact that they lagged considerably behind standard levels in the developed world (Oliveira et al. 2005: 216).

A considerable gap between aspirations and outcomes nevertheless remains. In particular, benefit standardisation was far less complete than one might expect, since while most of the old funds were dismantled, several were permitted to continue existing alongside the new one. The result is a large gap in care levels between those members of the funds that guarantee additional care (most notably civil servants, alongside other smaller groups) and the vast majority of the population with access only to the universal system (Toth 2010: 331). This inequity is then further aggravated by the fact that the groups with better coverage also tend to be better off more generally (Oliveira and Pinto 2005: 204-205). What is more, considerable variation in the quality of benefits available to individuals has led to a particularly large role for costly private healthcare (Guibentif 1996: 231).

Consequently, while the Portuguese system effectively covers the entire population and shares numerous similarities with the Italian one, the continued existence of several funds parallel to the universal system has limited benefit standardisation. As in the Greek case, this raises questions

6 It is worth noting that, in contrast to our other cases, doctors in Portugal were generally vocal proponents of reform (De Miguel 1977).

about the causes of divergence. Here it would appear that there are a number of complementary explanations at work. Most notably, Guibentif (1996: 232-233) points to financial difficulties at the time as well as the long-standing 1985-1995 centre-right government, led by parties that were quite content with the status quo. As we would expect, partisanship thus appears to be an important factor here. In addition, Guillén (2002: 55) highlights the especially underdeveloped nature of the preceding system, with its low level of health coverage (at 66%) further complicating reform.

The Spanish healthcare system, in turn, bears the closest resemblance to that in Italy. The arrangement which preceded universalisation was, as in Greece and Portugal, also a social health insurance scheme dating back to the 1930s. Over the subsequent decades, it evolved from a largely residual system to a far more extensive one, with reform primarily driven by opposition groups, civil servants, and economic growth (Rico 1996: 119). By the return of democracy in the 1970s, approximately 80% of the population was covered, with most of the uncovered individuals consisting of the unemployed, employers, or liberal professionals (Rico and Costa-Font 2005: 238). Polling from the time suggests that almost everyone (at just under 97% of the population) felt that it was the state's responsibility to ensure access to healthcare, but economic limitations and a division between those who preferred piecemeal and dramatic reform slowed policy change (Rico and Costa-Font 2005: 238).

Following several years of delay, Spanish universal healthcare was introduced in 1986 alongside considerable decentralisation to the regions, though it set out a surprisingly gradual reform of the system. Here again the process was driven by the governing Socialists, with, as in Italy, trade unions and the regional governments pressing for government reform; but the relative strength of the anti-reform faction (especially pharmaceutical companies and the institute in charge of managing healthcare) compared to pro-reform groups created a more tepid reform than initially envisioned (Guillén 2002: 60). What is more, divisions from the previous decade around the appropriate type of reform continued to persist: while public opinion and the major parties broadly favoured most elements of the reform, attitudes on the proper division between public and private provision were far more divided (Rico 1996: 121-122).

The resultant healthcare system generally resembles the Italian one, but with a few peculiarities. With regard to coverage, it is largely – though not fully – universal, as the very top income earners (about 0.5% of the population) are excluded from membership requirements (Toth 2010: 331). This is a holdover from the previous arrangement, and while it is affects a limited number of people, it does serve to undermine the system's universalism. As for benefit standardisation, broad equivalency makes the system more like the

Italian than the Greek case, but civil servants are able to opt for private care at no extra cost, and some regional variation has been slow to disappear (Ferrera 1996b: 24). Overall, then, the relative strength of the pro-status quo elements, alongside more prominent disagreement about the key features of the new system, seem to have contributed to several quirks in the Spanish system. The Spanish trajectory nonetheless generally reflects Italian developments: broad support for reform among the public, trade unions, and the regions combined together with leftist party strength to produce a quasi-universalising reform.

Overall, the Southern European healthcare systems are marked by general similarities regarding coverage extension alongside some variation in benefit standardisation. In general, the explanatory variables in Chapter 5 appear to be applicable here as well. The countries all shared the perception that the preceding system's inequities and lack of coordination were problematic, and the key role of leftist parties is also relatively consistent.[7] Variations in benefit standardisation, in turn, seem to reflect the entrenched power of pro-status quo interests and the comparative weakness of pro-reform coalitions (see Guillén 2002). Consequently, our additional Southern European cases provide considerable support for the conclusions drawn from the French-Italian comparison.

Examining Public Opinion

Having examined the policy trajectories across our additional case studies, we now turn to a brief discussion of public opinion. We begin by comparing French and Italian attitudes towards their respective healthcare systems before proceeding to the other cases. As mentioned above, because all of our key variables are national-level factors, we limit ourselves here to a descriptive discussion of attitudes across the countries. While this restricts our ability to draw conclusions, it provides us with an indication of attitudinal variation and serves as a first step towards the multi-level model analysis conducted at the beginning of Chapter 7.

The survey data is taken from the 1996 Eurobarometer, which contains the most relevant survey questions for our purposes and was conducted in the run-up to the introduction of the CMU. Note that in this instance there is unfortunately no single question that directly assesses our attitude of interest. We therefore combine an analysis of two questions that together allow us to best approach the aspects of public opinion discussed in the

7 As with our discussion of benefits for the unemployed, there was also corresponding desire to EC recommendations and just generally become more 'European' (Guillén 2002: 65).

previous chapter: first, that governments are responsible for ensuring access to healthcare (thereby addressing the role assigned to governments vis-à-vis welfare state outsiders); and second, that substantial reform of the healthcare system is required (thereby ascertaining the degree of reform thought to be necessary).

In the first instance, the following options listed for respondents (with answers recoded from 0 to 1, where 1 represents a strong belief in government responsibility):

1 The [national] government has to ensure that healthcare is provided to all people residing legally here, irrespective of their income.
2 The [national] government has to ensure that healthcare is provided only to people residing legally here with low incomes.
3 The [national] government does not have to ensure that healthcare is provided to people residing legally here, even those with low incomes.

For the second question, looking at satisfaction with the status quo versus the need for reform, respondents were in turn provided with the following options (with responses once again recoded from 0 to 1, where 1 represents a preference for fundamental transformation):

1 On the whole, healthcare in [this country] runs quite well.
2 There are some good things in the way healthcare in [this country] runs, and only minor changes would make it work better.
3 There are some good things in the way healthcare in [this country] runs, but only fundamental changes would make it work better.
4 Healthcare in [this country] runs so badly that we need to rebuild it completely.

Table 6.3 French and Italian Mean Survey Responses in Our Key Cases

	France	Italy
The government should ensure that all legal residents have access to healthcare: 0 to 1, where 1 signifies agreement	0.848 *(0.292)*	0.842 *(0.226)*
N	950	1014
Fundamental transformations of the healthcare system are required: 0 to 1, where 1 signifies agreement	0.362 *(0.282)*	0.702 *(0.267)*
N	964	1048

Source: Eurobarometer 2002
Own calculations using weights. Standard deviations are italicised in parentheses.

Table 6.3 summarises opinions from just after the introduction of the CMU, with the French notably more satisfied than their Italian counterparts with the status quo.[8] In fact, the Italian mean is, along with Portugal, the highest out of any of our cases. This is at least partly attributable to the debates that were occurring in Italy in the mid-1990s, with the survey conducted between the second (1992-1993) and third (1997-2000) rounds of major healthcare reform (Donatini et al. 2001: 92-94). Italians were nonetheless about as likely as the French to support a strong role for the public healthcare system.

Table 6.4 Mean Survey Responses in the Continental Cases

	Austria	Belgium	Germany
The government should ensure that all legal residents have access to healthcare: 0 to 1, where 1 signifies agreement	0.794 *(0.303)*	0.738 *(0.391)*	0.829 *(0.292)*
N	996	937	968
Fundamental transformations of the healthcare system are required: 0 to 1, where 1 signifies agreement	0.276 *(0.282)*	0.262 *(0.275)*	0.268 *(0.262)*
N	1002	976	974

Source: Eurobarometer 2002
Own calculations using weights. Standard deviations are italicised in parentheses.

Table 6.5 Mean Survey Responses in the Southern European Cases

	Greece	Portugal	Spain
The government should ensure that all legal residents have access to healthcare: 0 to 1, where 1 signifies agreement	0.916 *(0.235)*	0.828 *(0.297)*	0.939 *(0.198)*
N	987	914	926
Fundamental transformations of the healthcare system are required: 0 to 1, where 1 signifies agreement	0.636 *(0.272)*	0.682 *(0.280)*	0.499 *(0.307)*
N	983	931	921

Source: Eurobarometer 2002
Own calculations using weights. Standard deviations are italicised in parentheses.

8 Results of two tailed t-tests confirm that the difference is statistically significant ($p<.001$).

Tables 6.4 and 6.5 provide an indication of attitudes across the additional Continental and Southern European cases, respectively. The patterns broadly reflect those of the French-Italian comparison. The Continental countries are characterised by moderately strong beliefs in government responsibility for healthcare (with most respondents fully agreeing) and low preferences for serious reform of the system (with 75% to 80% of respondents believing that at most minor reform is required). The former result, at only moderately high levels, reflects the dominance of the insurance principle and the generally reduced role of governments in social health insurance systems, while the latter suggests much greater satisfaction with the status quo.

Southern European countries, by contrast, combine strong beliefs in government responsibility with a perceived need for serious reform. About two-thirds of respondents in each country believed that either minor or fundamental reform is necessary, while about 85% to 90% felt that the government has a responsibility to ensure access to healthcare for all. Spain is the only country with a somewhat lower mean response on the reform question (at 0.5), though it still remains notably above the Continental averages. The only cross-type overlap on the question of government responsibility is between Germany and Portugal, with mean responses in both countries around 0.83.

At first glance, these results might appear to contradict our expectations, but there are several complicating factors that necessitate a careful unpacking. First, attitudes about government responsibility are necessarily situated within a given healthcare framework. As a result, well-functioning social health insurance systems are likely to increase preferences for maintaining the insurance principle and a reasonable amount of autonomy for quasi-public programmes. Second, at least in the 1990s, the far more recently created Southern European (quasi-) universalist systems were considerably more in flux than their Continental counterparts. We take up these discussions in more detail in the next chapter, after including additional cases and controlling for potentially confounding national-level variables.

Conclusion

This chapter has offered a first step towards assessing the generalisability of our findings from the French-Italian comparison, paralleling the approach employed in our analysis of benefits for the unemployed. This entailed both an analysis of policy trajectories in our six additional Continental and Southern European cases and a discussion of attitudes in our broader universe of countries. We pause here to briefly recap the conclusions from this analysis before continuing on to quantitatively assess public opinion and policy-related outcomes.

Beginning with the case studies, the investigation suggests that the French and Italian trajectories generally reflect those in other similar countries, though with some important differences. With regard to the Continental countries, piecemeal extension was a common attribute, but the timing and means by which access was extended to those typically incapable of qualifying for insurance benefits differed substantially. In the Southern European cases, coverage extension was dramatic and appears to have had similar driving factors, though the degree of benefit standardisation differs. The reasons behind this variation seem to broadly reflect those discussed in the French-Italian comparison, with the comparative power of pro-status quo interests especially central.

The discussion of healthcare opinion across our cases, in turn, gave a sense of attitudinal cleavages in the two healthcare types. Because our key explanatory variables are national-level factors, we limited ourselves to a discussion of country-level descriptives. In doing so, we examined two sets of responses to the 1996 Eurobarometer survey, which was carried out in the run-up to the French CMU reform. These questions addressed attitudes about the role of government in healthcare provision and the need for dramatic reform of the system. A comparison of mean response values across the countries suggests that Southern Europeans are more likely to believe in both greater government responsibility for healthcare provision and a greater need for significant reform. Yet important country-level differences across the two cases complicate the conclusions one can draw from this analysis, necessitating more in-depth analysis.

In light of these limitations, the next chapter will address a number of missing elements in the analysis thus far: first, despite the more limited direct impact of public opinion in this policy domain, it will analyse the national-level determinants of attitudes towards healthcare via multi-level model analysis; second, and in line with our approach in Chapter 3, it will explore policy outcomes, employing both time-series and duration analysis.

7 Examining Healthcare Coverage across the OECD

Returning to our investigation of the generalisability of the findings of the French-Italian comparison, this chapter will explore the results of the healthcare analysis in the previous two chapters. Reflecting the approach of Chapter 4, it will do so using a combination of multi-level model, time-series, and duration analysis. Here again, the goal is to ascertain the factors (at both individual and national level) impacting popular attitudes towards welfare state programmes, couched within a more general exploration of the interplay between public opinion and national-level influences on policy decisions about how to address gaps in coverage. The latter aspect of this interplay will be analysed most notably through the use of duration analysis (designed in this case to uncover the determinants of universalisation), though we will also discuss incremental changes in healthcare coverage levels through time-series analysis.

Prior to laying out the results of this exploration, we will first delineate the dependent, explanatory, and control variables to be used in the proceeding statistical examination. The chapter will then proceed to sketch out the factors shaping public opinion, presenting the findings of multi-level model survey analysis looking at two survey questions from a 1996 Eurobarometer. Given our predictions about the impact of contextual factors on public preferences, which in turn create pressures/incentives for reform, the goal here will be to examine what factors lead individuals to feel that: (a) governments are responsible for ensuring access to healthcare; and (b) substantial reform of the healthcare system is required. In an attempt to link this analysis to actual outcomes, we will then turn to examining changes in coverage levels, once again using time-series and duration analysis, designed to analyse changes in coverage levels and policy, respectively. While the time-series analysis will examine all changes in coverage, the duration analysis will allow us to move beyond the typical approach and more precisely address our question of interest: namely, what factors push governments towards universalising their healthcare systems? We will then conclude by summarising the findings of the previous sections and laying out some general conclusions, tying the results of this analysis to those of previous chapters.

In brief, this chapter will present evidence suggesting that social health insurance systems shape public opinion in a way that impacts the likelihood of extending benefit access via residualisation instead of universalisation; this impact is noted both at the level of survey data and actual policy outcomes, though the lack of longitudinal survey data restricts us to analysing these issues separately. Similarly, structural constraints, taken as a proxy for lobby group strength, also appear to negatively impact the odds of reform. Finally, we also find some evidence to suggests that left-wing government presence and trade union density impact the odds of transformative healthcare reform, though it is more difficult to disentangle these effects (as they appear to counteract one another). Overall, the results suggest that the analysis carried out in the previous chapters has broader applicability, and the contrast between the results of the time-series and duration analysis once again stresses the value of examining policy change directly.

The Models

In setting up the proceeding analysis, this section will outline each of the variables to be used in the three stages of our investigation. We will begin by presenting the dependent variables utilised in each type of analysis. The explanatory variables, as indicated by the analysis of the French and Italian cases in Chapter 4, will then be presented in turn. Finally, the section will then conclude by noting the controls that will also be included in the subsequent multi-level, time-series, and duration analysis models.

Dependent Variables

The dependent variables we employ here generally reflect the approach taken in Chapter 4 with regard to benefits for the unemployed, though in this instance there are less issues with the coverage data. For the multi-level model survey analysis, we use the two 1996 Eurobarometer survey questions described in the previous chapter. To recapitulate, there is a first question looking at government responsibility for healthcare (with the answers recoded from 0 to 1, where 1 represents a strong belief in government responsibility):

1 The [national] government has to ensure that healthcare is provided to all people residing legally here, irrespective of their income.
2 The [national] government has to ensure that healthcare is provided only to people residing legally here with low incomes.
3 The [national] government does not have to ensure that healthcare is provided to people residing legally here, even those with low incomes.

The second question, in turn, looks at the extent of reform believed to be necessary (with responses once again recoded from 0 to 1, where 1 represents a preference for fundamental transformation):

1 On the whole, healthcare in [this country] runs quite well.
2 There are some good things in the way healthcare in [this country] runs, and only minor changes would make it work better.
3 There are some good things in the way healthcare in [this country] runs, but only fundamental changes would make it work better.
4 Healthcare in [this country] runs so badly that we need to rebuild it completely.

With regard to both of the survey questions, data are available only for fifteen European countries,[1] preventing us from including North America and the Antipodes in the analysis. Though ideally the two questions would have been combined, taken together they provide a reasonable starting-off point.

Within the time-series analysis, the model is constructed using *healthcare coverage levels* taken from the Organisation for Economic Co-operation and Development (OECD 2012a). The dataset contains 21 countries and typically covers the 1960 to 2010 period, with only the United States lacking a substantial number of yearly observations.[2] While this dataset does provide an indication of the prevalence of healthcare outsiders (i.e. those excluded from coverage), it fails to distinguish between coverage changes that are the result of policy and those that are artefacts of other changes. This is due to the nature of the OECD coverage data, which emphasises incremental changes rather than sweeping systemic ones. What is more, the data does not distinguish between system types. The issue here is not only that there is no indication as to whether the benefits are standardised, but also that a completion of coverage (say a ten-point rise from 90% to 100%) is more noteworthy for us from a theoretical perspective than an equivalent increase that does not lead to complete coverage (say a rise from 60% to 70%).

To deal with these limitations, a final, binary dependent variable was constructed for use in the duration analysis, this time indicating universalisation rather than residualisation (as was the case in Chapter 3).[3] We therefore

1 These are: Austria, Belgium, Denmark, Finland, France, Germany, Greece, Ireland, Italy, Luxembourg, the Netherlands, Portugal, Spain, Sweden, and the United Kingdom.

2 These are: Australia, Austria, Belgium, Canada, Denmark, Finland, France, Germany, Greece, Iceland, Ireland, Italy, the Netherlands, New Zealand, Norway, Portugal, Spain, Sweden, Switzerland, the United Kingdom, and the United States.

3 While we would ideally be able to analyse both types of changes, a dearth of cases prevents us from being able to examine residualisation.

code the introduction of *universally available, (generally) standardised healthcare* – this is to say, public healthcare systems with ostensibly equal access to standardised care (save for inevitable geographical variation of course). The universalisation measure was constructed for the 1960 to 2000 period using qualitative data derived primarily from the *Social Security Programs throughout the World* database.[4] Data was collected for the same twenty countries used in the time-series analyses, though the statistical requirements of duration analysis prevent a number of them from being included in the final analysis. The overall result is both a measure of the length of time countries took to develop universal, standardised healthcare and an indicator of countries that have not carried out such a reform.

As was the case with unemployment binary, this means that while the variable does capture the large policy changes that were underweighted or even missed in the coverage variable, differences between private and semi-public *non-standardised* systems are lost. Thus, a private system with low coverage, such as that of the United States, must be grouped in with a semi-public system with almost complete coverage, as in the case of France; the nature of duration analysis means that we unfortunately cannot incorporate different degrees of standardisation and/or coverage. Importantly, however, employing the binary variable allows us to directly address universalisation, thereby complementing the analysis looking at incremental changes in coverage.

The Explanatory Variables

In contrast to the issues surrounding variables used to analyse benefits for the unemployed in the last chapter, the models related to healthcare coverage are relatively simple to construct, with longitudinal data (taken from a variety of sources) available in all instances. For all of the variables, save for structural constraints, we expect a positive correlation – that is, higher values should increase coverage levels.

The first variable of interest, supported by both the broader literature (e.g. Navarro 1989; France and Taroni 2005) and the findings of Chapter 4, is *left-wing party strength in government*. The variable is measured as the percentage of left-wing party members in the cabinet, weighted by number of days in office during a given year. The data is taken from the Comparative Political Data Set I (Armingeon et al. 2011) and contains information on 23 OECD countries over the 1960 to 2009 period. Classification of parties, particularly when comparing leftist and centrist ones, must of course be

4 See US Social Security Administration 2012.

Figure 7.1 Mean Left Government Presence

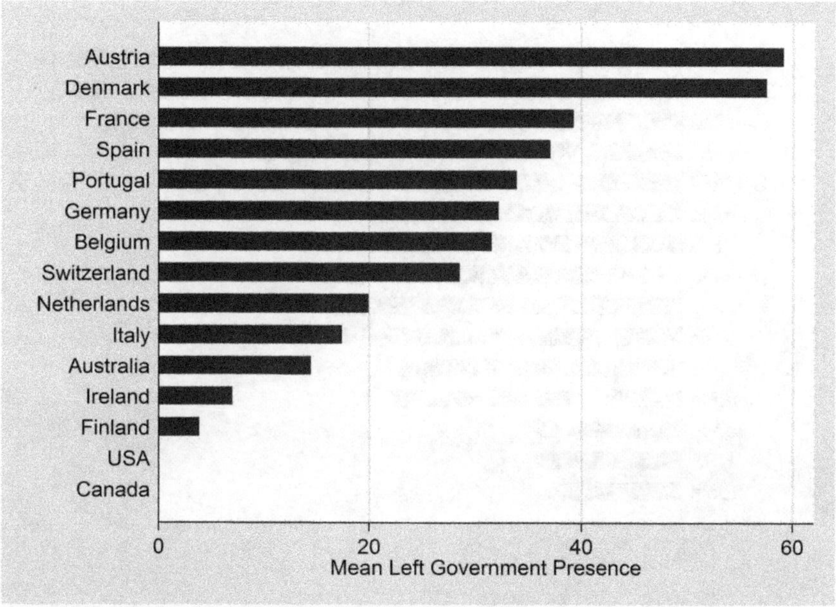

handled with care, especially since parties may shift positions over time.[5] Nevertheless, for our purposes we are interested in the impact of left-wing parties relatively broadly conceived, and given that the alternative, party manifesto-based approach is not without its own difficulties (e.g. Dinas and Gemenis 2010) we opt to use the Armingeon et al. data. For the multi-level model survey analysis, averages over the 20 years prior to the survey are used in order to roughly approximate the recent influence of left governments in a given country. For the duration analysis, in turn, the mean is taken for the period from 1960 either to the adoption of universal healthcare or, in cases where no reform has occurred, through to 2009. Figure 7.1 demonstrates the distribution of the latter variable, indicating considerable variance across cases.

The next variable, again supported by both the literature (particularly studies originating from the Power Resource theory perspective) and Chapter 5, is *trade union density*. This is measured using OECD data generally covering the 1960 to 2009 period, calculated as the percentage of union

5 In addition, the inclusion of ideological factors not related to a party's welfare state preference in the classification process may muddle the way the left-centre-right distinction reflects a party's potential policy impact (Schumacher 2011: 5-6).

Figure 7.2 Mean Trade Union Density

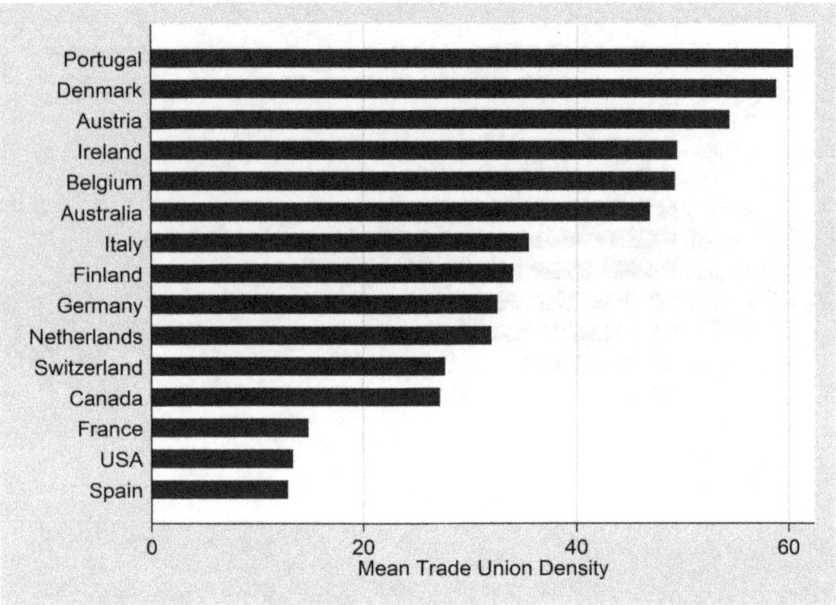

members in the labour force. While this data provides the most accurate proxy available for union influence, in a few instances, such as France, it unfortunately underestimates it, as well as the coverage of collective bargaining agreements more broadly. Note that the potential interaction between union density and left government is incorporated into the models as well. In addition, just as with left government, 20-year averages of trade union density are used to approximate trade union influence in the multi-level model analysis, while the duration analysis uses the pre-reform mean. Figure 7.2 demonstrates the considerable cross-country variance in the latter instance.

The third variable of interest is *decentralisation*, supported by our findings and studies such as those of Maioni (1997) and Guillén (2002). This is used in lieu of federalism in order to avoid obscuring, for example, the differences between the French and Italian contexts. This measure is taken from Armingeon et al. 2011. Data is available for OECD countries typically for our entire period of interest (1960 to 2009), with countries listed as having either having strong (coded 2), weak (coded 1), or no decentralisation (coded 0). While most of our cases fall into either the strongly decentralised (5 cases) or not at all decentralised (7 cases) categories for the entire period, a few countries do shift categories part way through

Figure 7.3 Mean Structural Constraints

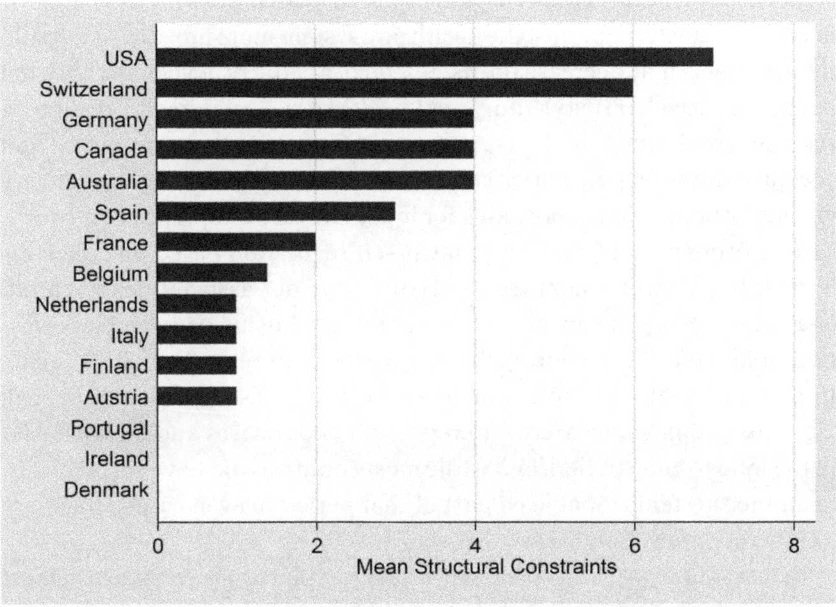

Fourth, we include a variable intended to capture potential lobby group impact. Note that this is a somewhat tricky concept to operationalise, but data on *structural constraints* offer a proxy for the prospective opportunities for lobby groups to impact policy outcomes (see Immergut 1992). This data comes once again from Armingeon et al. (2011), here updating work by Huber et al. (1993). The measure provides an indication of the number of constitutional veto points, calculated additively using information on the presence/absence of federalism, the type of government (parliamentary or presidential), the electoral system, bicameralism, and the frequency of referenda. A score for each of our countries is available during the 1960 to 2009 period, thereby providing contextual information on the extent to which lobby groups could more easily impact health policy decisions. Figure 7.3 notes considerable variation over the pre-reform/2009 period across our cases.

Finally, a dummy variable for *the existence of a social insurance healthcare system* is used in both the survey and duration analysis section.[6] The ex-

6 Since the existence of social health insurance is expected to impact the likelihood of dramatic shifts in access to healthcare (i.e. universalisation) rather than incremental changes, the variable is not included in the time series.

pectation here is that these Bismarckian systems may engender a different attitude towards both the role of the state in healthcare provision and the need for a transformation of the healthcare system more broadly. As a result, these systems may decrease the likelihood of a country developing national health service (NHS)-style universal healthcare. Social health insurance systems are defined by the connection between employment status and coverage (implying the potential prevalence of outsiders), service delivery via public or non-profit hospitals for inpatient care but private (for-profit) care in other sectors, and 'corporatist self-regulation based on collective bargaining between sickness funds and provider associations' (Schmid et al. 2010: 469).[7] This measure was constructed using country classifications laid out by Toth (2010: 328) – themselves compiled from Flora (1986), Immergut (1992), and Cutler and Johnson (2004) – as well as Schmid et al. (2010: 468-469). Values were entered for all of our cases and for each year in the 1960 to 2009 period, and while most countries did have social health insurance systems for at least part of that period (eleven cases), there are a few exceptions (four cases).

In total, then, we come to include five key explanatory variables[8] in most of the analysis (and four in the time series).[9]

7 Note that while this categorisation system does not capture the nuanced differences between the French and Italian systems pointed to in Chapter 5, it does mark an important, clear-cut distinction from other system types. The implications of this decision will be further discussed with reference to our findings.

8 We are unable to include a variable that adequately captures the potential impact of centre-right clientelistic networks in healthcare, due to measurement difficulties. The best available approximation – a dummy variable for Southern European welfare states – poses problems since the welfare state type is traditionally defined both by the prevalence of clientelism and a universalistic healthcare system (Ferrera 1996a). Thus, while it is likely that the variable shapes leftist party preferences, we are unfortunately unable to assess its impact quantitatively.

9 Note, however, that multicollinearity among some of these national-level variables complicates our ability to properly tease out the effects of the variables discussed in the previous two chapters. In particular, several pairwise comparisons reach particularly high levels of collinearity. Decentralisation and structural constraints (at 0.8) suffer most acutely from this problem – not surprisingly, given that the former forms a part of the latter measure. There is also a high degree of collinearity between the social health insurance dummy and the measures of decentralisation (at 0.65), structural constraints (at 0.54), and trade union density (at 0.56). Moving forward, we therefore are careful to point out the instances in which excluding the structural constraints and/or social health insurance variables notably impact the results.

Standard Variables

Turning now to our standard controls, the multi-level model survey analysis is carried out building on the analysis in the previous chapter. The basic individual-level variables discussed in the previous chapter are once again included: (1) *unemployment* (of potential import due to the nature of benefit coverage in social health insurance systems); (2) *family income* (in quartiles); (3) *gender*; (4) *education levels* (with three brackets, corresponding to leaving school: by the age of fifteen; between the ages of sixteen and nineteen; and after the age of nineteen); (5) being aged *65 and over*[10]; (6) *age bracket* (with brackets of 15-24, 35-39, 40-54, and 55 and over); and (7) *self-assessed health* (with five responses ranging from very bad to very good). At the national level, additional controls are also considered for the following variables: (8) *population 65 and over*, measured as a percentage of the total population; (9) *the percentage of the labour force that is female*, with increases in the size of the female workforce hypothesised to increase social service provision by changing popular attitudes towards the value of social services (see Huber and Stephens 2001: 56); (10) *health coverage levels*; and (11) the *mean inflation rates* and (12) *mean GDP* over the past three years (to indicate the general economic condition). All of these variables are taken from the OECD (2012a; 2012b; 2012c).

The time-series models, in turn, are built using previous research such as that carried out by Hicks (1999), Huber and Stephens (2001), Swank (2001), Allan and Scruggs (2004), and Soroka et al. (2006), as well as Korpi (1989) and Cutler and Johnson (2004). Presented in the order in which they are listed in the regression results, these standard variables are: (1) *the previous year's health coverage levels*, included to take into account the effects of potentially cumbersome welfare states or, conversely, institutional inertia; a variety of lagged economic factors – namely, (2) *GDP per capita*, (3) *inflation*; (4) *change in unemployment*; (5) *the percentage of the labour force that is female*, for the reasons noted above; and (6) *the share of the population over 64*. Once again, all data are derived from the OECD (2012a; 2012b; 2012c).

Findings

Having laid out the variables to be used, we now continue to the results of the empirical analysis. This section will begin with the multi-level model

10 This variable stands in for the unavailable retiree dummy measure, since the survey question that demarcates retirees unfortunately also includes those who are too ill to work.

survey analysis and then proceed to both the time-series and duration analysis. As mentioned above, the survey analysis will be carried out using Eurobarometer data from 1996, allowing us to build upon work in the previous chapters looking at attitudes in the run-up to the introduction of the Couverture Maladie Universelle (CMU). The time series will then be conducted on a sample of 21 OECD countries over varying segments (given data limitations) during the 1960 to 2009 period, while the duration analysis will cover the 1960 to 2000 period.

As in Chapter 4, the discussion of the results from these various models will focus on the ways in which the factors pointed to in the qualitative analysis may impact both attitudes and policy changes, with the effect on policy potentially mediated by the impact on attitudes.

Understanding Attitudes

Given our working assumption that contextual factors shape public opinion, which in turn may shapes policy changes by structuring electoral incentives, we begin by examining the individual- and national-level factors that may shape attitudes. Unlike the analysis surrounding unemployment coverage, however, none of the variables of interest highlighted in the qualitative analysis are located at the individual level. As such, the individual-level variables we include are all largely standard, designed principally as controls that assist us in determining the national-level factors impacting attitudes.

As stated above, our analysis of public opinion vis-à-vis healthcare is divided into two parts (with both questions coming from a 1996 Eurobarometer survey): the first relating to the government's responsibility in ensuring access to healthcare (addressing the issue of outsiders and measuring desire for change versus contentment with the status quo); and the second relating to the extent of healthcare reform judged necessary (assessing desire for more revolutionary reform). In both cases we once again build the multi-level models stepwise using generalised least squares (GLS) regression analysis (with country clusters),[11] with Model 1 including only the key explanatory variables, Model 2 adding individual-level controls, and Model 3 incorporating national-level controls as a robustness check. The limited number of country clusters means that we should be cautious when interpreting the effects of these national-level factors, but

11 Unfortunately, the complexity of the full models does not allow us to confirm that the same pattern of statistical significance is returned using a mixed-effects ordered logistic regression approach, but the simpler models do return similar results.

the approach serves as a solid starting point for the proceeding analysis of policy changes. We also confirm that various changes to the national-level variables included in the model do not alter the findings presented, referencing exceptions along the way where appropriate.

Starting off with the question of government responsibility, three potential answers were available to respondents, ranging from no government responsibility (coded 0), to government responsibility for low-income residents (coded 0.5), to government responsibility for all residents regardless of income (coded 1). Note that the latter two responses may be understood as support for residual and universalist approaches, respectively. Table 7.1 presents the results of the multi-level model analysis examining these attitudes, incorporating over 10,000 observations from thirteen European countries.[12] Dealing first with the controls, at the individual level, only family income and being male reach statistical significance, with both variables associated with a diminished belief in the government's responsibility to ensure access to healthcare. At the national level, the controls associated with older populations, greater female labour market participation, and higher GDP per capita are all correlated with a greater belief in government responsibility on the matter.

Of our variables of interest, those associated with Power Resource theory seem to clearly matter. In Model 2, which incorporates both the national-level variables of interest and the individual-level controls, both a history of left government and trade union density are associated with moderate decreases in assigned government responsibility – though an interaction effect between the two variables offsets this impact somewhat. Adding the battery of national-level economic controls in Model 3 alters these findings, however, changing the direction of union density's effect and causing the left-union interaction to lose significance.

12 These are: Austria, Belgium, Denmark, Finland, France, Germany, Greece, Ireland, Italy, Luxembourg, the Netherlands, Portugal, Spain, Sweden, and the United Kingdom. In the analysis of government responsibility, the total number of observations per country ultimately included in the regression analysis ranges from 317 (for Luxembourg) to 1662 (for Germany), with an overall average per country of 786.

Table 7.1 Predictors of Belief in Government Responsibility to Ensure Access to Healthcare across Countries

	Model 1	**Model 2**	**Model 3**
Mean Left Government (1977-1996)	**-0.008***** *(0.003)*	**-0.007***** *(0.0006)*	**-.004**** *(.002)*
Mean Trade Union Density (1977-1996)	-0.002 *(0.003)*	**-0.002***** *(0.0006)*	**.003**** *(.001)*
Left & Union Interaction	**0.0001**** *(0.00006)*	**0.0001***** *(0.00001)*	.00004 *(.00004)*
Structural Constraints	**0.044***** *(0.017)*	**0.044***** *(0.004)*	-.017 *(.017)*
Decentralisation	**-0.102***** *(0.031)*	**-0.089***** *(0.008)*	**-.070**** *(.028)*
Social Health Insurance Dummy	**0.092**** *(0.041)*	**0.069***** *(0.011)*	**.150***** *(.034)*
Unemployed	---	0.00009 *(0.010)*	-.002 *(.010)*
Family Income	---	**-0.013***** ***(0.002)***	**-.012***** *(.002)*
Male	---	**-0.013***** *(0.005)*	**-.013***** *(.005)*
Education Level	---	**0.007*** *(0.004)*	.005 *(.004)*
Aged over 64	---	-0.008 *(0.008)*	-.009 *(.008)*
Age Bracket	---	-0.002 *(0.003)*	-.003 *(.003)*
Self-Assessed Health	---	-0.006 *(0.011)*	-.004 *(.011)*
Health Coverage Level	---	---	-.00001 *(.001)*
Share of Population 64 and Over	---	---	**.016**** *(.007)*
Female Workforce	---	---	**.005***** *(0.001)*
Mean Inflation (1994-1996)	---	---	-.001 *(.009)*
Mean GDP per Capita (1994-1996)	---	---	**8.68e-08***** *(1.46e-08)*
Constant	0.923 *(0.124)*	0.968 *(0.031)*	.328 *(.108)*
Number of Observations	10218	10218	10218
Number of Groups	13	13	13

Note: Cells contain GLS random-effects regression coefficients with standard errors italicised in parentheses. Coefficients that reach significance ($p < .10$) are bolded.

* $p < .10$, ** $p < .05$, *** $p < .01$

Source: Eurobarometer 1996

Here we should be cautious in making too much of the findings in Model 3 on its own, given the high number of national-level variables and the low number of country clusters. On the one hand, the models tell a consistent story in which left-government presence negatively impacts the assignment of government responsibility. On the other, we are left wondering whether this effect might partly be offset by high levels of union density. At a theoretical level, this might be explained by a perception in countries with a greater left government presence that enough (or possibly too much) responsibility has already been assumed by the government vis-à-vis access to healthcare – a perception not entailed in higher trade union density. Yet in addition to the issues posed by the sheer number of variables included in Model 3, this is an instance in which correlation may be causing problems. Indeed, excluding the social health insurance dummy from the analysis results in a much more traditional story: left government presence and trade union density are both correlated with higher scores, although the interaction effect lessens the combined impact.

The other variables are more robust to these sorts of exclusions and more consistent across the models. Having a decentralised system of government is correlated with a lower belief in government responsibility (with moving from a federal to a centralised system associated with a drop of about 0.14, out of a total range of 1). Conversely, a social health insurance system is linked to increases in assigned responsibility (of about 0.15). Both of these findings may appear, prima facie, to be contrary to our expectations, but careful consideration suggests reasons to be less surprised. In the case of decentralisation, its predicted effect is expected primarily in the realm of non-attitudinal effects such as policy experimentation (despite some proposed impact on public opinion in Italy). In addition, the proposed policy impact is expected to relate to higher faith in regional versus central governments, but the survey question unfortunately refers only to the 'French government', 'Italian government', etc. As a result, the causal relationship is rather difficult for us to tease out in this instance.

The presence of a social health insurance system, by contrast, was more firmly expected to result in decreased responsibility assigned to the government (due to the central role for the social partners). The observed effect suggests the opposite relationship, perhaps due to reasons similar to those discussed with regard to left government: the typically stronger observed role of government in countries with NHS-style healthcare may lead residents of those countries to feel as though the government has already intervened enough, perhaps even overreaching. Already living in a universalist country, these individuals are likely less concerned with issues of excluded outsiders and more concerned with factors such as cost and quality of care. In addition, governments in these countries may generally also be the subjects of more criticism around their handling of healthcare, further undermining support for government responsibility.

Yet thus far we have limited ourselves to opinions about government responsibility in ensuring access to healthcare. Given that our ultimate interest is in pressures for transformative reform, we must consider the possibility that the two attitudes do not track well. It is possible, for example, that residents of countries with social health insurance believe more strongly in government responsibility (despite the system's weaker role for the state) while also being less interested in transformative reform – and indeed, this is what we find when we turn to our second question.

To recap, respondents were presented with four potential statements on healthcare from which to choose, essentially encapsulating: (a) no reform required; (b) minor changes required for improvement; (c) fundamental changes required for improvement; and (d) complete transformation required for improvement. We then recoded responses from 0 to 1 and analysed them in the same manner as those above. Table 7.2 presents the results, which once again include over 10,000 observations from (the same) thirteen European countries.[13] Looking first at the controls, at the individual level both family income and gender are no longer significant, while education, age (including being 65 and over), and self-assessed health all gain statistical significance. In all but the first instance, each of these variables is associated with decreased belief in the need for extensive reform. The effect of self-assessed health in particular is especially strong, perhaps because the increased exposure to the healthcare system experienced by ill persons increases their desire for stability in the system and/or their overall satisfaction with it.

At the national level, including the full battery of controls sees the size of the female workforce and GDP per capita maintaining their significance, but the direction of their effects is now reversed, with both variables associated with a weakened belief in the need for reform. The share of the population 65 and over, by contrast, is no longer significant. Most interestingly, health coverage level is now statistically significant, with higher coverage levels correlated with increased belief in the need for reform. This finding suggests that low coverage levels in and of themselves do not lead to increased belief in the need for reform.

13 The pattern of included observations is the same here as with the analysis of government responsibility, with the lowest number of observations in Luxembourg (316) and the highest in Germany (1634), and an overall average per country of 793.

Table 7.2 Predictors of Belief in the Need for Extensive Healthcare Reform across Countries

	Model 1	Model 2	Model 3
Mean Left Government (1977-1996)	-0.003 *(0.008)*	**-0.003***** *(0.0007)*	**-.017***** *(.002)*
Mean Trade Union Density (1977-1996)	-0.012 *(0.008)*	**-0.014***** *(0.0007)*	**-.025**** *(.002)*
Left & Union Interaction	0.00006 *(0.0002)*	**0.00009***** *(0.00001)*	**.0004***** *(.00004)*
Structural Constraints	-0.044 *(0.049)*	**-0.048***** *(0.004)*	**.084***** *(.019)*
Decentralisation	0.105 *(0.090)*	**0.106***** *(0.008)*	-.023 *(.030)*
Social Health Insurance Dummy	**-0.365***** *(0.117)*	**-0.421***** *(0.012)*	**-.335***** *(.037)*
Unemployed	---	-0.012 *(0.011)*	-.003 *(.011)*
Family Income	---	-0.0007 *(0.003)*	-.0004 *(.003)*
Male	---	-0.003 *(0.005)*	-.004 *(.005)*
Education Level	---	0.0002 *(0.004)*	**.010**** *(.004)*
Aged over 64	---	**-0.054***** *(0.009)*	**-.054***** *(.009)*
Age Bracket	---	**-0.010***** *(0.003)*	**-.007**** *(.003)*
Self-Assessed Health	---	**-0.118***** *(0.012)*	**-.109***** *(.012)*
Health Coverage Level	---	---	**.007***** *(.001)*
Share of Population 64 and Over	---	---	.009 *(.008)*
Female Workforce	---	---	**-.018***** *(0.001)*
Mean Inflation (1994-1996)	---	---	.015 *(.010)*
Mean GDP per Capita (1994-1996)	---	---	**-2.18e-07***** *(1.57e-08)*
Constant	1.117 *(0.361)*	1.315 *(0.034)*	.328 *(.108)*
Number of Observations	10310	10310	10310
Number of Groups	13	13	13

Note: Cells contain GLS random-effects regression coefficients with standard errors italicised in parentheses. Coefficients that reach significance ($p < .10$) are bolded.
* $p < .10$, ** $p < .05$, *** $p < .01$
Source: Eurobarometer 1996

Once we turn to our variables of interest, the somewhat surprising impact of high coverage levels begins to make more sense. While only the social health insurance dummy reaches significance in the null model, most of the other key variables attain significance once controls are added.[14] The consistent negative effect of having a social health insurance system suggests that satisfaction with the status quo in these countries – complete with their typically lower coverage levels – is notably higher (with an impact of about 0.34 out of a total range of 1). The exact nature of this relationship remains somewhat unclear, however, since social health insurance systems may engender decreased calls for reform or universal healthcare systems may engender greater calls for reform. Further research is required to clarify the exact nature of the relationship, but is beyond the scope of our task here.

As for the other variables referenced in Chapter 5, strong recent histories of left-wing government and trade union density are both associated with downward pressure on calls for reform. This is quite possibly due to the perception that desired reforms have already been carried out and/or the higher levels of satisfaction with those systems on the whole. (Note that the interaction of the two variables slightly counteracts this effect.) Decentralisation is not significant in this instance, but more structural constraints – contrary to our expectation – are correlated in Model 3 with a greater belief in the need for reform. Given that the variable's significance is sensitive to the included controls, however, the finding does not appear to be robust.

On the whole, these results indicate that the factors discussed in Chapter 5 appear to have a more general impact on attitudes (though this snapshot approach to public opinion makes it difficult to unpack the long-term direction of the effects). Interestingly, our results are also consistent with the discussion of the French CMU programme: the residualisation approach to coverage extension, with a strong role for government in insuring access to healthcare, appears consistent with public opinion in social health insurance systems. Nevertheless, there are limitations to the conclusions we can draw from this section alone. First, even with the combination of the two survey questions we are not completely able to assess opinions around the need for (and methods required to achieve) coverage extension. Second, dealing only with data from 1996, notwithstanding the period's relevance for the CMU, is overly restrictive given the *longue durée* nature of our argument. In addition, the 1996 data also limit our ability to analyse

14 In addition, multicollinearity does not appear to pose the same problems here as it did regarding the question about government responsibility.

the corporatist healthcare systems, particularly in Southern Europe, that did not survive all the way to the 1990s; this means that we are forced to compare attitudes in countries that have already universalised versus those that have opted for the residualisation approach. Finally, focusing on survey responses alone excludes many of the mechanisms discussed in Chapter 5.

As a result, we must now proceed to analyse actual changes in coverage, as we compensate for these shortcomings and round out our investigation.

Understanding Policy Changes (Part One)

As in Chapter 4, we follow up our analysis of public opinion by first taking the standard approach and examining the determinants of *gradual* changes in coverage levels via time-series analysis (using ordinary least squares (OLS) linear regressions with panel-corrected standard errors[15]). Table 7.3 presents the results of this analysis,[16] looking at healthcare benefit coverage levels in 21 countries.[17] The results here are somewhat surprising, with almost all variables – including lagged healthcare coverage levels – failing to reach or even near significance.[18] This is the case across the stepwise procession of the models, and even dropping the most correlated variables from the analysis has no notable effect.[19] Inflation is the only exception, with the higher levels surprisingly associated with increased coverage levels.[20]

15 The pairwise approach is utilised in the time-series analysis, due to a lack of time periods common to all panels.

16 Note that we are unable to ascertain the effect of social health insurance systems in the time-series model, since we expect its effect to manifest itself in one-off increases in coverage (rather than incrementally), leaving us to deal with the variable in the duration analysis below.

17 These are: Australia, Austria, Belgium, Canada, Denmark, Finland, France, Germany, Greece, Iceland, Ireland, Italy, the Netherlands, New Zealand, Norway, Portugal, Spain, Sweden, Switzerland, the United Kingdom, and the United States.

18 In no case does the removal of any given country substantially alter the results.

19 As in the previous section, no substantial differences arise when we include centre or right-wing parties in lieu of left-wing ones.

20 One explanation for this finding may be the rapid increases in coverage that occurred in a number of high-inflation countries – especially Greece, Italy, Portugal, and Spain, but also Finland in 1964, Australia in 1975, and Ireland in 1980). Yet irrespective of how we explain the apparent effect of inflation in the model, it is clearly not very effective at explaining gradual changes in healthcare coverage on the whole.

Table 7.3 Time Series Analysis – Healthcare Coverage Levels

	Model 1	Model 2	Model 3
Independent Variables			
DV $_{t-1}$	-0.0164	-0.0318	-0.035
	(0.0125)	*(0.0233)*	*(0.025)*
Union Density $_{t-1}$	-0.237	-0.423	-0.436
	(0.385)	*(0.384)*	*(0.408)*
Left Government $_{t-1}$	-0.204	-0.194	-0.195
	(0.294)	*(0.300)*	*(0.299)*
Left & Union Interaction $_{t-1}$	0.00360	0.00430	0.004
	(0.00449)	*(0.00452)*	*(0.005)*
Structural Constraints $_{t-1}$	-2.703	1.349	3.310
	(5.971)	*(4.382)*	*(4.815)*
Decentralisation $_{t-1}$	-1.221	-1.043	-2.983
	(5.859)	*(8.673)*	*(9.401)*
GDP $_{t-1}$	---	-0.0000182	-0.00002
		(0.0000139)	*(0.00002)*
Inflation $_{t-1}$	---	**2.433***	**3.454*****
		(1.064)	*(1.329)*
Δ Unemployment	---	-1.297	-1.350
		(6.353)	*(6.317)*
Female Workforce $_{t-1}$	---	---	1.272
			(1.808)
Population over 64 $_{t-1}$	---	---	1.750
			(2.086)
Constant	188.2	333.6	287.7
	(140.5)	*(251.0)*	*(235.3)*
N	700	700	700
Number of Panels	21	21	21
R^2	0.016	0.035	0.036

Note: Cells contain Random-effects GLS regression coefficients with standard errors italicised in parentheses. Coefficients that reach significance (p < .10) are bolded.
* p < .10, ** p < .05, *** p < .01

The lack of insight provided by this approach point to the limitations inherent in using healthcare coverage data in this way. It is true, of course, that time-series analysis might give us some indication of the determinants of smaller changes such as those that occurred via residualisation in France. But, crucially, this approach is incapable of distinguishing between changes that are political in origin and those that are not: for example, those that occur due to increased immigration in a non-universal system, or those that result from changes in the labour market. Coverage levels are therefore not an ideal dependent variable for getting at these sorts of changes. In order to specifically address changes of political origin – in particular universalisation – we must instead turn to analyse policy change directly through duration analysis.

Understanding Policy Changes (Part Two)

Analysing the factors shaping both public opinion about healthcare and gradual changes in coverage levels has provided only limited insights. Recall that many of the effects we noted in Chapter 5 related to revolutionary rather than incremental changes in coverage. As a result, duration analysis will better allow us to analyse whether or not the findings of the qualitative analysis can be generalised. So what happens when we directly examine policy change instead?

The findings of the duration analysis are presented in the same fashion employed in Chapter 4. The analysis here explores the factors driving a given country's probability of universalising its healthcare system – that is, of introducing universally available healthcare with at least ostensibly standardised benefits for citizens. Note that, in contrast to the approach taken in Chapter 4, duration analysis is used in this instance to examine the determinants of universalisation (rather than residualisation). In doing so, the investigation looks at the twentieth century from 1960 onward, the period during which most healthcare system changes occurred.[21]

To begin, Figure 7.4 presents a diagram of the timing of introductions of universal healthcare programmes. In this instance, after eliminating countries that had already developed the programme by 1960 (of which there were six), fifteen cases remain.[22] Once again, included within this set of countries are two cases (Spain and Portugal) that were not democratic for the entire period, so we confirm once again that changes in how these cases are considered do not affect the results.[23] In comparison with the introduction of social assistance discussed in Chapter 4, the progress in developing universal

21 A lack of control data prevents us from including pre-1960 developments, however.

22 The countries included in this analysis are: Australia, Austria, Belgium, Canada, Finland, France, Germany, Ireland, Italy, the Netherlands, Portugal, Spain, Switzerland, and the United States. Greece is excluded due to classificatory difficulties with its nominally universal system.

23 Neither including a democracy dummy variable nor excluding the non-democratic years from the analysis generally weakens the results. Both approaches introduce their own theoretical complications, however, as discussed in Chapter 3: excluding the non-democratic would lead us to equate (for example) the early 1960s with the late 1970s; and there is very limited variation in the democracy variable's value, as only Portugal and Spain have values not equal to 1. As such, we show results only for the standard approach.

Figure 7.4 Countries without Universal Healthcare

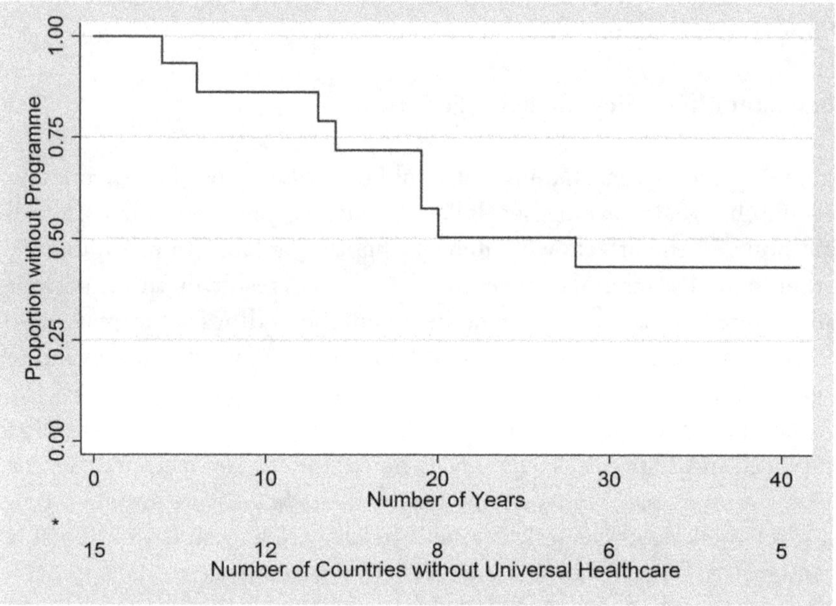

healthcare programmes has been quite distinct: here the changes are less evenly distributed – all of them occurred in the first 25 years, and most occurring during the expansionary welfare state phase – and far more of the countries fail to ever introduce the programme (eight as opposed to two).

How do our main variables of interest track alongside these changes? In the case of structural constraints, decentralisation, or trade union density, no clear pattern appears in the simple bivariate analysis. Yet as Figure 7.5 indicates, both the existence of a social health insurance system and above average left-wing government presence do appear to be related to the introduction of universal healthcare. In the case of the social health insurance dummy the graph indicates, in line with our anticipated results, that such systems are more resilient to change. Nevertheless, almost half of the countries with social health insurance switched to universal healthcare, indicating that the variable's presence is certainly not sufficient to subvert change. The effect of left-wing government presence in this simple, bivariate analysis, in turn, appears to be in the opposite direction we would expect, with the majority of reforms associated with countries that experienced below average exposure to left government. This can partly be explained by early adopting countries such as Canada and Ireland that had no history of left government, but without controls it is impossible to draw any firm conclusions.

Figure 7.5 Social Health Insurance, Left Government, and Programme Introduction

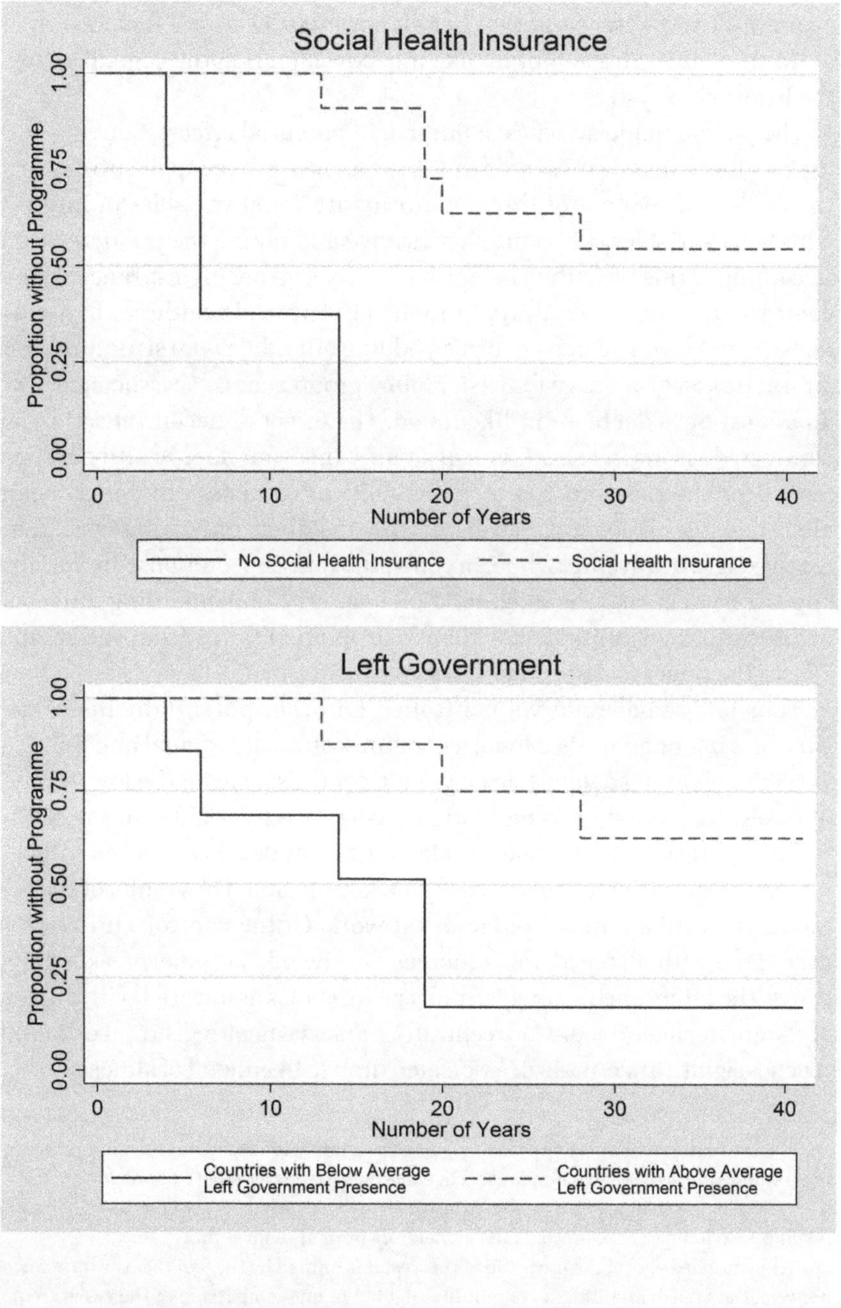

We therefore proceed to the results of the duration analysis. As in Chapter 4, given that collinearity and the small sample size lead to technical difficulties when too many variables are included, the models are once again built stepwise. Note that health coverage levels are included in all of the models in an attempt to take into consideration the general state of the healthcare system.[24]

The partial models suggest a number of potential effects. Starting with the results of Model 1 presented in Table 7.4, the findings appear to confirm the impact of two out of three of our institutional variables of interest, with both variables achieving significance and taking the predicted sign. According to this simplified model, having a social health insurance system decreases the odds of a country introducing universal healthcare by almost 100% in any given year. By contrast, adding one additional structural constraint (taken as a proxy for easier lobby group access) is associated with an almost 80% decrease in likelihood. The effect of decentralisation, by contrast, does not reach statistical significance, nor does health coverage level. Model 2 then incorporates the political variables of interest, again alongside health coverage levels. In this instance, only left government reaches significance. Yet while, in contrast to our expectations, the variable appears to decrease the likelihood of a country implementing universal healthcare, the finding is not robust: dropping France from the sample causes the effect to disappear entirely.

Thus far we have not yet controlled for other potentially important variables in our analysis. Model 3 combines our institutional and political variables of interest alongside economic controls.[25] Given the low number of cases, we exclude the most highly correlated variable that failed to reach significance in previous models – namely, decentralisation (though including the variable returns the same key results). The results of the full model indicate a number of factors at work. Of the controls, inflation is correlated with a considerable increase in the odds of reform, as moving across the interquartile range (from 3.38 to 7.64) is associated with an over 700% greater likelihood. More centrally, the social health insurance dummy reaches significance, with an associated drop in likelihood of almost 100%,[26]

24 Unfortunately, a similar approach was not possible with regard to minimum income programmes due to a lack of comparable coverage data (as discussed in Chapter 3).

25 Note that the results do not appear to be driven by any particular country, though in some instances excluding a case prevents the model from properly converging.

26 As mentioned above, the precision of this result is limited by the fact that the differences between the French and Italian systems highlighted in our comparison of the cases are not captured by the dummy variable (since the difference is arguably one of degree rather than

while structural constraints also appear to decrease the odds of reform. The effect of the two variables associated with Power Resource theory are more difficult to disentangle. Trade union density is associated with a lower likelihood of reform, yet this effect appears to be at least partly offset by left-wing party strength. We hesitate to draw too much from this result, however, as it the Power Resource variables are particularly susceptible to minor changes in model specification, suggesting that collinearity is likely an especially large problem here.

Table 7.4 Duration Analysis – Healthcare

	Model 1: Structural Model	**Model 2: Political Model**	**Model 3: Full Model**
Independent Variables			
Health Coverage Level	1.007 *(0.815)*	0.983 *(0.473)*	0.892 *(0.184)*
Social Health Insurance Dummy	$\mathbf{0.001}^{***}$ *(0.005)*	---	$\mathbf{2.70e\text{-}17}^{*}$ *(0.055)*
Structural Constraints	$\mathbf{0.204}^{***}$ *(0.038)*	---	$\mathbf{0.0005}^{*}$ *(0.069)*
Decentralisation	3.10 *(0.308)*	---	---
Union Density	---	1.000 *(0.998)*	$\mathbf{0.555}^{*}$ *(0.071)*
Left Government	---	$\mathbf{0.884}^{*}$ *(0.086)*	0.882 *(0.205)*
Left & Union Interaction	---	1.002 *(0.265)*	$\mathbf{1.008}^{*}$ *(0.063)*
Inflation	---	---	$\mathbf{2.818}^{**}$ *(0.032)*
GDP per Capita	---	---	1.000 *(0.121)*
N	15	15	15

Note: Cells contain survival analysis hazard ratios with p-values italicised in parentheses. Hazard ratios that reach significance (p < .10) are bolded.
* p < .10, ** p < .05, *** p < .01

kind). Yet insofar as the pre-SSN Italian system, for example, can be understood as somewhat of an impure social health insurance, these impurities could easily be understood as undermining the pro-status quo impact of the variable. Given that this description could likely be extended to other Southern European welfare states that switched over to universalist healthcare systems (see Toth 2010), the findings remain consistent with our expectations.

Summing Up

In presenting an overview of the preceding analysis, we draw attention to a number of key results.

Turning first to the multi-level modelling results, several of the factors discussed in the comparative case studies appear to have an impact on public opinion. While the effects of decentralisation and structural constraints were mixed and more difficult to unpack (for reasons discussed above), living in a country with social health insurance system is correlated with both a greater assigned role to government in ensuring access to healthcare *and* a lower perceived need for substantial reform. The variables associated with Power Resource theory, by contrast, appeared to be associated (on the whole) with a weaker belief in government responsibility and the need for transformative reform. This is possibly because a strong left government presence may lead people to feel that the government has already addressed its responsibilities in ensuring access. We cannot rule out, however, that multicollinearity issues are driving the impact on the power resource variables, particularly in the case of the question on government responsibility.

Yet despite the potential indirect impact of these factors on reforms (via public opinion), we cannot address our central theory without also more directly analysing the determinants of policy changes. Our first attempt to do so, looking at gradual changes in coverage levels via time-series analysis, yielded little of interest. We pointed to strong reasons that this should be the case: the use of time-series analysis does not actually allow us to directly address policy changes vis-à-vis access to coverage (whether through universalisation or residualisation), since in many instances changes may be artefacts of immigration, unemployment, or other non-policy factors.

The duration analysis, by contrast, is far more appropriate than the standard time-series approach to analysing coverage levels. Most notably, this method allows us to assess the direct impact of our variables of interest, as it looks directly at the decision to carry out universalisation. Both the presence of a social health insurance system and the number of structural constraints appear to have a generalisable effect. The variables associated with Power Resource theory point in somewhat opposite directions, however, with a negative effect of trade union density at least partly offset by left-wing government strength. Nevertheless, the sensitivity of these latter set of findings to small changes in model specification prevent us being able to draw firm conclusions on this question.

Taken as a whole, the findings presented in this chapter are consistent with our larger story, suggesting that certain structural factors (and in particular, the presence of a social health insurance system) likely shape popular opinion, which in turn impacts the likelihood of transformative reforms to address gaps in coverage.

Conclusion

This chapter has assessed the generalisability of the results of the qualitative analysis carried out in Chapter 5 by employing three types of complementary quantitative analysis in order to address different aspects of the issue. We began by laying out the variables to be used in the analysis. We then proceeded to the multi-level model survey analysis, which allowed us to assess the potential impact of key structural factors on public opinion. Two survey questions from a 1996 Eurobarometer survey were analysed: the first relating to government responsibility for ensuring access to healthcare (thereby getting at welfare state insider-outsider divides); and the second addressing the need for substantial reform of the system (thereby assessing the preferred scope of reforms). The results suggested, most notably, that living in a country with a social health insurance system is associated with an increased belief in the former and a decreased perceived need for the latter. While it is impossible to tease out our proposed causal relationship from a snapshot of public opinion, it is worth noting that these findings correspond well with the residualisation approach taken with the 1999 introduction of the CMU in France.

In order to link these determinants of public opinion with actual changes in outcomes, we then turned to the second step of our analysis. We began by using time-series analysis to assess the factors affecting gradual changes in coverage, and uncovered little of interest. When we examined transformative policy changes directly using duration analysis, however, the results were far more fruitful. Here again, this suggests that the use of time-series coverage data likely undermines quantitative attempts to explore certain types of policy reform. More substantively, the findings from this analysis suggest that the presence of a social health insurance system and increased structural constraints are correlated with a decreased likelihood of developing a universalist healthcare system. While a high degree of multicollinearity poses some challenges in interpreting the findings vis-à-vis the Power Resource variables, careful analysis finds support for the generalisability of several of the conclusions drawn from the French-Italian comparison.

In sum, as in the chapters analysing the determinants of different approaches to coverage extension regarding the unemployed, we have here again argued that structural factors – most notably the presence of a social health insurance system – impact public opinion, which in turn affects policy change through structuring parties' electoral incentives.[27]

27 As was the case with the quantitative analysis of benefits for the unemployed, analysing longitudinal survey results alongside policy change would obviously have been the ideal approach to determining a causal link, but a lack of necessary data prevent us from doing so. The complementary use of several additional case studies in Chapter 6 helps to offset some of the limitations inherent in this alternative approach, however.

8 Rectifying Coverage Gaps

This book set out to explore the when, why, and how governments extend benefit access to those without coverage. In particular, we have attempted to uncover the determinants driving governments to extend benefits to erstwhile outsiders – which in some instances has even entailed the standardisation of benefit levels.

This discussion has included a particular focus on leftist organisations, since coverage gaps in the age of austerity pose particularly difficult dilemmas for them. On the one hand, the broad leftist commitment to egalitarianism would suggest that this issue should be of considerable concern to left-wing parties and unions; pursuing the matter would contribute to both ideological consistency and a reaching out to labour market and welfare state outsiders. At the same time, however, fiscal and political constraints on welfare state scope and spending mean that any levelling of access and benefit generosity would almost certainly entail levelling down. It would therefore destroy many of the traditional privileges enjoyed by a variety of occupational groups – groups that often constitute a sizeable portion of the left's support base. What is more, the issue is often further complicated by organisational interests in maintaining certain social insurance institutions, with the goal of preserving sources of power and influence.

In light of the relevance of this issue in today's Europe, we have attempted to shed light on the ways this dilemma has played out vis-à-vis welfare state reform. A comparison of French and Italian reforms in the fields of benefits for the unemployed and healthcare provided the bulk of our framework for understanding the relationship of the left to benefit extension and standardisation. Given that there is no consistent attitude across either leftist parties or unions towards these types of reforms, the introduction laid out a number of general scenarios that might describe patterns of variation:

Scenario 1: The left may opt to maintain the backing of traditional (insider) supporters with pro-status quo preferences, leading partisanship to have a limited impact on the relevant party preferences. This decision may be based, for example, on the perceived feasibility of poaching more votes than might be lost by pursuing reform.

Scenario 2: The left may seek the support of outsiders where possible, but their preferences across countries may differ (being sometimes pro-reform, sometimes pro-status quo), with outcomes in line with those preferences. Outsider preferences might be shaped, for example, by the distribution of access to social programmes in society.

Scenario 3: The left may seek/oppose the extension and standardisation of benefits for reasons unrelated to insider/outsider cleavages – perhaps because it is of use to the leftist organisations themselves. This might be the case, for example, because leftist parties/unions prioritise the status quo to maintain political resources derived from the current institutional arrangement (or oppose it to undermine the political resources of rival parties/unions).

Scenario 4: Different relationships may dominate different policy domains. This could be the result of issues related to an issue inherent to the policy domain (e.g. is it dominated by life-cycle or redistributive characteristics?) or the specific institutional context of the relevant programme.

While the first and third scenarios stress the importance of party dynamics, the second points to potential variation in outsider preferences, and the fourth highlights intrinsic qualities of different policy domains. Insofar as institutional context factors into all of the scenarios, we might also group the scenarios into two categories, based on whether institutions shape party decisions indirectly (as in S2 and the first half of S4) or directly (as in S1, S3, and the latter half of S4). We will return to these scenarios in a moment, but before doing so we must first recap the findings of each of the preceding chapters so as to better situate our broader conclusions.

The first chapter served as an introduction to both the topic and the book as a whole, providing a review of related literatures and an outline of the methodology and structure of the subsequent chapters. It laid out the two goals of the book: to compensate for the dearth of systematic research on the relationship between partisanship and the extension (and in some instances standardisation) of benefit access under economic austerity; and to construct a more direct approach to analysing social policy reform quantitatively, in the process providing a critique of quantitative studies that use as their dependent variables time-series measures that poorly align with the actual policy changes in which they purport to be interested.

The book then turned to analyse the determinants of benefit extension and standardisation. Chapter 2 compared the reform of benefits for the unemployed in France and Italy, paying particular attention to the two minimum income (RMI) benefits that sought to residualise their respective systems and provide welfare state outsiders with access to (low-level) benefits. Since the Italian version of the scheme was adopted a full decade after the French programme and was cancelled within a few years, we explored differences between the two cases that might explain the divergence.

Various existing theories were considered, and it was argued that different outcomes were the result not of partisanship-based factors, but rather of contrasting levels of public pressure. The chapter posited that the divergence in public opinion was partly the result of the playing out (in Italy) of institutional factors typically associated with Southern European welfare states (see Ferrera 2005): namely, the prevalence of informal work, limited administrative capacity, and the central role of the family unit. Both the prevalence of informal work and the centrality of the family decreased the perceived precariousness of being unemployed with no direct access to unemployment benefits. In addition, the latter factor also decreased demands for reform from young adults who would otherwise have had no benefit recourse. Limited administrative capacity, in turn, contributed to the perception that an RMI-style programme was simply not feasible – especially in light of the complications that arise from the prevalence of informal employment. The result of this decreased demand for reform then played out at the policy level by removing electoral incentives for vote-seeking parties. These findings were then supported using an examination of public opinion in Italy and a few other countries.

The next two chapters then tested the generalisability of these conclusions. This process began in Chapter 3 with an assessment of our additional Continental and Southern European cases. Here we focused on policy trajectories and public opinion across the countries in order to assess just how typical the French and Italian cases are. While the Continental cases were characterised by considerable variation in their approaches to benefit extension and standardisation, the case studies highlighted three very different policy trajectories vis-à-vis outsider access to benefits, thereby offering insights on our central questions about benefit standardisation and universalisation. Specifically, we contrasted Austria's 'smoothed dualisation', Belgium's (largely union-driven) expansion of access to a gradually weakened unemployment insurance system, and Germany's more traditional dualisation. The Southern European cases, in turn, displayed a clear cleavage between countries that were able to implement successful reforms (Portugal and, to a much lesser extent, Spain) and those that were not (Greece and Italy). The same issues influencing extension in the Italian case were present in the others, but the success of the Portuguese reform in the face of these challenges was particularly instructive. Here we suggested that the focus on social exclusion and activation requirements, yoking benefit extension with welfare state modernisation, did considerable work in making the minimum income programme viable in the long term.

Chapter 4 then set out extend this analysis of public opinion and policy change in a more systematic way. It opened by building on the survey analysis with which the previous chapter ended, using multi-level model analysis to investigate the impact of the institutional factors highlighted above. Here we found most of our variables of interest to be of generalisable import. Since we care about public opinion not in and of itself but for its potential impact on policy, we then shifted our focus to outcomes: first through the use of time-series analysis (using coverage levels as its dependent variable), then through an examination of policy change directly. While a focus on gradual interest revealed little of interest, studying reforms directly suggested that both the size of the informal economy and the median age at which youth leave home impact the odds of reform. These findings served as support for both the conclusions of Chapter 2 and our broader argument about the importance of properly defining the dependent variable when seeking to assess policy changes.

In Chapter 5, we shifted our attention to reforms in the field of healthcare, concentrating on the 1978 Servizio Sanitario Nazionale (SSN) in Italy and the 1999 Couverture Maladie Universelle (CMU) in France. In this instance, the French once again pursued a residualising approach, whereas the Italians universalised their system (a stark contrast to their failure to act vis-à-vis benefits for the unemployed). As in Chapter 2, various pre-existing theories were delineated, and while they generally contributed to our understanding of the divergence, we also find that institutional arrangements shaped preferences for or against reform. In this instance, however, the direct impact of institutions on party preferences was seen to play a more crucial role than was the case in the chapter on benefits for the unemployed. In France, the institutional structure of healthcare attracted support for the status quo from both the public and the left (with a substantial role for workers' representatives), making a complete overhaul of the system less likely. In Italy, by contrast, these sources of support were missing. A universal healthcare system had long been a pet-project of the Italian Communist Party (PCI), and a broad popular movement in the 1970s eventually suggested a shift in public opinion towards reforming the system. Furthermore, the clientelistic resources that the Christian Democrats (DC) derived from the health insurance system also gave the PCI strong incentives to work to completely dismantle the system when its influence was at its peak. Here again, then, we note the importance of certain defining institutional features of Southern European welfare states (see Ferrera 1996b). The end result was a dramatic transformation of healthcare in

Italy, despite the fact that access to benefits for the unemployed has remained broadly unreformed.

Chapters 6 and 7 then examined whether these findings might be exportable to other contexts, with the approach reflecting that taken with regard to benefits for the unemployed. In examining policy trajectories across our additional Continental and Southern European cases, Chapter 6 revealed that the French and Italian cases generally reflected developments within their case sets. In Continental Europe, piecemeal extension was able to incorporate the vast majority of the population, but approaches to those falling outside of the primary system varied in both timing and style: within Austria and Germany, healthcare access for the vulnerable outside of the primary system was traditionally provided directly via social assistance (giving rise to various issues); while in Belgium, the early extension of access to the primary system nevertheless left in place various de facto barriers to care. The debates and reforms seeking to address these issues thus provided some parallels to the French reform. In Southern Europe, dramatic benefit extension appeared to have similar causes across the cases, with a shared perception that the preceding system's inequities and lack of coordination were problematic and a key role for the left. What is more, variation in benefit extension also seemed to be shaped by similar factors to those discussed in the French-Italian comparison – especially with regard to the entrenched power of pro-status quo interests. A brief discussion of country-level public opinion about healthcare across the cases also revealed considerable clustering.

Chapter 7 then began by using these same survey questions to assess the determinants of attitudinal differences regarding government responsibility to provide access to healthcare and the need for dramatic reform. While these results suggested a potential effect of numerous factors discussed in Chapter 5, it was impossible to unpack the proposed direction of the effects using only a snapshot of public opinion. To address this limitation, the chapter then proceeded to the longitudinal analyses, looking first at healthcare coverage levels and then at the universalising reforms themselves. The strongest support for our earlier findings came once again from this final analysis, performed using duration analysis to examine the likelihood of reform introduction. Results suggested that both the presence of a social health insurance system and the number of structural constraints negatively impact the odds of reform. We also found mixed support for the impact of variables associated with Power Resource theory (trade union density and left government), though collinearity made it particularly difficult to disentangle the effects. Overall, the chapter, considered alongside

Chapter 6, offers considerable support for the generalisability of Chapter 5's conclusions.

Taken together, what do these findings tell us about our broader question? Most generally, they support the position that there is no consistent relationship between the left and welfare state dualisation across countries and policy domains – either in the form of supporting or opposing benefit extension. Contra Rueda's findings on labour market reform (2007), we note that left-wing parties do not consistently hunker down and pursue the exclusive interests of their insider support base; rather, they often extend benefits through residualisation, and sometimes even pursue universalisation. They do appear to be more inclined towards the former approach than the latter, but this inclination does not rely simply on the attractiveness of pursuing the votes of outsiders at the potential expense of lost insider votes. While vote-seeking behaviour may spur a party towards action, it is not enough to determine what type of reform they carry out.

To begin with the first part of the opinion-policy equation, this book has stressed the central role of institutions in shaping outsider opinions, which in turn can incentivise vote-seeking parties to pursue benefit reform. Dualised welfare states would normally be expected to inculcate different attitudes towards reform, with (in general) insiders pro-status quo and outsiders pro-extension. Institutional arrangements can diminish public pressures for reform across both groups, and the chapters highlight common mechanisms through which this might occur: they might do so by suggesting that welfare state outsiders might not truly be outsiders, since they could have access to indirect benefits (through the family) or under-the-table work – leading the public as a whole to be more pro-status quo; they might legitimately provide outsiders with indirect access to benefits, thereby making them less pro-reform than they would otherwise be; or they might give trade unions a central role in the system, making leftists and trade unionists more pro-status quo. As such, and in line with Scenario 2, even where the left seeks outsider support, that attempt will have different implications in different contexts – a conclusion that complements Emmenegger's (2009) findings on labour market preferences. Coupled with the impact of institutions on broader public opinion, these sorts of contextual factors appear to shape whether or not benefit coverage is extended at all – through either residualisation or universalisation – by shaping electoral incentives.

The manner in which dualised welfare states are reformed, on the other hand, appears to be tied to both public opinion *and* the organisational preferences of leftist parties. By providing some parties with a valuable political resource, an institutional arrangement may give other parties an added incentive to overhaul the system. We can therefore see Scenarios 3 and 4 at work in two key ways: the first sees the adoption of a pro-status quo position on the left in situations where unions are key social partners (since that ostensibly provides workers with institutionalised input); and the second sees the adoption of a pro-reform stance where political rivals derive substantial political resources from the status quo (as through clientelism). Where there is a dualised welfare state and a fiscal or political limitation preventing the extension of generous benefits to all, these sorts of considerations are likely to condition the choice between residualist and universalist approaches to reform.

Note that in both policy domains, many of the relevant factors shaping public opinion and party preferences are either associated with Mediterranean countries or constitute defining characteristics of the Southern European welfare state typology (see Ferrera 1996b; 2000; 2005; Martin 1996; Rhodes 1996; Naldini 2003). We can observe this in the case of both benefits of the unemployed (where the size of the informal economy, a lack of municipal administrative capacity, and the role of the family were central) and healthcare (where clientelism played an important role). This makes sense, given that Southern European welfare states tend to combine weak or absent social assistance with universal healthcare – and the mechanisms discussed throughout this book may well help to explain this rather counterintuitive combination of low- and high-coverage programmes.

We would therefore stress this institutionalist explanation in accounting for the differences across the policy domains, rather than basing our argument on differences between life-cycle and redistributive policies (cf. Jensen 2012). Inherent in the life-cycle/redistributive distinction is the idea that policies in the former grouping involve redistribution along health status and age divisions – which, given that most people can easily envision themselves aging and/or falling ill, creates a limited sense of conflict. We would argue, however, that in systems that create groups of excluded outsiders and where benefits are not standardised across occupational groups, altering the distribution of benefits does indeed entail redistribution that is not simply based on health status or age. Insofar as a levelling down for certain groups is inevitable, reforms under these circumstances do in fact involve redistributional struggles – and the pro- and anti-universalisation cleavages in a number of our cases support this conclusion.

These findings provide a framework for future examinations of the relationship between partisanship and welfare state dualism. They also suggest that any future attempts to uncover a uniform relationship between partisanship and welfare state generosity *writ large* are unlikely to be successful. In addition, our variegated approach to testing the generalisability of our comparative analysis has illustrated the potential pitfalls of using coverage-level data to analyse policy reforms. Instead, we have suggested that the timing of policy reforms themselves serve as a more appropriate dependent variable, and that such an approach is possible using duration analysis.

Most centrally, this book has attempted to shift the attention from retrenchment and segmentation to benefit extension and standardisation, in order to shed light on the conditions in which governments have extended coverage in the post-expansionary age. This focus is of particular relevance in today's Europe, given that coverage gaps persist and can contribute to a cycle of exclusion that will long outlast the current crisis. Outsiders on the European periphery are especially at risk in this regard, and welfare state dualism complicates attempts to extend protection to these individuals. This is because, as Rueda (2014) argues, the insider-outsider cleavage has the potential to dramatically weaken responses to economic crises where insider protection is already firmly established.

Our investigation unfortunately supports this rather pessimistic view, while highlighting a number of further complications. First, although familialism may serve as a protective measure against hardship during economic downturns, it also is likely to quell long-term pressure to implement and maintain benefit extension. Nevertheless, the fact that researchers have found familialism to be on the decline, especially in Spain and Portugal (see Moreno and Marí-Klose 2013), suggests that the situation is not immutable. Second, external pressures for benefit extension, of the sort found in Italy, have a hard time substituting entirely for internal pressures. Where internal demand was weak, these programmes have tended to either disappear with limited fanfare or be otherwise undermined by subsequent governments. Finally, the organisational incentives that shape preferences among leftist unions and parties, couched as they are in sticky institutional arrangements, tend to be rather difficult to reconfigure. Yet more optimistically, we hope that by flagging potential confounders of benefit extension, our investigation will help those seeking to uncover possible routes forward.

Appendix: A Brief Methodological Note

The French and Italian case studies benefited from a series of interviews conducted in 2011 and 2012 at various French and Italian parties and unions that can broadly be categorised as either leftist or centre-left. What follows is a brief outline of how the interviewees were selected and how the interviews themselves were conducted.

The first step was of course the selection of the organisations to be contacted. In the case of political parties, I sought interviews at parties that held seats when the reforms I focus upon were passed: in Italy, this led me to contact the Partito Democratico, Italia dei Valori, Partito della Rifondazione Comunista, and Partito dei Comunisti Italiani; in France, the relevant parties were the Parti Socialiste, Parti Radical de Gauche, Europe Écologie – Les Verts, and Parti Communiste Français. Given the relevance of labour unions, I also sought interviews with officials at the three large union confederations in each country: in Italy, these were the Italiana Sindacati Lavoratori, Unione Italiana del Lavoro, and Confederazione Generale Italiana del Lavoro; while in France, they were the Confédération Française Démocratique des Travailleurs, Force Ouvrière, and Confédération Générale du Travail.

I then contacted the national headquarters of the parties and unions. After outlining my research project, I asked to make an appointment with someone in the relevant section of the organisation, so as to inquire about the organisation's positions on the relevant topics and policies. Although I was unable to obtain interviews in all instances, I was able to speak with individuals at the Partito Democratico, Italia dei Valori, Partito della Rifondazione Comunista, Partito dei Comunisti Italiani, Europe Écologie – Les Verts, Parti Communiste Français, Confederazione Generale Italiana del Lavoro, Force Ouvrière, and Confédération Générale du Travail.[1] Interview subjects tended to be national directors or presidents of the relevant sections, though in some cases I was given interviews with former or current elected politicians, national secretaries, and editors-in-chief of party reviews. On a few occasions I was able to interview more than one subject at a given organisation.

1 In the case of the Partito Democratico and Italia dei Valori, my unsolicited interview requests were not successful, but I was nevertheless able to obtain interviews through connections.

The interviews were then conducted in a semi-structured manner, with scripts tailored to organisation type and country.[2] The script incorporated questions covering general positions (e.g. regarding welfare state dualisation, universalism, etc.), stances regarding key policies, and related interactions with other key organisations/interest groups. Interviews were held in two rounds: the first exploratory round was conducted in 2011, so as to gain insights that might inform archival research; and the second round in 2012, which gave me the opportunity to ask more specific questions. In most instances, interviews were conducted with the same subject on both occasions.

2 While I had a general script, I would ask additional questions where appropriate and ended each interview with open-ended questions that allowed subjects to add general comments.

Bibliography

Allan, J.P., and Scruggs, L. (2004). Political Partisanship and Welfare State Reform in Advanced Industrial Societies. *American Journal of Political Science, 48*(3), 496-512.

Altenstetter, C., and Busse, R. (2005). Health Care Reform in Germany: Patchwork Change within Established Governance Structures. *Journal of Health Politics, Policy and Law, 30*(1-2), 121-142.

Alti, T. (2001). The Predicament of Activation in the Italian Minimum Insertion Income. Paper presented at the European Sociological Association, Helsinki.

Armingeon, K., Weisstanner, D., Engler, S., Potolidis, P., Gerber, M., and Leimgruber, P. (2011). *Comparative Political Data Set I (23 OECD Countries).*

Arriba, A., and Moreno, L. (2005). Spain: Poverty, Social Exclusion, and 'Safety Nets'. In M. Ferrera, ed., *Welfare State Reform in Southern Europe: Fighting Poverty and Social Exclusion in Italy, Spain, Portugal and Greece* (pp. 110-162). New York: Routledge.

Arts, W., and Gelissen, J. (2001). Welfare States, Solidarity and Justice Principles: Does the Type Really Matter? *Acta Sociologica, 44,* 283-299.

Austria (2014). *Social Protection in Austria.* Vienna: Sozialministerium.

Baccaro, L., Hamman, K., and Turner, L. (2003). The Politics of Labour Movement Revitalization: The Need for a Revitalized Perspective. *European Journal of Industrial Relations, 9*(1), 119-133.

Baglioni, S., Della Porta, D., and Graziano, P. (2008). The Contentious Politics of Unemployment: The Italian Case in Comparative Perspective. *European Journal of Political Research, 47,* 827-851.

Bahle, T., Hubl, V., and Pfeifer, M. (2011). *The Last Safety Net: A Handbook of Minimum Income Protection in Europe.* Chicago: The Policy Press.

Baldini, M., Bosi, P., and Toso, S. (2002). Targeting Welfare in Italy: Old Problems and Perspectives on Reform. *Fiscal Studies, 23*(1), 51-75.

Bambra, C. (2005). Worlds of Welfare and the Health Care Discrepancy. *Social Policy & Society, 4*(1), 31-41.

Barbier, J.-C., and Fargion, V. (2004). Continental Inconsistencies on the Path to Activation: Consequences for Social Citizenship in Italy and France. *European Societies, 6*(4), 437-460.

Barbier, J.-C., and Théret, B. (2001). Welfare-to-Work or Work-to-Welfare. In N. Gilbert and R. Van Voorhis, eds, *Activating the Unemployed: A Comparative Appraisal of Work-oriented Policies* (pp. 135-184). New Brunswick, NJ: Transaction Publishers.

Barbier, J.-C., and Théret, B. (2003). The French System of Social Protection: Path Dependencies and Societal Coherence. In N. Gilbert and R.A. Van Voorhis, eds, *Changing Patterns of Social Protection* (pp. 119-168). New Brunswick, NJ: Transaction Publishers.

Bec, C. (1995). Assistance and Equality in the French Social Welfare System. In D. Bouget and B. Palier, eds, *Comparing Social Welfare Systems in Nordic Europe and France* (Vol. 4, pp. 127-139). Paris, France: MIRE-DREES.

Béland, D. (2001). Does Labor Matter? Institutions, Labor Unions and Pension Reform in France and the United States. *Journal of Public Policy, 21*(2), 153-172.

Béland, D., and Hansen, R. (2000). Reforming the French Welfare State: Solidarity, Social Exclusion and the Three Crises of Citizenship. *West European Politics, 23*(1), 47-64.

Belorgey, J.-M. (1988). *La Gauche et les Pauvres.* Paris: Syros.

Benassi, C., and Vlandas, T. (2016). Union Inclusiveness and Temporary Agency Workers: The Role of Power Resources and Union Ideology. *European Journal of Industrial Relations, 22*(1), 5-22.

Bentolila, S., and Ichino, A. (2008). Unemployment and Consumption Near and Far Away from the Mediterranean. *Journal of Population Economics, 21*, 255-280.

Berlinguer, E. (1977). *Austerità: Occasione per transformare l'Italia*. Rome: Riuniti.

Bernardi, F., and Garrido, L. (2008). Is There a New Service Proletariat? Post-industrial Employment Growth and Social Inequality in Spain. *European Sociological Review, 24*(3), 299-313.

Berger, S., & Piore, M.J. (1980). *Dualism and Discontinuity in Industrial Societies*. New York, NY: Cambridge University Press.

Berton, F., Richiardi, M., and Sacchi, S. (2009). Flessibilità del Lavoro e Precarietà dei Lavoratori in Italia: Analisi Empiriche e Proposte di Policy. *Rivista Italiana di Politche Pubbliche, 1*, 33-70.

Berton, F., Richiardi, M., and Sacchi, S. (2012). *The Political Economy of Work Security and Flexibility: Italy in Comparative Perspective*. Chicago: The Policy Press.

Billari, F., Philipov, D., and Baizán, P. (2001). Leaving Home in Europe: The Experience of Cohorts Born around 1960. MPIDR Working Paper. Max Planck Institute for Demographic Research.

Blanchard, O., and Landier, A. (2002). The Perverse Effects of Partial Labour Market Reform: Fixed-Term Contracts in France. *The Economic Journal, 112*(480), 214-244.

Blekesaune, M., and Quadagno, J. (2003). Public Attitudes toward Welfare State Policies: A Comparative Analysis of 24 Nations. *European Sociological Review, 19*(5), 415-427.

Blendon, R.J., Kim, M., and Benson, J.M. (2001). The Public versus the World Health Organization on Health System Performance. *Health Affairs, 20*(3), 10-20.

Bleses, P., and Seeleib-Kaiser, M. (2004). *The Dual Transformation of the German Welfare State*. New York, NY: Palgrave.

Boeri, T., Brugiavini, A., Calmfors, L., Booth, A.L., Burda, M., Checchi, D., Ebbinghaus, B., Freeman, R., Garibaldi, P., Holmlund, B., Naylor, R., Schludi, M., Verdier, T., Visser, J. (2001a). Unions' Involvement in the Welfare State. In T. Boeri, A. Brugiavini, and L. Calmfors, eds, *The Role of Unions in the Twenty-First Century: A Report to the Fondazione Rodolfo Debenedetti* (pp. 163-186). Oxford: Oxford University Press.

Boeri, T., Börsch-Supan, A., and Tabellini, G. (2001b). Would You Like to Shrink the Welfare State? A Survey of European Citizens. *Economic Policy, 16*(32), 9-50.

Bonoli, G. (1997). Classifying Welfare States: a Two-dimension Approach. *Journal of Social Policy, 26*(3), 351-372.

Bonoli, G., and Haüsermann, S. (2009). Who Wants What from the Welfare State? Socio-structural Cleavages in Distributional Politics: Evidence from Swiss Referendum Votes. *European Societies, 11*(2), 211-232.

Bonoli, G., and Palier, B. (1996). Reclaiming Welfare: The Politics of French Social Protection Reform. *South European Society and Politics, 1*(3), 240-259.

Booth, A.L., Francesconi, M., and Frank, J. (2002). Temporary Jobs: Stepping Stones or Dead Ends? *The Economic Journal, 112*(480), 189-213.

Bouget, D. (1998). The Juppé Plan and the Future of the French Social Welfare System. *Journal of European Social Policy, 8*(2), 155-172.

Brooks, C., and Manza, J. (2007). *Why Welfare States Persist: The Importance of Public Opinion in Democracies*. Chicago: University of Chicago Press.

Brown, L.D. (1984). Health Reform, Italian-style. *Health Affairs, 3*(3), 75-101.

Bruto da Costa, A. (2003). Minimum Guaranteed Income and Basic Income in Portugal. In G. Standing, ed., *Minimum Income Schemes in Europe* (pp. 73-104). Geneva: International Labour Office.

Burau, V., and Blank, R.H. (2006). Comparing Health Policy: An Assessment of Typologies of Health Systems. *Journal of Comparative Policy Analysis: Research and Practice, 8*(1), 63-76.

Burgoon, B. (2001). Globalization and Welfare Compensation: Disentangling the Ties That Bind. *International Organization, 55*(3), 509-551.

Burgoon, B., and Dekker, F. (2010). Flexible Employment, Economic Insecurity and Social Policy Preferences in Europe. *Journal of European Social Policy, 20*(2), 126-141.

Busemeyer, M.R., Goerres, A., and Weschle, S. (2009). Attitudes towards Redistributive Spending in an Era of Demographic Ageing: The Rival Pressures from Age and Income in 14 OECD Countries. *Journal of European Social Policy, 19*(3), 195-212.

Busse, R., and Blümel, M. (2014). Germany: Health System Review. *Health Systems in Transition, 16*(2):1-296.

Busse, R., and Riesberg, A. (2004). Health Care Systems in Transition: Germany. Copenhagen: WHO Regional Office for Europe on Behalf of the European Observatory on Health Systems and Policies.

Capucha, L., Bomba, T., Fernandes, R., and Matos, G. (2005). Portugal: A Virtuous Path towards Minimum Income? In M. Ferrera, ed., *Welfare State Reform in Southern Europe: Fighting Poverty and Social Exclusion in Italy, Spain, Portugal and Greece* (pp. 204-265). London: Routledge.

Castles, F.G. (2004). *The Future of the Welfare State: Crisis Myths and Crisis Realities*. Oxford: Oxford University Press.

Catrice-Lorey, A., and Steffen, M. (2006). Implementation of Health Care Reforms in the Bismarckian Systems: Unequal Capacities. *Revue Française des Affaires Sociales, 6*, 163-182.

CGIL (1956). Rassegna Sindacale: Settimanale della CGIL.

Clasen, J., and Clegg, D. (2006). Beyond Activation: Reforming European Unemployment Protection Systems in Post-Industrial Labour Markets. *European Societies, 8*(4), 527-553.

Clegg, D. (2007). Continental Drift: On Unemployment Policy Change in Bismarckian Welfare States. *Social Policy & Administration, 41*(6), 597-617.

Clegg, D. (2010). From Insurance or Insertion to Rights and Responsibilities: The Shifting Logics of Unemployment Policy in France. In A. Neville, ed., *Human Rights and Social Policy: A Comparative Analysis of Values and Citizenship in OECD Countries* (pp. 83-100). Cheltenham: Edward Elgar.

Clegg, D. (2011). France: Integration versus Dualization. In J. Clasen and D. Clegg, eds, *Regulating the Risk of Unemployment: National Adaptations to Post-Industrial Labour Markets in Europe* (pp. 34-54). Oxford: Oxford University Press.

Clegg, D. (2012). Solidarity or Dualization? Social Governance, Union Preferences, and Unemployment Benefit Adjustment in Belgium and France. In P. Emmenegger, S. Haüsermann, B. Palier, and M. Seeleib-Kaiser, eds, *The Age of Dualization: The Changing Face of Inequality in Deindustrializing Societies* (pp. 253-279). Oxford: Oxford University Press.

Clegg, D., Graziano, P., and Van Wijnbergen, C. (2010). Between Sectionalism and Revitalisation: Trade Unions and Activation Policies in Europe. Working Papers on the Reconciliation of Work and Welfare in Europe. Edinburgh.

Collettivo dell'Istituto Superiore di Sanità (1971). *La Salute e il Potere in Italia*. Bari: De Donato.

Conference Board (2015). The Conference Board Total Economy Database™, September. http://www.conference-board.org/data/economydatabase/.

Cutler, D.M., and Johnson, R. (2004). The Birth and Growth of the Social Insurance State: Explaining Old Age and Medical Insurance across Countries. *Public Choice, 120*(1-2), 87-121.

D'Addio, A.C., and Rosholm, M. (2005). Temporary Employment in Europe: Characteristics, Determinants and Outcomes. *Brussels Economic Review, 48*(1/2), 13-41.

D'Alimonte, R. (1999). Party Behavior in a Polarized System: The Italian Communist Party and the Historic Compromise. In W.C. Muller and K. Strom, eds, *Policy, Office, or Votes? How Political Parties in Western Europe Make Hard Decisions* (pp. 141-171). New York: Cambridge University Press.

Da Conceicao-Heldt, E. (2008). Pension Reforms in France: The Role of Trade Unions and the Timing of the Electoral Cycle. *Policy Studies, 29*(1), 19-34.

Dahl, R.A. (1961). *Who Governs? Democracy and Power in an American City.* New Haven, CT: Yale University Press.

Dallinger, U. (2010). Public Support for Redistribution: What Explains Cross-national Differences? *Journal of European Social Policy, 20*(4), 333-349.

Davaki, K., and Mossialos, E. (2005). Plus ça Change: Health Sector Reforms in Greece. *Journal of Health Politics, Policy and Law, 30*(1-2), 143-168.

Davidsson, J., and Naczyk, M. (2009). *The Ins and Outs of Dualisation: A Literature Review.* Working Papers on the Reconciliation of Work and Welfare in Europe. Edinburgh.

Davidsson, J.B., and Emmenegger, P. (2013). Defending the Organisation, Not the Members: Unions and the Reform of Job Security Legislation in Western Europe. *European Journal of Political Research, 52*(3), 339-363.

Dell'Aringa, C., and Lodovici, M.S. (1996). Policies for the Unemployed and Social Shock Absorbers: The Italian Experience. *South European Society and Politics, 1*(3), 172-197.

De Miguel, J.M. (1977). Policies and Politics of the Health Reforms in Southern European Countries: A Sociological Critique. *Social Science and Medicine, 11,* 379-393.

De Vito, A., and Giliberto, F. (1975). Quando il Malato è Sano. *La Stampa,* 5 February.

Dinas, E., and Gemenis, K. (2010). Measuring Parties' Ideological Positions with Manifesto Data: A Critical Evaluation of Competing Methods. *Party Politics, 16*(4), 427-450.

Donatini, A., Rico, A., D'Ambrosio, M.G., Lo Scalzo, A., Orzella, L., Cicchetti, A., and Profili, S. (2001). Health Care Systems in Transition: Italy. Copenhagen: WHO Regional Office for Europe on Behalf of the European Observatory on Health Systems and Policies.

Downs, A. (1957). *An Economic Theory of Democracy.* New York: Harper.

Emmenegger, P. (2009). Barriers to Entry: Insider/Outsider Politics and the Political Determinants of Job Security Regulations. *Journal of European Social Policy, 19*(2), 131-146.

Emmenegger, P., Haüsermann, S., Palier, B., and Seeleib-Kaiser, M. (2012). *The Age of Dualization.* Oxford, UK: Oxford University Press.

Enns, P.K., and Wlezien, C., eds. (2011). *Who Gets Represented?* New York: Russell Sage Foundation.

Erikson, R.S., MacKuen, M., and Stimson, J.A. (2002). *The Macro Polity.* New York: Cambridge University Press.

Esping-Andersen, G. (1990). *The Three Worlds of Welfare Capitalism.* Cambridge: Polity Press.

Esping-Andersen, G. (1999a). Politics without Class? Post-Industrial Cleavages in Europe and America. In H. Kitschelt, P. Lange, G. Marks, and J.D. Stephens, eds, *Continuity and Change in Contemporary Capitalism* (pp. 293-316). New York: Cambridge University Press.

Esping-Andersen, G. (1999b). *Social Foundations of Postindustrial Economies.* New York: Oxford University Press.

ESS Round 4: European Social Survey Round 4 Data (2008).

Estevez-Abe, M. (2006). Gendering the Varieties of Capitalism: A Study of Occupational Segregation by Sex in Advanced Industrial Societies. *World Politics, 59*(1), 142-175.

Eurobarometer (1996). *Eurobarometer 44.3: Health Care Issues and Public Security,* February-April.

Eurobarometer (2002). *Eurobarometer 57.2: Health Issues, Cross-Border Purchases, and National Identities,* April-June.

European Union (2010) *Household Structure in the EU.* Luxembourg: Publications Office of the European Union.

Eurostat (2009). *Youth in Europe – A Statistical Portrait.* Luxembourg: Publications Office of the European Union.

Eurostat (2010). *Combating Poverty and Social Exclusion: A Statistical Portrait of the European Union.* Luxembourg: Eurostat Statistical Books.

Eurostat (2012). *Income and Living Conditions Dataset.*

Evans, R.G. (2005). Fellow Travelers on a Contested Path: Power, Purpose, and the Evolution of European Health Care Systems. *Journal of Health Politics, Policy and Law, 30*(1-2), 277-293.

EVS (2008). *European Values Study.*

EVS (2011). *European Values Study 1999 – Integrated Dataset.*

Fantozzi, R. (2012) Interview, 16 May. Translation by Anthony Kevins.

Fargion, V. (2003). Half Way through the Ford: The Italian Welfare State at the Start of the New Century. In N. Gilbert and R.A. Van Voorhis, eds, *Changing Patterns of Social Protection* (pp. 309-338). New Brunswick, NJ: Transaction Publishers.

Ferrera, M. (1986). Italy. In P. Flora, ed., *Growth to Limits: The Western European Welfare States since World War II – Vol. 2, Germany, United Kingdom, Ireland, Italy* (pp. 385-482). Berlin: Walter de Gruyter & Co.

Ferrera, M. (1989). The Politics of Health Reform: Origins and Performance of the Italian Health Service in Comparative Perspective. In G. Freddi and J. W. Bjorkman, eds, *Controlling Medical Professionals: The Comparative Politics of Health Governance* (pp. 116-129). London: Sage.

Ferrera, M. (1993). *Modelli di Solidarietà: Politica e Riforme Sociali nelle Democrazie.* Bologna: Il Mulino.

Ferrera, M. (1995). The Rise and Fall of Democratic Universalism: Health Care Reform in Italy, 1978-1994. *Journal of Health Politics, Policy and Law, 20*(2), 275-302.

Ferrera, M. (1996a). La partitocrazia della salute. In M. Cotta and P. Isernia, eds, *Il gigante dai piedi di argilla: La crisi del regime paritocratico in Italia* (pp. 53-72). Bologna: Il Mulino.

Ferrera, M. (1996b). The 'Southern Model' of Welfare in Social Europe. *Journal of European Social Policy, 6*(1), 17-37.

Ferrera, M. (2000). Reconstructing the Welfare State in Southern Europe. In S. Kuhnle, ed., *Survival of the European Welfare State* (pp. 166-181). London: Routledge.

Ferrera, M., ed. (2005). *Welfare State Reform in Southern Europe: Fighting Poverty and Social Exclusion in Italy, Spain, Portugal and Greece.* New York: Routledge.

Ferrera, M., Fargion, V., and Jessoula, M. (2012). *Alle Radici del Welfare all'Italiana: Origini e Futuro di un Modello Sociale Squilibrato.* Venice: Marsilio.

Flora, P., ed. (1986). *Growth to Limits: The European Welfare States since World War II.* Berlin: De Gruyter.

France (1945). *Ordonnance no. 45/2454 du 19 octobre 1945.*

France (1986). *Journal Officiel de la République Française: Débats Parlementaires.* http://archives.assemblee-nationale.fr/7/qst/7-qst-1986-01-27.pdf.

France (1988). *Loi no. 88-1088 du 1 décembre 1988 relative au revenu minimum d'insertion.*

France (1999). *Loi no. 99-641 du 27 juillet 1999 portant création d'une couverture maladie universelle.* http://www.legifrance.gouv.fr/affichTexte.do;jsessionid=1F2171974681233EA23E9E23DA26D6F8.tpdjo10v_1?cidTexte=JORFTEXT000000198392&categorieLien=id.

France, G., and Taroni, F. (2005). The Evolution of Health-Policy Making in Italy. *Journal of Health Politics, Policy and Law, 30*(1-2), 169-187.

Freeman, R. (2000). *The Politics of Health in Europe.* New York: Manchester University Press.

Freeman, R., and Frisina, L. (2010). Health Care Systems and the Problem of Classification. *Journal of Comparative Policy Analysis: Research and Practice, 12*(1-2), 163-178.

Gabaglio, E. (2012) Interview, 16 May. Translation by Anthony Kevins.

Gagliarducci, S. (2005). The Dynamics of Repeated Temporary Jobs. *Labour Economics, 12*(4), 429-448.

Gallup Organization (2007). *Flash Eurobarometer Series #202: Youth Survey among People Aged between 15-30, in the European Union.*

Garrett, G. (1998). *Partisan Politics in the Global Economy.* New York: Cambridge University Press.

Gash, V. (2008). Bridge or Trap? Temporary Workers' Transitions to Unemployment and to the Standard Employment Contract. *European Sociological Review, 24*(5), 651-668.

Gash, V., and McGinnity, F. (2007). Fixed-term Contracts – The New European Inequality? Comparing Men and Women in West Germany and France. *Socio-Economic Review, 5*(3), 467-496.

Gaston, N., and Rajaguru, G. (2008). The Rise (and Fall) of Labour Market Programmes: Domestic vs. Global Factors. *Oxford Economic Papers, 60,* 619-648.

Gerkens, S., and Merkur, S. (2010). Belgium: Health System Review. *Health Systems in Transition, 12*(5), 1-266.

Giuliano, P. (2007). Living Arrangements in Western Europe: Does Cultural Origin Matter? *Journal of the European Economic Association, 5*(5), 927-952.

Godt, P.J. (1987). Confrontation, Consent, and Corporatism: State Strategies and the Medical Profession in France, Great Britain, and West Germany. *Journal of Health Politics, Policy and Law, 12*(3), 459-480.

Gordon, D.M., Edwards, R., and Reich, M. (1982). *Segmented Work, Divided Workers: The Historical Transformation of Labor in the United States.* Cambridge: Cambridge University Press.

Gough, I. (1996). Social Assistance in Southern Europe. *South European Society and Politics, 1*(1), 1-23.

Graziano, P.R., and Jessoula, M. (2011). 'Eppur si muoveva...': The Italian Trajectory of Recent Welfare Reforms: From 'Rescued by Europe' to Euro-scepticism. In P.R. Graziano, S. Jacquot, and B. Palier, eds, *The EU and the Domestic Politics of Welfare State Reforms: Europa, Europae* (pp. 148-174). Basingstoke: Palgrave Macmillan.

Green, D.P., and Citrin, J. (1994). Measurement Error and the Structure of Attitudes: Are Positive and Negative Judgments Opposites? *American Journal of Political Science,* 38(1), 256-281.

Green-Pedersen, C. (2003). Still There but for How Long? The Counter-Intuitiveness of the Universal Welfare Model and the Development of the Universal Welfare State in Denmark. *Revue Française des Affaires Sociales, 57*(4), 105-120.

Guibentif, P. (1996). The Transformation of the Portuguese Social Security System. *South European Society and Politics, 1*(3), 219-239.

Guillén, A.M. (2002). The Politics of Universalisation: Establishing National Health Services in Southern Europe. *West European Politics, 25*(4), 49-68.

Hacker, J.S. (2004). Privatizing Risk without Privatizing the Welfare State: The Hidden Politics of Social Policy Retrenchment in the United States. *American Political Science Review, 98*(2), 243-260.

Hall, P.A. (1993). Policy Paradigms, Social Learning and the State: The Case of Economic Policy in Britain. *Comparative Politics, 25*(3), 275-296.

Hassenteufel, P. (1996). The Medical Profession and Health Insurance Policies: A Franco-German Comparison. *Journal of European Public Policy, 3*(3), 461-480.

Hassenteufel, P., and Palier, B. (2007). Towards Neo-Bismarckian Health Care States? Comparing Health Insurance Reforms in Bismarckian Welfare States. *Social Policy & Administration, 41*(6), 574-596.

Häusermann, S. (2010a). *The Politics of Welfare State Reform in Continental Europe: Modernization in Hard Times*. Cambridge: Cambridge University Press.

Haüsermann, S. (2010b). Solidarity with Whom? Why Organised Labour Is Losing Ground in Continental Pension Politics. *European Journal of Political Research, 49*(2), 223-256.

Haüsermann, S., and Palier, B. (2008). The Politics of Employment-friendly Welfare Reforms in Post-industrial Economies. *Socio-Economic Review, 6*, 559-586.

Haüsermann, S., and Schwander, H. (2011). Who Are the Outsiders and What Do They Want? Welfare State Preferences in Dualized Societies. *Les Cahiers européens de Sciences Po, 1*.

Haüsermann, S., and Schwander, H. (2012). Varieties of Dualization? Labor Market Segmentation and Insider-Outsider Divides across Regimes. In P. Emmenegger, S. Haüsermann, B. Palier, and M. Seeleib-Kaiser, eds, *The Age of Dualization: The Changing Face of Inequality in Deindustrializing Societies* (pp. 27-51). Oxford: Oxford University Press.

Hicks, A. (1999). *Social Democracy and Welfare Capitalism: A Century of Income Security Politics*. Ithaca, NY: Cornell University Press.

Hofmarcher, M.M. (2013). Austria: Health System Review. *Health Systems in Transition, 15*(7), 1-291.

Holian, D.B. (2004). He's Stealing my Issues! Clinton's Crime Rhetoric and the Dynamics of Issue Ownership. *Political Behavior, 26*(2), 95-124.

Huber, E., Ragin, C., and Stephens, J.D. (1993). Social Democracy, Christian Democracy, Constitutional Structure, and the Welfare State. *American Journal of Sociology, 99*(3), 711-749.

Huber, E., and Stephens, J.D. (2001). *Development and Crisis of the Welfare State: Parties and Policies in Global Markets*. Chicago: University of Chicago Press.

Iacovou, M. (2011). *Leaving Home: Independence, Togetherness and Income in Europe*. New York: UN Department of Economic and Social Affairs, Population Division.

Immergut, E.M. (1990). Institutions, Veto Points, and Policy Results: A Comparative Analysis of Health Care. *Journal of Public Policy, 10*(4), 391-416.

Immergut, E.M. (1992). *Health Politics: Interests and Institutions in Western Europe*. New York: Cambridge University Press.

International Social Survey Programme (2008). *ISSP 2006 –"Role of Government IV" – ZA No. 4700*. http://www.gesis.org/issp/modules/issp-modules-by-topic/role-of-government/2006/.

ISTAT (2011). La Popolazione Straniera Residente in Italia. https://www.istat.it/it/archivio/39726

Italy (1947). *Costituzione della Repubblica Italiana*. http://www.governo.it/Governo/Costituzione/CostituzioneRepubblicaItaliana.pdf.

Italy (1978). *Legge 23 dicembre 1978, n.833*. http://www.normativasanitaria.it/jsp/dettaglio.jsp?id=21035.

Italy (2003). *Piano di Azione Nazionale contro la Povertà e l'Esclusione Sociale 2003-2005*. Rome. http://db.formez.it/StoricoArchivioNews.nsf/a26f42aa355bd33dc1256ebc003de13e/5535745adfd9d78dc1256d900058541e?OpenDocument.

Jacobs, L.R., and Skocpol, T. (2005). *Inequality and American Democracy: What We Know and What We Need to Learn*. New York: Russell Sage Foundation.

Jæger, M.M. (2006). Welfare Regimes and Attitudes towards Redistribution: The Regime Hypothesis Revisited. *European Sociological Review, 22*(2), 157-170.

Javeline, D. (1999). Response Effects in Polite Cultures: A Test of Acquiescence in Kazakhstan. *Public Opinion Quarterly, 63*(1), 1-28.

Jensen, C. (2012). Labour Market- versus Life Course-related Social Policies: Understanding Cross-programme Differences. *Journal of European Public Policy, 19*(2), 275-291.

Jessoula, M., Graziano, P., and Madama, I. (2010). 'Selective Flexicurity' in Segmented Labor Markets: The Case of Italian 'Mid-Siders'. *Journal of Social Policy, 39*(4), 561-583.

Jessoula, M., Kubisa, J., Madama, I., and Zielenska, M. (2014). Understanding Convergence and Divergence: Old and New Cleavages in the Politics of Minimum Income Schemes in Italy and Poland. *Journal of International and Comparative Social Policy, 30*(2), 128-146.

Jessoula, M., and Vesan, P. (2011). Italy: Limited Adaptation of an Atypical System. In J. Clasen and D. Clegg, eds, *Regulating the Risk of Unemployment: National Adaptations to Post-Industrial Labour Markets in Europe* (pp. 142-163). New York: Oxford University Press.

Juppé, A. (1995). Déclaration de Politique Générale de M. Alain Juppé, Premier Ministre, sur son Plan de Réforme de la Protection Sociale, à l'Assemblée nationale le 15 novembre 1995. France: Vie Publique.

Kalleberg, A.L. (2000). Nonstandard Employment Relations: Part-time, Temporary and Contract Work. *Annual Review of Sociology, 26,* 341-365.

Karamessini, M. (2008). Continuity and Change in the Southern European Social Model. *International Labour Review, 147*(1), 43-70.

Kevins, A. (2015). Political Actors, Public Opinion, and the Extension of Welfare Coverage. *Journal of European Social Policy, 25*(3), 303-15.

King Baudouin Foundation (1995). *Rapport général sur la pauvreté.*

King, D., and Rueda, D. (2008). Cheap Labor: The New Politics of 'Bread and Roses' in Industrial Democracies. *Perspectives on Politics, 6*(2), 279-297.

Kingdon, J.W. (1984). *Agendas, Alternatives and Public Policies.* Boston: Little, Brown & Co.

Kitschelt, H. (1994). *The Transformation of European Social Democracy.* New York: Cambridge University Press.

Kitschelt, H. (2001). Partisan Competition and Welfare State Retrenchment: When Do Politicians Choose Unpopular Policies? In P. Pierson, ed., *The New Politics of the Welfare State* (pp. 265-301). New York: Oxford University Press.

Kittel, B., and Obinger, H. (2003). Political Parties, Institutions, and the Dynamics of Social Expenditure in Times of Austerity. *Journal of European Public Policy, 10*(1), 20-45.

Korpi, W. (1980). Social Policy and Distributional Conflict in the Capitalist Democracies: A Preliminary Comparative Framework. *West European Politics, 3*(3), 296-316.

Korpi, W. (1989). Power, Politics, and State Autonomy in the Development of Social Citizenship: Social Rights during Sickness in Eighteen OECD Countries since 1930. *American Sociological Review, 54*(3), 309-328.

Korpi, W. (1995). Un État-Providence Contesté et Fragmenté. Le Développement de la Citoyenneté Sociale en France. Comparaisons avec la Belgique, l'Allemagne, l'Italie et la Suède. *Revue française de science politique, 45*(4), 632-667.

Korpi, W., and Palme, J. (2003). New Politics and Class Politics in the Context of Austerity and Globalization: Welfare State Regress in 18 Countries, 1975-95. *American Political Science Review, 97*(3), 425-446.

Lafore, R. (2008). Droit et Pauvreté: Les Métamorphoses du Modèle Français. *Revue de droit sanitaire et social,* 111-126.

Lalioti, V. (2016). The Curious Case of the Guaranteed Minimum Income (GMI): Highlighting Greek 'Exceptionalism' in a Southern European Context. *Journal of European Social Policy, 26*(1), 80-93.

Laparra, M., and Aguilar, M. (1996). Social Exclusion and Minimum Income Programmes in Spain. *South European Society and Politics, 1*(3), 87-114.

Le Duigou, J.-C. (2012). Interview. Translation by Anthony Kevins.

León, M., and Migliavacca, M. (2013). Italy and Spain: Still the Case of Familistic Welfare Models? *Population Review, 52*(1).

Levy, J.D. (1999). Vice into Virtue? Progressive Politics and Welfare Reform in Continental Europe. *Politics & Society, 27*(2), 239-273.

Levy, J.D. (2001). Partisan Politics and Welfare Adjustment: The Case of France. *Journal of European Public Policy, 8*(2), 265-285.

Levy, J.S. (2003). Applications of Prospect Theory to Political Science. *Synthese, 135*, 215-241.

Le Soir (2007). Petits Risques, mais Gros Coût pour les Indépendants. *Le Soir*, 14 November. http://archives.lesoir.be/petits-risques-mais-gros-co%FBt-pour-les-independants_t-20071114-00DTF4.html?query=sdi&queryor=sdi&firstHit=20&by=10&when=-1&sort=date desc&all=238&pos=23&all=256&nav=1

Lindbeck, A., and Snower, D.J. (1988). *The Insider-Outsider Theory of Employment and Unemployment*. Cambridge, MA: MIT Press.

Lindbeck, A., and Snower, D.J. (2001). Insiders versus Outsiders. *Journal of Economic Perspectives, 15*(1), 165-188.

LIS (2013). Luxembourg Income Study Database, 1998-2001.

Lobo, M.C., and Magalhães, P.C. (2004). The Portuguese Socialists and the Third Way. In G. Bonoli and M. Powell, eds, *Social Democratic Party Policies in Contemporary Europe* (pp. 83-101). London: Routledge.

Lodovici, M.S., and Semenza, R. (2008). The Italian Case: From Employment Regulation to Welfare Reforms? *Social Policy & Administration, 42*(2), 160-176.

Lupu, N., and Pontusson, J. (2011). The Structure of Inequality and the Politics of Redistribution. *American Political Science Review, 105*(2), 316-336.

L'Unità (1962). L'editoriale. *L'Unità*, 8 September, p. 12. http://archiviostorico.unita.it/cgi-bin/highlightPdf.cgi?t=ebook&file=/archivio/uni_1962_09/19620908_0012.pdf&query=%22sistema sanitario%22.

L'Unità (1963). La Riforma Sanitaria: Proposte e Azione del PCI. *L'Unità*, 20 April, p. 13.

L'Unità (1974). Nel Decreto per i Debiti delle Mutue Inganno a Favore dei 'Carrozzini'. *L'Unità*, 22 July, p. 2. http://archiviostorico.unita.it/cgi-bin/highlightPdf.cgi?t=ebook&file=/archivio/uni_1974_07/19740722_0002.pdf&query=%22sistema sanitario%22 mutue.

Maarse, H., and Paulus, A. (2003). Has Solidarity Survived? A Comparative Analysis of the Effect of Social Health Insurance Reform in Four European Countries. *Journal of Health Politics, Policy and Law, 28*(4), 585-614.

Mailly, J.-C. (2008). *Qu'est-ce que Force Ouvrière?* Paris: L'Archipel.

Maino, F. (2001). *La Politica Sanitaria*. Bologna: Il Mulino.

Maioni, A. (1997). Parting at the Crossroads: The Development of Health Insurance in Canada and the United States, 1940-1965. *Comparative Politics, 29*(4), 411-431.

Manow, P. (2001). Comparative Institutional Advantages of Welfare State Regimes and New Coalitions in Welfare State Reforms. In P. Pierson, ed., *The New Politics of the Welfare State* (pp. 146-164). New York: Oxford University Press.

Maresso, A., et al., eds. (2015). *Economic Crisis, Health Systems, and Health in Europe: Country Experiences*. Brussels: European Observatory on Health Systems and Policies.

Martin, A., Ross, G., Baccaro, L., Daley, A., Fraile, L., Howell, C., Locke, R.M., Mahon, R., and Silvia, S.J. (1999). *The Brave New World of European Labor: European Trade Unions at the Millennium.* New York: Berghahn.

Martin, C. (1996). Social Welfare and the Family in Southern Europe. *South European Society and Politics, 1*(3), 23-41.

Martin, C.J., and Thelen, K. (2007). The State and Coordinated Capitalism Contributions of the Public Sector to Social Solidarity in Postindustrial Societies. *World Politics, 60*(1), 1-36.

Marx, I. (2003). Mass Joblessness, the Bismarckian Model and the Limits to Gradual Adaptation: The Case of Belgium. In G. Standing, ed., *Minimum Income Schemes in Europe* (pp. 219-242). Geneva: International Labour Office.

Marx, I., and Nelson, K. (2013). A New Dawn for Minimum Income Protection? In I. Marx and K. Nelson, eds, *Minimum Income Protection in Flux* (pp. 1-27). London: Palgrave Macmillan.

Marx, P. (2014). Labour Market Risks and Political Preferences: The Case of Temporary Employment. *European Journal of Political Research, 53*(1), 136-159.

Matsaganis, M. (2005). Greece – Fighting with Hands Tied Behind the Back: Anti-poverty Policy without a Minimum Income. In M. Ferrera, ed., *Welfare State Reform in Southern Europe: Fighting Poverty and Social Exclusion in Italy, Spain, Portugal and Greece* (pp. 24-64). New York: Routledge.

Matsaganis, M. (2015). Η αντιμετώπιση της 'ανθρωπιστικής κρίσης' και άλλα παραμύθια… [Addressing the 'humanitarian crisis' and other tales…]. *Protagon*, 9 March. http://www.protagon.gr/?i=protagon.el.article&id=39945.

Matsaganis, M., Ferrera, M., Capucha, L., and Moreno, L. (2003). Mending Nets in the South: Anti-poverty Policies in Greece, Italy, Portugal and Spain. *Social Policy & Administration, 37*(6), 639-655.

Maynard, A. (1975). *Health Care in the European Community.* London: Croom Helm.

Meguid, B.M. (2005). Competition between Unequals: The Role of Mainstream Party Strategy in Niche Party Success. *American Political Science Review, 99*(03), 347-359.

Milanovic, B. (2000). The Median-Voter Hypothesis, Income Inequality, and Income Redistribution: An Empirical Test with the Required Data. *European Journal of Political Economy, 16*(3), 367-410.

Milio, S. (2007). Can Administrative Capacity Explain Differences in Regional Performances? Evidence from Structural Funds Implementation in Southern Italy. *Regional Studies, 41*(4), 429-442.

Mingione, E. (1995). Labour Market Segmentation and Informal Work in Southern Europe. *European Urban and Regional Studies, 2*(2), 121-143.

Ministero del Lavoro e delle Politiche Sociali (2013). *Piano di azione nazionale contro la povertà e l'esclusione sociale 2003-2005.* Rome, Italy

Mitlacher, L.W. (2007). The Role of Temporary Agency Work in Different Industrial Relations Systems: A Comparison between Germany and the USA. *British Journal of Industrial Relations, 45*(3), 581-606.

Mitterrand, F. (1988). Lettre à tous les Français. *Libération,* 7 April.

Moran, M. (2000). Understanding the Welfare State: The Case of Health Care. *British Journal of Politics and Industrial Relations, 2*(2), 135-160.

Moreira, A. (2008). *The Activation Dilemma: Reconciling the Fairness and Effectiveness of Minimum Income Schemes in Europe.* Bristol: The Policy Press.

Moreno, L., and Marí-Klose, P. (2013). Youth, Family Change and Welfare Arrangements: Is the South Still so Different? *European Societies, 15*(4), 493-513.

Morin, A. (2011). Interview, 27 May. Translation by Anthony Kevins.

Mossialos, E., and Allin, S. (2005). Interest Groups and Health System Reform in Greece. *West European Politics, 28*(2), 420-444.

Naldini, M. (2003). *The Family in the Mediterranean Welfare State.* London: Frank Cass.

Naldini, M., and Jurado, T. (2013). Family and Welfare State Reorientation in Spain and Inertia in Italy from a European Perspective. *Population Review, 52*(1).

Navarro, V. (1989). Why Some Countries Have National Health Insurance, Others Have National Health Services, and the U.S. Has Neither. *Social Science and Medicine, 28*(9), 887-898.

Negri, N., and Saraceno, C. (1996). *Le Politiche contro la Povertà in Italia.* Bologna: Il Mulino.

Nelson, K. (2010). Social Assistance and Minimum Income Benefits in Old and New EU Democracies. *International Journal of Social Welfare, 19*(4), 367-378.

Nikolentzos, A., and Mays, N. (2008). Can Existing Theories of Health Care Reform Explain the Greek Case (1983-2001)? *Journal of European Social Policy, 18*(2), 163-176.

Norton, E.C., Wang, H., and Ai, C. (2004). Computing Interaction Effects and Standard Errors in Logit and Probit Models. *Stata Journal, 4,* 154-167.

Nys, H. (2010). *Medical Law in Belgium.* Bedfordshire: Kluwer Law International.

Obinger, H., Starke, P., and Kaasch, A. (2012). Responses to Labor Market Divides in Small States since the 1990s. In P. Emmenegger, S. Haüsermann, B. Palier, and M. Seeleib-Kaiser, eds, *The Age of Dualization: The Changing Face of Inequality in Deindustrializing Societies* (pp. 176-200). Oxford: Oxford University Press.

OECD (1987). Financing and Delivering Health Care: A Comparative Analysis of OECD Countries. Paris: OECD.

OECD (2012a). *Employment and Labour Market Statistics Dataset.*

OECD (2012b). *Health Data Dataset.*

OECD (2012c). *National Accounts Statistics Dataset.*

OECD (2014a). *International Migration Outlook 2014.* OECD Publishing. http://dx.doi.org/10.1787/migr_outlook-2014-en

OECD (2014b). *Health Dataset.*

Oliveira, M.D., Magone, J.M., and Pereira, J.A. (2005). Nondecision Making and Inertia in Portuguese Health Policy. *Journal of Health Politics, Policy and Law, 30*(1-2), 211-230.

Oliveira, M.D., and Pinto, C.G. (2005). Health Care Reform in Portugal: An Evaluation of the NHS Experience. *Health Economics, 14*(S1), S203-S220.

Paci, M. (1987). Pubblico e Privato nel sistema Italiano di Welfare. In P. Lange and M. Regini, eds, *Stato e Regolazione Sociale: Nuove Prospettive sul Caso Italiano* (pp. 271-294). Bologna: Il Mulino.

Paci, M. (1989). *Pubblico e Privato nei Moderni Sistemi di Welfare.* Naples: Liguori Editore.

Palier, B. (2002). Re-Negotiating the Continental European Welfare States: The Case of France in the 1990's. Unpublished manuscript. CEVIPOF. Paris.

Palier, B. (2004a). French Welfare Reform in Comparative Perspective. *Revue Française des Affaires Sociales, 45* (supplement), 97-124.

Palier, B. (2004b). *La Réforme des Systèmes de Santé.* Paris: Presses Universitaires de France.

Palier, B., and Martin, C. (2007). From 'a Frozen Landscape' to Structural Reforms: The Sequential Transformation of Bismarckian Welfare Systems. *Social Policy & Administration, 41*(6), 535-554.

Palier, B., and Thelen, K. (2010). Institutionalizing Dualism: Complementarities and Change in France and Germany. *Politics & Society, 38*(1), 119-148.

Parti Socialiste (1988). *Comité Directeur, 2 juillet 1988.*

Patto per l'Italia (2002). *Accordo Interconfederale 5 Luglio 2002 – Patto per l'Italia Contratto per il Lavoro – Intesa per la Competitività e i'Inclusione Sociale.* http://www.confetra.it/it/prontuari/PattoItalia-2002.pdf.

Patucchi, M. (2013). Fondo Povertà o Reddito Minimo. *La Repubblica,* 27 November. http://www.repubblica.it/economia/rubriche/il-commento/2013/11/27/news/l_importanza_dei_nomi_la_chiarezza_conta_di_marco_patucchi-72086191/

Paugam, S. (1993). La Société Française et ses Pauvres: L'expérience du Revenu Minimum d'Insertion. Paris, France: Presses Universitaires de France.

Pempel, T.J. (1998). *Regime Shift: Comparative Dynamics of the Japanese Political Economy.* Ithaca, NY: Cornell University Press.

Pennings, P. (1999). European Social Democracy between Planning and Market: A Comparative Exploration of Trends and Variations. *Journal of European Public Policy, 6*(5), 743-756.

Petrocik, J.R. (1996). Issue Ownership in Presidential Elections, with a 1980 Case Study. *American Journal of Political Science, 40*(3): 825-850.

Pfeifer, M. (2009). Public Opinion on State Responsibility for Minimum Income Protection: A Comparison of 14 European Countries. *Acta Sociologica, 52*(2), 117-134.

Picot, G. (2012). *Politics of Segmentation: Party Competition and Social Protection in Europe.* New York: Routledge.

Pierson, P. (1994). *Dismantling the Welfare State? Reagan, Thatcher, and the Politics of Retrenchment.* Cambridge: Cambridge University Press.

Pierson, P. (1996). The New Politics of the Welfare State. *World Politics, 48*(2), 143-179.

Pierson, P. (2001a). Coping with Permanent Austerity: Welfare State Restructuring in Affluent Democracies. In P. Pierson, ed., *The New Politics of the Welfare State* (pp. 410-456). New York: Oxford University Press.

Pierson, P. (2001b). Post-industrial Pressures on the Mature Welfare States. In P. Pierson, ed., *The New Politics of the Welfare State* (pp. 80-104). New York: Oxford University Press.

Piperno, A. (1983). Medici e Stato in Italia. In P. Donati, ed., *La Sociologia Sanitaria* (pp. 141-164). Milan: Franco Angeli.

Pizzorno, A. (1978). Political Exchange and Collective Identity in Industrial Conflict. In C. Crouch and A. Pizzorno, eds, *The Resurgence of Class Conflict in Western Europe Since 1968: Vol. 2, Comparative Analyses* (pp. 277-298). New York: Holmes & Meier.

Privat, P. (2012). Interview, 17 April. Translation by Anthony Kevins.

Przeworski, A., and Sprague, J. (1986). *Paper Stones: A History of Electoral Socialism.* Chicago: University of Chicago Press.

Putnam, R. (1993). *Making Democracy Work: Civic Traditions in Modern Italy.* Princeton, NJ: Princeton University Press.

Raitano, M. (2007). The Italian Pension System and Social Inclusion. In T. Meyer, P. Bridgen, and B. Riedmuller, eds, *Private Pensions versus Social Inclusion? Non-state Provision for Citizens at Risk in Europe* (pp. 168-192). Cheltenham: Edward Elgar.

Rauch, F. (2012). Interview, 20 April. Translation by Anthony Kevins.

Reif, K., and Marlier, E. (1998). *Eurobarometer 44.3: Health Care Issues and Public Security, February-April 1996.* http://dx.doi.org/10.3886/ICPSR06752.v1.

Rhodes, M. (1996). Southern European Welfare States: Identity, Problems and Prospects for Reform. *South European Society and Politics, 1*(3), 1-22.

Rico, A. (1996). Regional Decentralization and Health Care Reform in Spain (1976-1996). *South European Society and Politics, 1*(3), 115-134.

Rico, A., and Costa-Font, J. (2005). Power Rather Than Path Dependency? The Dynamics of Institutional Change under Health Care Federalism. *Journal of Health Politics, Policy and Law, 30*(1-2), 231-252.

Riz, S. (2002). Palazzo Chigi e il Ministero del... *Corriere della Sera*, 9 December.

Robb, J.H. (1986). The Italian Health Services: Slow Revolution or Permanent Crisis? *Social Science and Medicine, 22*(6), 619-627.

Rochaix, L., and Wilsford, D. (2005). State Autonomy, Policy Paralysis: Paradoxes of Institutions and Culture in the French Health Care System. *Journal of Health Politics, Policy and Law, 30*(1-2), 97-119.

Rodwin, V.G., and Le Pen, C. (2004). Health Care Reform in France: The Birth of State-Led Managed Care. *The New England Journal of Medicine, 351*(22), 2259-2262.

Ross, F. (2000). 'Beyond Left and Right': The *New Partisan* Politics of Welfare. *Governance, 13*(2), 155-183.

Ross, G. (2000). Labor versus Globalization. *Annals of the American Academy of Political and Social Science, 570*, 78-91.

Rueda, D. (2005). Insider-Outsider Politics in Industrialized Democracies: The Challenge to Social Democratic Parties. *American Political Science Review, 99*(1), 61-74.

Rueda, D. (2006). Social Democracy and Active Labour-Market Policies: Insiders, Outsiders and the Politics of Employment Promotion. *British Journal of Political Science, 36*(3), 385-406.

Rueda, D. (2007). *Social Democracy Inside Out: Partisanship and Labor Market Policy in Industrialised Democracies*. New York: Oxford University Press.

Rueda, D. (2014). Dualization, Crisis and the Welfare State. *Socio-Economic Review, 12*(2), 381-407.

Ruscoe, J. (1982). *The Italian Communist Party, 1976-81: On the Threshold of Government*. London: Macmillan.

Sacchi, S., and Bastagli, F. (2005). Italy – Striving Uphill but Stopping Halfway: The Troubled Journey of the Experimental Minimum Insertion Income. In M. Ferrera (Ed.), *Welfare State Reform in Southern Europe: Fighting Poverty and Social Exclusion in Italy, Spain, Portugal and Greece* (pp. 84-140). New York, NY: Routledge.

Saint-Paul, G. (1996). Exploring the Political Economy of Labour Market Institutions. *Economic Policy, 11*(23), 263-315.

Saint-Paul, G. (1998). A Framework for Analyzing the Political Support for Active Labor Market Policy. *Journal of Public Economies, 67*, 151-165.

Saltman, R., Busse, R., and Figueras, J. (2004). *Social Health Insurance Systems in Western Europe*. Maidenhead: McGraw-Hill International.

Sandier, S., Paris, V., and Polton, D. (2004). Health Care Systems in Transition: France. Copenhagen: WHO Regional Office for Europe on Behalf of the European Observatory on Health Systems and Policies.

Saraceno, C., and Negri, N. (1994). The Changing Italian Welfare State. *Journal of European Social Policy, 4*(1), 19-34.

Scarpa, S. (1973). Prima il Profitto poi la Salute nel Progetto di Legge Governativo. *L'Unità*, 31 January, p. 6. http://archiviostorico.unita.it/cgi-bin/highlightPdf.cgi?t=ebook&file=/archivio/uni_1973_01/19730131_0006.pdf&query=%22sistema sanitario%22

Scarpa, S. (1974). Quanto Costa non Fare la Riforma Sanitaria? *L'Unità*, 29 August, p. 3.

Scharpf, F.W. (2000). The Viability of Advanced Welfare States in the International Economy: Vulnerabilities and Options. *Journal of European Public Policy, 7*(2), 190-228.

Scherer, S. (2004). Stepping-Stones or Traps? The Consequences of Labour Market Entry Positions on Future Careers in West Germany, Great Britain and Italy. *Work, Employment & Society, 18*(2), 369-394.

Schickler, E. (2001). *Disjointed Pluralism: Institutional Innovation and the Development of the U.S. Congress*. Princeton, NJ: Princeton University Press.

Schmid, A., Cacace, M., Gotze, R., and Rothgang, H. (2010). Explaining Health Care System Change: Problem Pressure and the Emergence of 'Hybrid' Health Care Systems. *Journal of Health Politics, Policy and Law, 35*(4), 455-486.

Schmidt, V.A. (2000). Values and Discourse in the Politics of Adjustment. In F.W. Scharpf and V.A. Schmidt, eds, *Welfare and Work in the Open Economy: Vol. 1, From Vulnerability to Competitiveness* (pp. 229-309). Oxford: Oxford University Press.

Schneider, F. (2005). Shadow Economies around the World: What Do We Really Know? *European Journal of Political Economy, 21*(3), 598-642.

Schneider, F., Buehn, A., and Montenegro, C.E. (2010). Shadow Economies All over the World: New Estimates for 162 Countries from 1999 to 2007. Policy Research Working Paper. Washington, DC: The World Bank.

Schneider, F., and Hofreither, M. (1986). Measuring the Size of the Shadow Economy: Can the Obstacles Be Overcome? *Economic Affairs, 7*(2), 18-23.

Schrijver, F. (2006). *Regionalism after Regionalisation: Spain, France and the United Kingdom*. Amsterdam: Amsterdam University Press.

Schumacher, G. (2011). Why Not to Use Left-Right scales in Welfare State Research: Introducing a New Measure for Cabinet Partisanship. Paper presented at the annual conference of the European Consortium on Political Research, Reykjavik, Iceland.

Schwander, H. (2013). Are Social Democratic Parties Really Insider Parties? Social Democratic Electoral Strategy in Western Europe. Paper presented at the Conference for European Studies, Amsterdam, The Netherlands.

Schwander, H., and Häusermann, S. (2013). Who Is In and Who Is Out? A Risk-based Conceptualization of Insiders and Outsiders. *Journal of European Social Policy, 23*(3), 248-269.

Scruggs, L. (2004). *Welfare State Entitlements Data Set: A Comparative Institutional Analysis of Eighteen Welfare States, Version 1.2.*

Scruggs, L., and Allan, J.P. (2006). Welfare-State Decommodification in 18 OECD Countries: a Replication and Revision. *Journal of European Social Policy, 16*(1), 55-72.

Silver, H. (1994). Social Exclusion and Social Solidarity: Three Paradigms. *International Labour Review, 133*(5-6), 531-578.

Smith, T.B. (2004). *France in Crisis: Welfare, Inequality, and Globalization since 1980*. Cambridge: Cambridge University Press.

Solow, R.M. (1985). Insiders and Outsiders in Wage Determination. *The Scandinavian Journal of Economics, 87*(2), 411-428.

Soroka, S., Johnston, R., and Banting, K. (2006). Immigration and Redistribution in a Global Era. In S. Bowles, P. Bardhan, and M. Wallerstein, eds, *Globalization and Egalitarian Redistribution* (pp. 261-268). Princeton, NJ: Princeton University Press and Russell Sage Foundation.

Soroka, S.N., Johnston, R., Kevins, A., Banting, K., and Kymlicka, W. (2016). Migration and Welfare State Spending. *European Political Science Review, 8*(2), 174-193.

Soroka, S.N., and Wlezien, C. (2010). *Degrees of Democracy: Politics, Public Opinion, and Policy*. New York: Cambridge University Press.

Sorum, P.C. (2005). France Tries to Save Its Ailing National Health Insurance System. *Journal of Public Health Policy, 26*(2), 231-245.

Spence, R. (1996). Italy. In A. Wall, ed., *Health Care Systems in Liberal Democracies* (pp. 47-75). New York: Routledge.

Starke, P. (2006). The Politics of Welfare State Retrenchment: A Literature Review. *Social Policy & Administration, 40*(1), 104-120.

Steffen, M. (2010). The French Health Care System: Liberal Universalism. *Journal of Health Politics, Policy and Law, 35*(3), 353-387.

Stella, G.A. (2010). L'Italia dei Finti Assunti e del Lavoro Nero. *Corriere della Sera*, 6 February.

Streeck, W., and Thelen, K., eds. (2005). *Beyond Continuity: Institutional Change in Advanced Political Economies*. Oxford: Oxford University Press.

Swank, D. (2001). Political Institutions and Welfare State Restructuring: The Impact of Institutions on Social Policy Change in Developed Democracies. In P. Pierson, ed., *The New Politics of the Welfare State* (pp. 197-237). New York: Oxford University Press.

Taylor-Gooby, P. (2011a). Does Risk Society Erode Welfare State Solidarity? *Policy & Politics, 39*(2), 147-161.

Taylor-Gooby, P. (2011b). Security, Equality and Opportunity: Attitudes and the Sustainability of Social Protection. *Journal of European Social Policy, 21*(2), 150-163.

Testai, C. (1971). Dal 'Medico della Mutua' a una 'Medicina Nuova'. *L'Unità*, 8 August, p. 7.

Thelen, K. (2003). How Institutions Evolve: Insights from Comparative-Historical Analysis. In J. Mahoney and D. Rueschemeyer, eds, *Comparative Historical Analysis in the Social Sciences* (pp. 208-240). New York: Cambridge University Press.

Threlfall, M. (1997). Spain in Social Europe: A Laggard or Compliant Member State? *South European Society and Politics, 2*(2), 1-33.

Tibaldi, D. (2011). Interview. Translation by Anthony Kevins.

Torres, A., Coelho, B., and Cabrita, M. (2013). Bridge over Troubled Waters: Family, Gender and Welfare in Portugal in the European Context. *European Societies, 15*(4), 535-556.

Toth, F. (2010). Is there a Southern European Healthcare Model? *West European Politics, 33*(2), 325-343.

Touadi, J.-L. (2012). Interview, 21 May. Translation by Anthony Kevins.

Treisman, D. (2002). Defining and Measuring Decentralization: A Global Perspective. Unpublished manuscript.

Treves, C. (2012). Interview, 22 May. Translation by Anthony Kevins.

Trifiletti, R. (1999). Southern European Welfare Regimes and the Worsening Position of Women. *Journal of European Social Policy, 9*(1), 49-64.

United Nations (2009). *Trends in International Migrant Stock: The 2008 Revision.* [New York]: United Nations Population Division. http://www.un.org/esa/population/migration/UN_MigStock_2008.pdf.

US Social Security Administration (2012). Social Security Programs throughout the World. http://www.ssa.gov/policy/docs/progdesc/ssptw/.

Vail, M.I. (2010). *Recasting Welfare Capitalism: Economic Adjustment in Contemporary France and Germany*. Philadelphia: Temple University Press.

Van de Geuchte, I., Maulet, N., Willems, S., Roland, M., and De Maeseneer, J. (2007). Recherche sur les Initiatives Mises en Place en Matière d'inégalités Socio-économiques de Santé Belgique 1995-2006. King Baudouin Foundation.

Van Oorschot, W. (2006). Making the Difference in Social Europe: Deservingness Perceptions among Citizens of European Welfare States. *Journal of European Social Policy, 16*(1), 23-42.

Vicarelli, G. (1995). Welfare Systems and Social Change: One Hundred Years of Health and Social Policies in Italy. In B. Palier, ed., *Comparing Social Welfare Systems in Southern Europe, Vol. 3* (pp. 109-133). Paris: MIRE.

Vis, B. (2010). *Politics of Risk-taking: Welfare State Reform in Advanced Democracies*. Amsterdam: Amsterdam University Press.

Wendt, C., Frisina, L., and Rothgang, H. (2009). Healthcare System Types: A Conceptual Framework for Comparison. *Social Policy & Administration, 43*(1), 70-90.

Williams, R. (2009). Using Heterogeneous Choice Models to Compare Logit and Probit Coefficients across Groups. *Sociological Methods & Research, 37*(4), 531-559.

Wilsford, D. (1994). Path Dependency, or Why History Makes It Difficult but Not Impossible to Reform Health Care Systems in a Big Way. *Journal of Public Policy, 14*(3), 251-283.

World Health Organization (2000). *The World Health Report 2000: Health Systems: Improving Performance*. Geneva: World Health Organization.

Zipponi, M. (2012). Interview, 23 May. Translation by Anthony Kevins.

Index